Springer Series in Behavior Modification
THEORY / RESEARCH / APPLICATION

Cyril M. Franks / Series Editor

Volume 1
Multimodal Behavior Therapy
Arnold A. Lazarus

Arnold A. Lazarus, Ph.D., a prominent authority on behavioral methods of treatment whose multifaceted approach to therapy has attracted wide attention, is professor of psychology at the Graduate School of Applied and Professional Psychology, Rutgers University. Previously, he was Director of Clinical Training at Yale University. He has also held teaching posts at Temple University Medical School and at Stanford University, and has several consultant positions in addition to his private practice. A Fellow of the American Psychological Association, Dr. Lazarus is a former president of the Association for Advancement of Behavior Therapy and a Diplomate of the American Board of Professional Psychology. His lectures, invited addresses, and workshops, here and abroad, number in the hundreds. He is the author of numerous articles as well as several books, of which the best known is *Behavior Therapy and Beyond*.

MULTIMODAL BEHAVIOR THERAPY

ARNOLD A. LAZARUS

With Eleven Contributors

SPRINGER PUBLISHING COMPANY

New York

Springer Publishing Company, Inc.
200 Park Avenue South
New York, N.Y. 10003

76 77 78 79 80 / 10 9 8 7 6 5 4 3 2 1

Library of Congress Cataloging in Publication Data

Main entry under title:

Multimodal behavior therapy.

  (Springer series in behavior modification)
  Includes bibliographical reference and index.
  1. Behavior therapy—Addresses, essays, lectures.
I. Lazarus, Arnold A. [DNLM: 1. Behavior therapy.
WM420 M961]
RC489.B4M84   616.8'914   76-4464
ISBN 0-8261-2160-8

Printed in the United States of America

Composition by Topel Typographic Corporation, New York City

Contents

Foreword

For reasons relating both to the field as a whole and to the key individuals concerned, it is doubtful whether a single definitive history of behavior therapy could ever be written; thus, we will have to rest content with an ongoing series of minisurveys, each written from the vantage point of the particular commentator. As I read or hear about not-so-long-past developments in the saga of behavior therapy—in many instances relating to occasions when I was physically present—the essential subjectivity of most eyewitnesses becomes apparent (excluding myself, of course). Even such seemingly factual matters as who first coined and placed on record the term "behavior therapy" are open to dispute, and so it is hardly surprising that complex issues become subject to grievous, albeit unwitting, distortion by usually careful and sincere observers.

These hazards notwithstanding, it is still possible to detect certain trends in the evolution of behavior therapy and to arrive at tentative conclusions with which few observers would take serious issue. Overwhelmingly, there seems to be a movement away from the understandably overdetermined restrictions of the narrow S-R models of the early sixties and toward a conceptual sophistication that embraces the complexity of man in his total internal and external environment. Whether this signifies a systematic evolution into something that can still be meaningfully classified under the original rubric of behavior therapy, or whether we are witnessing a transition into some radically different framework—Kuhn would call it a paradigm shift—remains to be seen. Perhaps both of these processes are at work at different levels. It will be of interest to see what future historians of behavior therapy make of these mid-seventies stirrings.

In either case—orderly progression or paradigm shift—two clear trends are unmistakable. Early behavior therapists overreacted to Freudian insistence upon the primary nature of mysterious inner forces in the government of man's life and rejected almost anything that went beyond the constraints of basic S-R conditioning. Modern-day behavior therapy, more secure and sensitive to the evidence, recognizes that the inner man is significant, but repudiates the mentalistic and superfluous superstructure imposed on its study by Freudian theory. Whether the label be cognitive restructuring, rational therapy, or cognitive behavior therapy, it comes to pretty much the same thing: contemporary behavior therapy, with its emphasis upon self-control and biofeedback, cognition, imagery, and the like, is no longer consonant with the radical behaviorism of an earlier era.

In similar fashion, behavior therapy is extending its domain outward, beyond the individual to the group and the group process, and beyond the group process to society at large, with its many socioecological and other interwoven systems. Of necessity, this entails contact with disciplines far removed from traditional S-R psychology, and a willingness at least to consider approaches to data accumulation and interpretation at variance with the more conventional canons of the laboratory scientist.

What is particularly encouraging about these exciting developments is that they are being accomplished with due regard for those clearly delineated principles of scientific rigor that first led concerned behavioral pioneers to break away from the traditional psychodynamic mold. Regardless of the direction, it is this allegiance to data, controlled study, replication, and external validation—coupled with a healthy skepticism and conservatism with respect to inference, conclusion, and generalization—that characterizes behavior therapy now, as then. This is the true strength of behavior therapy, rather than any impressive list of therapeutic successes or techniques generated (important as these are). And it is by these criteria that any broadly behavioral innovation, including the subject matter of the present book, must be evaluated.

If any individual can be said to personify these developments, that individual is Arnold A. Lazarus. Rejecting the ineffective techniques of psychodynamic procedures in favor of the seemingly more promising model of early S-R conditioning therapy, Lazarus (along with others) became disenchanted with both the many clinical failures and the blinkered outlook of behavior therapy as it then was. Gradually, painstakingly, he carved out a series of fresh clinical strategies, one leading naturally to the next, and always in accord with social learning theory or some offshoot thereof. Thus, we were introduced, through *Behavior Therapy and Beyond,* to the concept of broad-spectrum behavior therapy, to the doctrine of technical eclecticism, and finally to the complex and highly sophisticated system of assessment and therapy that is the subject matter of this, his latest book. Taken together, the BASIC ID and the multimodal approach constitute what is probably the most comprehensive behavioral system of therapy in existence today.

And just as behavior therapy itself is constantly changing in response to the data and the *Zeitgeist,* so it is with Arnold Lazarus. It is within this context that the present volume must be savored and appreciated for what it is, the culmination of Lazarus' thinking at this time. It is not so much a static theoretical product as a combination of working guide for the present and blueprint for the future. And, as with all pioneering routes to important places, the road it charts is uneven and often hard to travel, with many a cul-de-sac and jolt on the way. Some of the contributed chapters in Lazarus' book are less rigorously conceived than others and Lazarus himself cautions us against a too-facile acceptance of his system. We can look with confidence to an orderly progression in Lazarus' thinking and general clinical strategies as further data are adduced.

The rational approach to behavior therapy entails a rigorous process of deduction from general and independently established laws. It is Lazarus' contention that while this is viable as a research strategy, it is relatively ineffective for the advancement of clinical practice. For Lazarus, empiricism is the royal road to clinical success, and this outlook presupposes a readiness to deploy any technique of promise, regardless of theoretical origins (if any), as long as there is demonstrable empirical support for its use. Contrary to the beliefs of some of his critics, Lazarus repeatedly voices his rejection of the purely notional, the hunch, the whim, and the whimsy, the technique supported by no more than persuasion, hearsay, and emotional appeal. His constant concern with the need for caution and validation of data is clearly expressed in his Concluding Commentary; if followers of his multimodal approach should slip from the path of empiricism to the sheltered but treacherous slopes of the notional, it will not be for lack of a caveat from Lazarus.

To my way of thinking, this book represents a sampling of the best that modern developments in broad-spectrum behavior therapy have to offer, a culmination of years of thinking by one of the foremost practitioners in our field. It can be used wisely as a basis for further research and controlled clinical investigation or, less prudently, as a blanket authorization to engage in any esoteric practices that seem intuitively to work or that strike the clinician's fancy. It is my considered opinion—which I am sure is shared by Arnold Lazarus—that the former approach will prevail.

Cyril M. Franks
Graduate School of Applied and
Professional Psychology
Rutgers University

Multimodal Behavior Therapy is the first volume in Springer's new series in behavior modification. It is most propitious to have a distinguished author of the rank of Arnold Lazarus to introduce the series. The scope of this volume may be seen as a reflection of the current state of behavior modification. At a time when critics are voicing the potential dangers of a too rigid, mechanistic application of behavior modification, this book clearly reveals a breadth and depth of approach that should assuage the skeptics. The authors accord a full tribute to the totality of the human personality, reflecting the concern among behavior therapists for humanistic values that inspires this new series. The other novel extension of behavior therapy shown in this book—namely, that of attending to the social context of the individual, as well as to groups in the therapy setting—also points to new paths of orientation and intervention explored by multimodal therapists. This is indeed a splendid book, both in its own right and as the inaugurator of the Springer Series in Behavior Modification.

C. M. F.

Acknowledgments

I acknowledge with thanks the following publishers, who generously granted permission for me to reprint papers and articles: Academic Press, Brunner/Mazel, *Psychological Reports, Psychotherapy: Theory, Research and Practice,* the Williams and Wilkins Company, World Institute Council, and Ziff-Davis Publishing Company.

Louisa Kessel deserves special thanks for typing several drafts of the manuscript, and especially for helping me wield a vigorous editorial pen in translating the various contributions (including my own) from "Psychology" into "English."

Contributors

Dan W. Briddell, Ph.D.
Clinical psychologist,
Munson Medical Center,
Traverse City, Michigan

Allen Fay, M.D.
Private practice, New York, New York.
Department of psychiatry,
Mount Sinai School of Medicine
    (C.U.N.Y.)
Graduate School of Applied and
    Professional Psychology,
Rutgers University,
New Brunswick, New Jersey

Vito Guarnaccia, Ph.D.
Supervising psychologist,
    Assistant professor,
Mental Retardation Institute,
New York Medical College,
    Flower and Fifth Avenue Hospitals,
Valhalla, New York.
Co-director, New York Association
    for Training in Multimodal Therapy,
White Plains, New York

Robert A. Karlin, Ph.D.
Assistant professor,
Department of psychology,
University College,
Rutgers University,
New Brunswick, New Jersey

Donald B. Keat II, Ph.D.
Coordinator, Child Counseling Program,
Pennsylvania State University,
University Park, Pennsylvania.
Private practice in child psychotherapy,
State College, Pennsylvania

Sandra Risa Leiblum, Ph.D.
Clinical assistant professor of psychiatry,
College of Medicine and Dentistry
    of New Jersey,
Rutgers Medical School,
Piscataway, New Jersey.
Adjunct assistant professor,
Graduate School of Applied and
    Professional Psychology,
Rutgers University

Patricia McKeon, M.Ed.
Research assistant,
Center of Alcohol Studies,
Rutgers University,
New Brunswick, New Jersey.
Research associate,
Center for Policy Research,
New York, New York

William L. Mulligan, Ph.D.
Clinical psychologist,
    private practice,
Virginia Beach, Virginia

Carole Pearl, M.A.
Psychologist and coordinator,
Multimodal Therapy Program, M.R.I.,
New York Medical College,
    Flower and Fifth Avenue Hospitals,
Valhalla, New York.
Co-director, New York Association for
    Training in Multimodal Therapy,
White Plains, New York

Frank C. Richardson, Ph.D.
Assistant professor,
Department of educational psychology,
University of Texas at Austin

Robert L. Woolfolk, Ph.D.
Assistant professor,
Department of psychology,
University College,
Rutgers University,
New Brunswick, New Jersey

Part One

Some Theoretical and Clinical Foundations

Chapter 1 provides a brief clinical and conceptual perspective of multimodal behavior therapy. I have endeavored to provide a differentiation between the multimodal orientation and other eclectic approaches. The main differences between "behavior therapy," "broad-spectrum behavior therapy," and "multimodal behavior therapy" are delineated.*

Chapter 2, my first published paper on multimodal behavior therapy, adds further depth and detail to the preceding chapter and provides a case illustration of how multimodal behavior therapy was applied to a 24-year-old woman diagnosed as an undifferentiated schizophrenic.

Chapter 3 is a brief report by Robert Woolfolk which places the multimodal model into a general decision-making framework. It centers on the way in which the multimodal orientation facilitates the systematic processing of information in the therapeutic context.

In Chapter 4 I have described the type of questions and procedures employed when assessing various problem areas across each modality. Precise and specific multimodal assessment techniques are outlined in considerable detail.

In Chapter 5 Robert Woolfolk discusses the "affective modality" in

---

* We have assumed that our readers are familiar with general principles of therapy, and more specially behavior therapy. In this connection, in addition to one of my earlier books—*Behavior Therapy and Beyond* (New York: McGraw-Hill, 1971)—I would recommend three truly outstanding volumes: O'Leary and Wilson's *Behavior Therapy: Application and Outcome* (New York: Prentice-Hall, 1975); Rimm and Masters' *Behavior Therapy: Techniques and Empirical Findings* (New York: Academic Press, 1974); and Goldfried and Davison's *Clinical Behavior Therapy* (New York: Holt, Rinehart and Winston, 1976).

the light of experimental and empirical evidence. An appreciation of affective processes is crucial since each therapist's explicit or implicit theory of emotion seems to dictate which methods he or she applies or withholds in every case.

In Chapter 6 Allen Fay has compartmentalized the plethora of "psychiatric drugs" in a manner that will enable both medical and nonmedical practitioners to appreciate significant nuances of the "drug modality."

Chapter 7 addresses itself to some conceptual problems in the area of "personality theory," emphasizes the limitations of most theories of personality, and argues for a multimodal theory and therapy of "personality disorders."

Chapter 1

Introduction and Overview

Arnold A. Lazarus

Many therapists waste time. They tend to ask irrelevant questions and apply techniques of dubious validity. For example, while watching a colleague at work with a couple behind a one-way mirror, it became evident to the observers that both husband and wife criticized each other as people instead of aiming their remarks at one another's specific behaviors. Correction of this error seemed essential, but the therapist directed his attention to the supposition that the husband was like his father (argumentative) and the wife was like her mother (irascible). Regardless of the possible accuracy of this interpretation, it provided the couple with no way of monitoring and correcting their ongoing difficulties. They went home with their vicious tactics uncorrected and doubtless wrought further havoc during the week.

One would assume that all therapists are interested in applying efficient and effective procedures that will yield rapid and durable results. This seems not to be the case. Many are primarily interested in theorizing, in understanding, and in tapping putative dynamics. Some believe that the very act of delving into antecedent processes is curative (an unproven hypothesis) and they eschew direct methods of intervention in the here-and-now.

As soon as one identifies with a particular theory or subscribes to a definite school of thought, one develops vested interests in strengthening and confirming that system's basic theoretical underpinnings. Almost inevitably, one's selectivity of perception comes into play, so that pet theories become blessed with all sorts of confirming "data" and substantiating "evidence."

A multimodal orientation presupposes no identification with any

I am grateful to William L. Mulligan for help in preparing some of the material used in this introduction.

specific school of psychological thought. Nor is it a separate school in itself. Its practitioners are pragmatists who endorse scientific empiricism and logical positivism without succumbing to unnecessary reductionistic reasoning. Conceptually, the positivist position is taken in combination with the stance of a creative synthesist. Technical eclecticism (as opposed to theoretical eclecticism) is espoused (Lazarus, 1971a). This implies a full awareness that methods and techniques used in therapy may be effective for reasons other than those their originators propound. A metaphysical and mystical theorist may invent a new method of meditation based upon esoteric and spiritual beliefs. He may also provide convincing evidence that this technique significantly ameliorates pervasive anxiety in more than 80 per cent of anxious sufferers who practice it twice daily for two weeks. Disregarding the guru's untestable ideas about how and why his technique proves effective, we would test it out on our clients. If it seemed to work with them, we would note that as an empirical observation. At the same time, we would also narrow the specific focus so that we could modify the technique to better suit our clients' purposes, and thereby establish the precise indications and contraindications for its implementation. Yet, by borrowing and administering this technique, we would in no way be subscribing to any of the guru's unprovable tenets.

Although as multimodal therapists we do not subscribe to any particular theory, our findings and observations do have a place in a broad theoretical framework. This lies within the province of learning principles and, more especially, social learning, cognitive processes, and behavioral principles for which there is experimental evidence. We assume that a major portion of therapy is educational, and that the questions of how and why people learn and unlearn adaptive and maladaptive responses are crucial for effective therapeutic intervention. Thus, the major thrust in multimodal therapy is didactic. Our primary assumption is that the more people learn in therapy, the broader their coping responses become, the less likely are they to relapse.

Descriptively, we are beings who move, feel, sense, imagine, think, and relate. When psychological disturbances are present, they affect each of these functions. The way we move or behave can become adversely influenced by our imagination, by our cognitions, by our emotions and sensations, and by the way other people react to us. Similarly, if we change any facet of our interpersonal relationships, this change will alter our cognitions, emotions, sensations, self-image, and the way we behave in general. A change in any one area of our being will affect every other dimension. However, complete therapy requires that attention be devoted to *each* modality. The therapist needs to examine the client's salient behaviors, affective processes, each of his/her five senses, basic images, cognitions, and interpersonal relations.

How is this done? The content of each diagnostic inquiry depends upon the vicissitudes of the individual case; nonetheless, there is an overall structural framework that has general applicability. We are interested in discovering the client's intrusive behavior patterns (tics, compulsions, habits, mannerisms, etc.), negative emotions (times, places, and situations that elicit anger, anxiety, depression, etc.), unpleasant sensations (aches and pains, dizziness, flushing, etc.), intrusive images (disturbing recollections of unpleasant events or scenes), faulty cognitions (self-defeating values, attitudes, and beliefs), and interpersonal shortcomings (overcompetitive strivings, aggressive responses, childish demands, etc.). In addition to these maladaptive responses, we are also concerned with the client's *deficits* across each modality—the *absence* of useful behaviors, pleasant feelings, good sensations. Thus, the major assessment framework examines responses within each modality that are best *decreased*, as well as those that are best *increased*.

The model employed may be viewed as "actualization," "growth," or "educational" rather than as one based upon disease analogies, medicine, or pathology. Everyone can benefit from a change in behavior that eliminates unwanted or surplus reactions while stepping up the frequency, duration, and intensity of useful, creative, fulfilling responses. Similarly, the control or absence of unpleasant emotions coupled with an increase in positive feelings is a most worthy goal. In the sensory modality, while applying techniques to eliminate negative sensations (ranging from terrifying hallucinations to mild but chronic muscular tension), the growth-enhancing elements concern precise ways of deriving more pleasure and meaning from each of our five senses. Imagery—the most versatile modality, limited only by the constraints of our wildest fantasies—refers to the wide range of "mental pictures" which ultimately coalesce in a series of "self-images" which we try to make overridingly positive rather than negative. Faulty assumptions and irrational cognitions clearly undermine our day-to-day living, and are replaced by as many reality-oriented, factual, and rational assumptions as can be mustered. And good, close, and rewarding interpersonal relationships call for specific skills and an elaborate series of prosocial interactions which everyone would do well to cultivate.

We have referred to behavior, affect, sensation, imagery, cognition, and interpersonal processes. These six modalities may be said to constitute human "personality." These specific dimensions are all interactive and yet sufficiently discrete to preserve their own locus of control. In my opinion they are the mainstay of "psychology." The study of behavior, sensation, perception, cognition, and emotion is basic to academic psychology. More recently, especially within the province of "social psychology," the study of interpersonal processes has become central. Indeed, psychology—the scientific study of *behavior*—is essentially a body of knowledge in which data have been accumulated about various active, reactive, and interactive effects of sensation, perception, cognition, and affective responses (intrapersonal and interpersonal). But there is a non-psychological modality that cannot be ignored. Neurological and bio-chemical factors obviously influence behavior, affective responses, sensations, images, cognitions, and interpersonal responses. If we subsume these organic or physiological processes under the term "Drugs," as a generic symbol for this biological substrate, a useful acronym emerges. The first letter taken from *Behavior, Affect, Sensation, Imagery, Cognition, Interpersonal,* and *Drugs* spells BASIC ID. The mnemonic advantages of this acronym are extremely useful. It serves as a constant compass to orient therapists towards the client's entire network of interactive modalities.

Multimodal therapy is an extension and refinement of broad-spectrum behavior therapy, which in its turn evolved out of the original limited range of behavior therapy techniques and strategies. From the start behavior therapy stood in dramatic contrast to other psychotherapeutic approaches. Instead of applying untested and ill-defined methods to vague and general diagnostic labels with unspecified outcomes, behavior therapists attempted to use experimentally tested principles and techniques to achieve systematic and measurable results. A behavioral approach is exemplified by the *specificity* with which problems are identified and goals are delineated. Global presenting problems are dissected into precise maladaptive habits and response deficits. Once a careful analysis has elucidated the treatment objectives, specific techniques are selected to ameliorate particular problems. However, in their zeal for experimental rigor, and in their desire to circumvent the quagmire of internal or subjective phenomena, many behavior therapists have limited themselves to a rather narrow range of human experience (i.e., methods that can be conceptualized within a learning theory framework).

Broad-spectrum behavior therapy (Lazarus, 1965; 1971a) was developed to broaden the legitimate scope of behavioral inquiry and intervention. An increased repertoire of techniques was used to modify "private events," "covert processes," or "cognitions," in addition to overt behaviors. This approach has emphasized that the implementation of effective techniques can proceed independently of all theoretical explanations (cf. London, 1972). However, broad-spectrum behavior therapy is vulnerable to the criticism that few guidelines are provided for the selection of specific techniques under specifiable conditions.

Multimodal behavior therapy provides a more comprehensive and systematic assessment-therapeutic modus operandi. It was developed when follow-up studies revealed that behavior therapy, and even broad-spectrum behavior therapy, is subject to as much as a 40 per cent relapse rate within one to three years after treatment (Lazarus, 1971a; 1971b). To delineate the differences between ''behavior therapy,'' ''broad-spectrum behavior therapy,'' and ''multimodal behavior therapy,'' let us consider how each of these approaches might deal with a man who requested therapy for ''alcohol addiction.''

Behavior therapy: Following a detailed life history and the administration of tests such as the Willoughby Neurotic Inventory and a Fear Checklist (Wolpe, 1969), the patient's major hypersensitivities and social inadequacies would be elucidated. A regimen of aversion therapy, probably using electrical stimulation and negative imagery (e.g., picture yourself feeling nauseated after imbibing your favorite alcoholic beverage) would be supplemented by systematic desensitization, assertive training, relaxation therapy, and various ancillary methods where necessary— thought stopping, role playing, positive imagery, etc.

Broad-spectrum behavior therapy: In addition to the foregoing, various maintaining factors would be sought within several interpersonal transactions, and conjoint or family therapy would probably be implemented. Furthermore, cognitive processes would be parsed beyond the correction of obvious misconceptions, (i.e. fundamental irrational viewpoints and unadaptive self-talk would be disputed and replaced by ''internal sentences'' that undermine needless anxiety and anger). Close therapeutic attention would also be paid to leisure and recreational pursuits, vocational guidance, the development of ''self-worth,'' and to a host of environmental contingencies.

Multimodal behavior therapy: A meticulous inquiry into each of the modalities covered by the BASIC ID will usually uncover elements of behavior that elude the usual diagnostic scrutiny embodied in history-taking and the functional analysis of behavior. Thus, for instance, by examining in great detail the exact *sensory* stimuli that usually precede or accompany drinking behaviors, one may be in a position to teach the client how to extirpate a range of subtle sensations that, when combined with specific affective reactions, make excessive drinking likely. Similarly, a detailed assessment of salient behaviors, images, cognitions, etc., may be expected to shed light on several significant aspects of the patient's problem areas.

How does multimodal therapy differ from the methods employed by eclectic therapists who apply a multifaceted treatment approach? Most eclectic therapists draw on a variety of techniques from different disciplines, but when their actual treatment sessions are observed, it becomes evident that they generally do *not* cover the BASIC ID. Many therapists have their favorite modalities. I know several clinicians who deal solely with one or two modalities and ignore the other modalities of the BASIC ID or treat them *en passant*. Of course, through the "ripple effect," a change in one modality will influence all the other modalities to some extent, but our follow-up data suggest that durable outcomes call for specific interventions across all modalities. And the usual multifaceted, eclectic therapists do not devote the amount of time and attention to each area of the BASIC ID that we deem necessary. It may be slightly uncharitable to state that they often practice *multimuddle* rather than multimodal therapy!

Although other therapies—notably "cognitive behavior therapy" and "Gestalt therapy"—do cover each modality more extensively than does the traditional eclectic practitioner, they have their shortcomings. Broad-spectrum behavior therapists do not delve as thoroughly into sensory and imagery modalities as we are advocating; nor are they inclined to identify certain unexpressed emotions. Most Gestalt therapists tend to examine each modality quite thoroughly with the exception of the cognitive domain (which they are inclined to neglect in favor of "gut reactions") and they may overlook certain behavioral deficits (for which they lack the precise and disciplined retraining procedures employed by behavior therapists). While multimodal therapy draws heavily from rational-emotive therapy, Gestalt therapy, and behavior therapy, we hope to show that the present approach transcends each of these systems. And without falling prey to any theoretical befuddlement, as multimodal therapists we draw on Berne's transactional analysis, Mowrer's integrity therapy, and many other direct methods of application and intervention (Cf. Jurjevich, 1973). The pre-eminent consideration is to include each significant area of the BASIC ID.

References

Jurjevich, R. M. (Ed.) *Direct psychotherapy*. Vols. I and II. Coral Gables, Fla.: University of Miami Press, 1973.

Lazarus, A. A. Towards the understanding and effective treatment of alcoholism. *South African Medical Journal,* 1965, *39,* 736-741.

Lazarus, A. A. *Behavior therapy and beyond*. New York: McGraw-Hill, 1971. (a)

Lazarus, A. A. Notes on behavior therapy, the problem of relapse and some tentative solutions. *Psychotherapy: Theory, Research and Practice,* 1971, *8,* 192-194. (b)

London, P. The end of ideology in behavior modification. *American Psychologist,* 1972, *27,* 913-920.

Wolpe, J. *The practice of behavior therapy*. New York: Pergamon, 1969.

Chapter 2

Multimodal Behavior Therapy: Treating the BASIC ID

Arnold A. Lazarus

Progress in the field of psychotherapy is hindered by a factor that is endemic in our society: an item is considered newsworthy, and accolades are accorded when claims run counter to the dictates of common sense. Thus everything from megavitamins to anal lavages and primal screams gains staunch adherents who, in their frenetic search for a panacea, often breed confusion worse confounded. The present paper emphasizes that patients are usually troubled by a multitude of *specific* problems which should be dealt with by a similar multitude of *specific* treatments. The approach advocated herein is very different from those systems which cluster presenting problems into ill-defined constructs and then direct one or two treatment procedures at these constructs. The basic assumption is that durable (long-lasting) therapeutic results depend upon the amount of effort expended by patient and therapist across at least six or seven parameters.

Research into the interaction between technique and relationship variables in therapy has shown that an effective therapist "must be more than a 'nice guy' who can exude prescribed interpersonal conditions—he must have an armamentarium of scientifically derived skills and techniques to supplement his effective interpersonal relations" (Woody, 1971, p. 8). Deliberately excluded from the present formulation is the empathic, non-judgmental warmth, wit, and wisdom which characterize those therapists who help rather than harm their clients (Bergin, 1971). If this were an

From The *Journal of Nervous and Mental Disease, 156,* 404-411. Copyright 1973, The Williams & Wilkins Company. Reprinted by permission.

Several colleagues made incisive criticisms of the initial draft. I am especially grateful to Bob Karlin, Bill Mulligan, Carole Pearl, and Terry Wilson.

article on surgical techniques and procedures, we would presuppose that individuals who apply the prescribed methods are free from pronounced tremors and possess more than a modicum of manual dexterity. Thus, it is hoped that multimodal behavioral procedures will attract nonmechanistic therapists who are flexible, empathic, and genuinely concerned about the welfare of their clients.

The main impetus for all forms of treatment probably stems from the general urgency of human problems and the need for practical assistance. This has lent acceptance to technically faulty work that would not pass muster in other fields, and every informed practitioner is all too well aware of the fragmentary and contradictory theories that hold sway in the absence of experimental evidence. Apart from the plethora of different techniques, systems, and theories, we have conflicting models and paradigm clashes as exemplified by the differences between radical behaviorists and devout phenomenologists. Attempts to blend divergent models into integrative or eclectic harmony may often result in no more than syncretistic muddles (Reisman, 1971; Woody, 1971). And yet without general guiding principles that cut across all systems of therapy, we are left with cabalistic vignettes in place of experimental data or even clinical evidence. Multimodal behavior therapy encompasses: (1) specification of goals and problems; (2) specification of treatment techniques to achieve these goals and remedy these problems; and (3) systematic measurement of the relative success of these techniques.

Since all patients are influenced by processes that lie beyond the therapist's control and comprehension, the field of psychological treatment and intervention is likely to foster superstitious fallacies as readily as well-established facts. The tendency to ascribe causative properties to the *last* event in any sequence is all too well known (e.g., her stomach pains must be due to the sausage she just ate for lunch). Thus a patient, after grappling with a problem for years, starts massaging his left kneecap while plucking his right ear lobe and experiences immediate and lasting relief from tenacious symptoms. If a therapist happens to be close at hand, a new technique is likely to be born and placed alongside the parade of other "breakthroughs" with the screamers, confronters, disclosers, relaxers, dreamers, and desensitizers. And if the therapist happens to be sufficiently naive, enthusiastic, and charismatic, we will probably never convince him, his students, or his successful patients that the knee-and-ear technique per se is not the significant agent of change. To guard against this penchant, we must insist upon the precise specification of the operations by which systematic assessment of the efficacy of a treatment for a specific problem is made on a regular basis.

The foregoing variables plus the power struggle between psychiatrists and psychologists and the various schools therein tend to hamper progress.

The field, over the span of the past eight years, is described by two leading research clinicians as "chaotic" (Colby, 1964; Frank, 1971). Part of the confusion may also be ascribed to the fact that there is a human (but unscientific) penchant to search for unitary treatments and cures. How nice if insight alone or a soul-searing scream could pave the way to mental health. How simple and convenient for countless addicts if aversion therapy afforded long-lasting results. And what a boon to phobic sufferers if their morbid fears were enduringly assuaged by systematic desensitization and assertive training methods. But while short-lived relief is available to most, we must concur with Lesse that for most syndromes "there is very little proof at this time that any one given technique is superior to another in the long-range therapy of a particular type of psychogenic problem" (1972, p. 330).

Notwithstanding the biases that lead to theoretical befuddlement, most clinicians would probably agree with the pragmatic assumption that the more a patient learns in therapy, the less likely he is to relapse afterwards. Thus, an alcoholic treated only by aversion therapy would be more likely to relapse than his counterpart who had also received relaxation therapy (Blake, 1965). The benefits that accrue from aversion therapy plus relaxation training would be further potentiated by the addition of assertive training, family therapy, and vocational guidance (Lazarus, 1965). This general statement implies that *lasting change* is at the very least a function of combined *techniques, strategies,* and *modalities*. This vitiates the search for a panacea, or a single therapeutic modality. But a point of diminishing returns obviously exists. If two aspirins are good for you, ten are not five times better. When and why should we stop pushing everything from transcendental meditation to hot and cold sitz baths at our clients? Conversely, how, when, where, and why do we infer that in a given instance, meditation plus sensitivity training is preferable to psychodrama and contingency contracting? Above all, how can we wield Occam's razor to dissect the chaos of these diverse psychotherapeutic enterprises into meaningful and congruent components?

Seven Modalities

An arbitrary division created *sui generis* would simply turn back the clock on the composite theories and facts that psychologists have amassed to date. It is no accident that ever since the publication of Brentano's *Psychologie vom empirischen Standpunkte* in 1874, acts like ideation, together with feeling states and sensory judgments, have constituted the main subject matter of general psychology. In other words, psychology as the scientific study of behavior has long been concerned with sensation, imagery, cognition, emotion, and interpersonal relationships. If we examine psychotherapeutic processes in the light of each of these basic modalities, seemingly disparate systems are brought into clearer focus, and the necessary and sufficient conditions for long-lasting therapeutic change might readily be discerned.

Every patient-therapist interaction involves *behavior* (be it lying down on a couch and free associating, or actively role-playing a significant encounter), *affect* (be it the silent joy of nonjudgmental acceptance, or the sobbing release of pent-up anger), *sensation* (which covers a wide range of sensory stimuli from the spontaneous awareness of bodily discomfort to the deliberate cultivation of specific sensual delights), *imagery* (be it the fleeting glimpse of a childhood memory, or the contrived perception of a calm-producing scene), and *cognition* (the insights, philosophies, ideas, and judgments that constitute our fundamental values, attitudes, and beliefs). All of these take place within the context of an *interpersonal* relationship, or various interpersonal relationships. An added dimension with many patients is their need for medication or *drugs* (e.g., phenothiazine derivatives and various antidepressants and mood regulators). Taking the first letter of each of the foregoing italicized words, we have the acronym BASIC ID. Obviously, the proposed seven modalities are interdependent and interactive.

If we approach a patient *de novo* and inquire in detail about his salient behaviors, affective responses, sensations, images, cognitions, interpersonal relationships, and his need for drugs or medication, we will probably know more about him than we can hope to obtain from routine history taking and psychological tests. Whether or not these general guidelines can provide all that we need to know in order to be of therapeutic service is an empirical question.*

Other Systems

While it is important to determine whether the BASIC ID and the various combinations thereof are sufficiently exhaustive to encompass most vagaries of human conduct, it is perhaps more compelling first to view, very briefly, a few existing systems of therapy in the light of these modalities. Most systems touch lightly on the majority of modalities; very

---

* Some may argue that the absence of a "spiritual" dimension is an obvious hiatus, although in the interests of parsimony, it can be shown that cognitive-affective interchanges readily provide the necessary vinculum.

few pay specific and direct attention to each particular zone. Psycho-analysis deals almost exclusively with cognitive-affective interchanges. The neo-Reichian school of bioenergetics (Lowen, 1967) focuses upon behavior (in the form of "body language"), and the sensory-affective dimension. Encounter groups and Gestalt therapy display a similar suspicion of the "head" and are inclined to neglect cognitive material for the sake of affective and sensory responses. Gestalt therapists also employ role-playing and imagery techniques. The Masters and Johnson (1970) sex-training regimen deals explicitly with sexual behavior, affective processes, the "sensate focus," various re-educative features, and the correction of misconceptions, all within a dyadic context, preceded by routine medical and laboratory examinations. They do not avail themselves of imagery techniques (e.g., desensitization, self-hypnosis, or fantasy projection), a fact which may limit their overall success rate. (See the final chapter of this book for further elaboration on this point.)

Perhaps it is worth stressing at this point that the major hypothesis, backed by the writer's clinical data, is that *durable results are in direct proportion to the number of specific modalities deliberately invoked by any therapeutic system*. Psychoanalysis, for instance, is grossly limited because penetrating insights can hardly be expected to restore effective functioning in people with deficient response repertoires—they need explicit training, modeling, and shaping for the acquisition of adaptive social patterns. Conversely, nothing short of coercive manipulation is likely to develop new response patterns that are at variance with people's fundamental belief systems. Indeed, insight, self-understanding, and the correction of irrational beliefs must usually precede behavior change whenever faulty assumptions govern the channels of manifest behavior. In other instances, behavior change must occur before "insight" can develop (Lazarus, 1971a). Thus, cognitive restructuring and overt behavior training are often reciprocal. This should not be misconstrued as implying that a judicious blend of psychoanalysis and behavior therapy is being advocated. Psychoanalytic theory is unscientific and needlessly complex; behavioristic theory is often mechanistic and needlessly simplistic. The points being emphasized transcend any given system or school of therapy. However, adherence to social learning theory (Bandura, 1969) as the most elegant theoretical system to explain our therapeutic sorties places the writer's identification within the province of behavior therapy—hence "multimodal behavior therapy." Perhaps the plainest way of expressing our major thesis is to stress that comprehensive treatment at the very least calls for the correction of irrational beliefs, deviant behaviors, unpleasant feelings, intrusive images, stressful relationships, negative sensations, and possible biochemical imbalance. To the extent that problem identification (diagnosis) systematically explores each of these modalities, whereupon therapeutic intervention remedies whatever deficits and maladaptive patterns emerge, treatment outcomes will be positive and long-lasting. To ignore any of these modalities is to practice a brand of therapy that is incomplete. Of course, not every case requires attention to each modality, but this conclusion can only be reached after each area has been carefully investigated during problem identification (i.e., diagnosis). A similar position stressing comprehensive assessment and therapy has been advocated by Kanfer and Saslow (1968).

Problem Identification

Faulty problem identification (inadequate assessment) is probably the greatest impediment to successful therapy. The major advantage of a multimodal orientation is that it provides a systematic framework for conceptualizing presenting complaints within a meaningful context. A young man with the seemingly monosymptomatic complaint of "claustrophobia" was seen to be troubled by much more than "confined or crowded spaces" as soon as the basic modalities had been scanned. The main impact upon his *behavior* was his inability to attend social gatherings, plus the inconvenience of avoiding elevators, public transportation, and locked doors. The *affective* concomitants of his avoidance behavior were high levels of general anxiety and frequent panic attacks (e.g., when a barber shop became crowded, and at the check-out counter of a supermarket). The *sensory* modality revealed that he was constantly tense and suffered from muscle spasms. His *imagery* seemed to focus on death, burials, and other morbid themes. The *cognitive* area revealed a tendency to catastrophize and to demean himself. At the *interpersonal* level, his wife was inclined to mother him and to reinforce his avoidance behavior. This information, *obtained after a cursory 10- to 15-minute inquiry,* immediately underscored crucial antecedent and maintaining factors that warranted more detailed exploration as a prelude to meaningful therapeutic intervention.

In contrast with the foregoing case, little more than *sensory unawareness* in a 22-year-old woman seemed to be the basis for complaints of pervasive anxiety, existential panic, and generalized depression. She was so preoccupied with lofty thoughts and abstract ideation that she remained impervious to most visual, auditory, tactile, and other sensory stimuli. Treatment was simply a matter of instructing her to attend to a wide range of specific sensations. "I want you to relax in a bath of warm water and to examine exact temperature contrasts in various parts of your body and study all the accompanying sensations." "When you walk into a room I want you to pay special attention to every object, and afterwards, write down a description from memory." "Spend the next ten minutes listening to all the sounds that you can hear and observe their effects upon you." "Pick up that orange. Look at it. Feel its weight, its texture, its temperature. Now start peeling it with that knife. Stop peeling and smell the orange. Run your tongue over the outside of the peel. Now feel the difference between the outside and the inside of the peel. . . ." These simple exercises in sensory awareness were extraordinarily effective in bringing her in touch with her environment and in diminishing her panic, anxiety, and depression. She was then amenable to more basic therapy beyond her presenting complaints.

The multimodal approach to therapy is similar to what is called "the problem-oriented record approach." This emphasis upon problem specification is just coming into its own in psychiatry as evidenced in an article by Hayes-Roth, Longabaugh, and Ryback (1972). In medicine this approach to record keeping and treatment is slightly older, being best illustrated by Weed's work (1968). Multimodal behavior therapy not only underscores the value of this new approach, but also provides a conceptual framework for its psychiatric implementation. Let us now turn to a case illustration of its use.

Case Illustration

A case presentation should lend substance to the string of assertions outlined on the foregoing pages.

Mary Ann, aged 24, was diagnosed as a chronic undifferentiated schizophrenic. Shortly after her third admission to a mental hospital, her parents referred her to the writer for treatment. According to the hospital reports, her prognosis was poor. She was overweight, apathetic, and withdrawn, but against a background of lethargic indifference, one would detect an ephemeral smile, a sparkle of humor, a sudden glow of warmth, a witty remark, an apposite comment, a poignant revelation. She was heavily medicated (Trilafon 8 mg. t.i.d., Vivactil 10 mg. t.i.d., Cogentin 2 mg. b.d.), and throughout the course of therapy she continued seeing a psychiatrist once a month who adjusted her intake of drugs.

A life history questionnaire, followed by an initial interview, revealed that well-intentioned but misguided parents had created a breeding ground for guilty attitudes, especially in matters pertaining to sex. Moreover, an older sister, five years her senior, had aggravated the situation "by tormenting me from the day I was born." Her vulnerability to peer pressure during puberty had rendered her prone to "everything but heroin."

Nevertheless, she had excelled at school, and her first noticeable break-down occurred at age 18, shortly after graduating from high school. "I was on a religious kick and kept hearing voices." Her second hospital admission followed a suicidal gesture at age 21, and her third admission was heralded by her sister's sudden demise soon after the patient turned 24.

Since she was a mine of sexual misinformation, her uncertainties and conflicts with regard to sex became an obvious area for therapeutic intervention. The book *Sex Without Guilt* by Albert Ellis (1965 Grove Press edition) served as a useful springboard toward the correction of more basic areas of sexual uncertainty and anxiety. Meanwhile, careful questioning revealed the Modality Profile given below.

The Modality Profile may strike the reader as a fragmented or mechanistic barrage of techniques that would call for a disjointed array of therapeutic maneuvers. In actual practice, the procedures follow logically and blend smoothly into meaningful interventions.

During the course of therapy, as more data emerged and as a clearer picture of the patient became apparent, the Modality Profile was constantly revised. Therapy was mainly a process of devising ways and means to remedy Mary Ann's shortcomings and problem areas throughout the basic modalities. The concept of "technical eclecticism" came into its own (Lazarus, 1967). In other words, a wide array of therapeutic methods drawn from numerous disciplines was applied, but to remain theoretically consistent, the active ingredients of every technique were sought within the province of social learning theory.

In Mary Ann's case, the array of therapeutic methods selected to restructure her life included familiar behavior therapy techniques such as desensitization, assertive training, role-playing, and modeling, but many additional procedures were employed such as time projection, cognitive restructuring, eidetic imagery, and exaggerated role-taking as described in some of the writer's recent publications (1971a, 1972). The empty chair technique (Perls, 1969) and other methods borrowed from Gestalt therapy and encounter group procedures were added to the treatment regimen. Mary Ann was also seen with her parents for eight sessions, and was in a group for 30 weeks.

During the course of therapy she became engaged and was seen with her fiancé for premarital counseling for several sessions.

The treatment period covered the span of 13 months at the end of which time she was coping admirably without medication and has continued to do so now for more than a year. This case was chosen for illustrative purposes because so often, people diagnosed as "psychotic" receive little more than chemotherapy and emotional support. Yet, in the writer's experience, once the florid symptoms are controlled by medication, many people are amenable to multimodal behavior therapy. It is tragic

Modality	Problem	Proposed Treatment
Behavior	Inappropriate withdrawal responses	Assertive training
	Frequent crying	Nonreinforcement
	Unkempt appearance	Grooming instructions
	Excessive eating	Low calorie regimen
	Negative self-statements	Positive self-talk assignments
	Poor eye contact	Rehearsal techniques
	Mumbling of words with poor voice projection	Verbal projection exercises
	Avoidance of heterosexual situations	Re-education and desensitization
Affect	Unable to express overt anger	Role playing
	Frequent anxiety	Relaxation training and reassurance
	Absence of enthuaism and spontaneous joy	Positive imagery procedures
	Panic attacks (Usually precipitated by criticism from authority figures)	Desensitization and assertive training
	Suicidal feelings	Time projection techniques
	Emptiness and aloneness	General relationship building
Sensation	Stomach spasms	Abdominal breathing and relaxing
	Out of touch with most sensual pleasures	Sensate focus method
	Tension in jaw and neck	Differential relaxation
	Frequent lower back pains	Orthopedic exercises
	Inner tremors	Gendlin's focusing method (Lazarus, 1971a, p.232)
Imagery	Distressing scenes of sister's funeral	Desensitization
	Mother's angry face shouting "You fool!"	Empty chair technique
	Performing fellatio on God	Blow up technique (implosion)
	Recurring dreams about airplane bombings	Eidetic imagery invoking feelings of being safe
Cognition	Irrational self-talk: "I am evil." "I must suffer." "Sex is dirty." "I am inferior."	Deliberate rational disputation and corrective self-talk
	Syllogistic reasoning, overgeneralization	Parsing of irrational sentences
	Sexual misinformation	Sexual education
Interpersonal relationships	Characterized by childlike dependence	Specific self-sufficiency assignments
	Easily Exploited /submissive	Assertive training
	Overly suspicious	Exaggerated role taking
	Secondary gains from parental concern	Explain reinforcement principles to parents and try to enlist their help
	Manipulative tendencies	Training in direct and confrontative behaviors

that large numbers of people who can be reached and helped by multimodal behavior therapy are often left to vegetate.

Conclusions

Those who favor working with one or two specific modalities may inquire what evidence there is to support the contention that multimodal treatment is necessary. At present, the writer's follow-up studies have shown that relapse all too commonly ensues after the usual behavior therapy programs, despite the fact that behavioral treatments usually cover more modalities than most other forms of therapy. Of course, the run-of-the-mill behavior therapist does not devote as much attention to imagery techniques as we are advocating (even when using covert reinforcement procedures and imaginal desensitization), nor does he delve meticulously enough into cognitive material, being especially neglectful of various philosophical values and their bearing on self-worth.

Another fact worth emphasizing is that in order to offset "future shock," multimodal therapy attempts to anticipate areas of stress that the client is likely to experience in time to come. Thus, one may use imaginal rehearsal to prepare people to cope with the marriage of a child, a possible change in occupation, the purchase of a new home, the process of aging, and so forth. In my experience, these psychological "fire drills" can serve an important preventive function.

As one investigates each modality, a clear understanding of the individual and his interpersonal context emerges. Even with a "simple phobia," new light is shed, and unexpected information is often gleaned when examining the behavioral, affective, sensory, imaginal, cognitive, and interpersonal consequences of the avoidance responses. Whenever a plateau is reached in therapy and progress falters, the writer has found it enormously productive to examine each modality in turn in order to determine a possibly neglected area of concern. More often than not, new material emerges and therapy proceeds apace.

References

Bandura, A. *Principles of behavior modification*. New York: Holt, Rinehart and Winston, 1969.

Bergin, A. E. The evaluation of therapeutic outcomes. In Bergin, A. E., & Garfield, S. L. Eds. *Handbook of psychotherapy and behavior change*, pp. 217-270. New York: Wiley, 1971.

Blake, B. G. The application of behavior therapy to the treatment of alcoholism. *Behavior Research and Therapy*, 1965, *3*, 75-85.

Colby, K. M. Psychotherapeutic processes. *Annual Review of Psychology*, 1964, *15*, 347-370.

Frank, J. D. Therapeutic factors in psychotherapy. *American Journal of Psychotherapy*, 1971, *25*, 350-361.

Hayes-Roth, F., Longabaugh, R., & Ryback, R. The problem-oriented medical record and psychiatry. *British Journal of Psychiatry*, 1972, *121*, 27-34.

Kanfer, F. H., & Saslow, G. Behavioral diagnosis. In C. M. Franks, Ed. *Behavior therapy: Appraisal and status*, pp. 417-444. New York: McGraw-Hill, 1969.

Lazarus, A. A. Towards the understanding and effective treatment of alcoholism. *South African Medical Journal*, 1965, *39*, 736-741.

Lazarus, A. A. In support of technical eclecticism. *Psychological Reports*, 1967, *21*, 415-416.

Lazarus, A. A. *Behavior therapy and beyond*. New York: McGraw-Hill, 1971. (a)

Lazarus, A. A. Notes on behavior therapy, the problem of relapse and some tentative solutions. *Psychotherapy: Theory, Research & Practice*, 1971, *8*, 192-196. (b)

Lazarus, A. A., Ed. *Clinical behavior therapy*. New York: Brunner/Mazel, 1972.

Lesse, S. Anxiety—Its relationship to the development and amelioration of obsessive-compulsive disorders. *American Journal of Psychotherapy*, 1972, *26*, 330-337.

Lowen, A. *The betrayal of the body*. New York: Macmillan, 1967.

Masters, W. H., & Johnson, V. E. *Human sexual inadequacy*. Boston: Little Brown, 1970.

Perls, F. S. *Gestalt therapy verbatim*. Lafayette, California: Real People Press, 1969.

Reisman, J. M. *Toward the integration of psychotherapy*. New York: Wiley, 1971.

Weed, L. L. Medical records that guide and teach. *New England Journal of Medicine*, 1968, *278*, 593-600.

Woody, R. H. *Psychobehavioral counseling and therapy*. New York: Appleton-Century-Crofts, 1971.

Chapter 3

The Multimodal Model as a Framework for Decision-Making in Psychotherapy

Robert L. Woolfolk

Psychotherapy, from beginning to end, entails a series of explicit and implicit decisions on the part of the therapist. These decisions essentially govern the planning, implementation, and evaluation of various therapeutic strategies. In order to be of value to clinicians, any conceptual basis for therapy must enrich one's repertoire of effective problem-solving decisions. All systems attempt to do this to a greater or lesser degree, but among present systems virtually all fall into one of two categories: (1) those with great decision-making power across a narrowly restricted range of clinical areas, e.g., operant approaches, (2) those with little decision-making power across a wide range of clinical areas, e.g., psychodynamic psychotherapy.

General Systems Theory (Churchman, 1968; Stufflebeam, et al., 1971) provides us with criteria against which any decision-making system can be measured or compared. Although there are many obvious differences between therapeutic cases and most contexts in which management science has been developed, basic concepts of systems theory can nevertheless have direct relevance to the therapeutic situation.

If decisions in therapy are to be specifiable, repeatable, and arguable on some basis other than intuition, they must flow from, and have as their basis, an objective procedure of evaluation. Here a process of evaluation refers simply to an "information system" for gathering and analyzing data with respect to clearly stated goals and objectives. Thus, a conceptual framework for therapy which permits systematic decision-making must

From *Psychological Reports*, 1974, *34*, 831-834. Reprinted by permission.

include provisions for the setting of objectives and the evaluation of activities designed to accomplish those objectives. More specifically, four basic conditions which would facilitate the systematic processing of information in therapy are: (1) assessment should yield direct implications for treatment, (2) therapeutic objectives should be specified in measurable terms, (3) therapeutic techniques should be specified for each objective (these techniques must be recognizable and replicable), and (4) the process and outcome of therapy should be evaluated.

One formulation which attempts to achieve greater systematization in treating the full range of psychological problems of living is the Multimodal Therapy of Lazarus (1973). This model attempts to extend the specificity and empirical method of behavioral approaches to the broader arena of general practice. Its further aim is in the integration of various techniques of disparate schools of psychotherapy and the provision of a framework to structure their implementation.

It is not within the scope of this paper to examine Lazarus' claims concerning therapeutic efficacy which results from the utilization of this schema. Instead, we shall attempt to examine the *formal* characteristics of Multimodal Therapy as a system—"a set of parts coordinated to accomplish a set of goals" (Churchman, 1968). In so doing we shall attempt to answer the question: "Does the multimodal method facilitate the systematic processing of information within the therapeutic context?"

With respect to assessment, the multimodal approach seems to allow for not only a clear nexus between diagnosis and treatment but also a suitable level of comprehensiveness. Early in therapy, diffuse, general, and specific presenting complaints are analyzed across each of the modalities.

The importance here of the BASIC ID is that *all* data inputs can be analyzed across this schema. The assessment inquiry is thus structured so that an exploration of presenting problems may lead to the uncovering of elements which might be overlooked by other systems.

For example, the following Modality Profile is that of a woman who was unable to produce assertive behavior in interactions with her husband. Such individuals often have been diagnosed as "lacking in assertiveness" and treated by the standard role-playing techniques.

The construction of a Modality Profile requires the integration of the processes of assessment, the setting of objectives, and the specification of treatment techniques. It must be stressed here that in the multimodal system, diagnosis does not focus upon the identification of personality traits or dwell upon the discovery of historical antecedents but is essentially a problem-centered endeavor which aims to identify specific and crucial areas of psychological malfunction. This identification and precise specification of each problem within a particular modality certainly aids in the fashioning of therapeutic objectives. In clear cases of behavioral excesses or deficits (Kanfer & Saslow, 1969), the therapeutic objectives are obvious. In the Modality Profile below, for example, the objective for treatment of lack of eye contact would be the increase of this behavior. In the very complex interpersonal realm this kind of precision in objectives is not easily achieved, but it is always the goal.

Modality	Problem	Proposed Treatment
Behavior	Speech nonfluency Lack of eye contact Low volume	Behavior rehearsal (employing modeling and videotaped feedback
Affect	Fear in presence of husband Attenuated anger	Desensitization Gestalt awareness exercises
Sensory	Muscular tension	Relaxation training
Imagery	Unrealistic scenes of retaliation	Self-hypnosis with success imagery
Cognition	Defeatist self-verbalization Irrational beliefs concerning inferiority of women	Modification of content of self-talk Rational disputation and bibliotherapy
Interpersonal relationships	Lack of interpersonal sensitivity Control of husband through passivity and withholding Reinforcement of passive role by husband	Train in perception of nonverbal cues Relationship therapy focused on negotiation of needs Train husband to recognize and reinforce assertive behavior
Drugs	Periodic depression	If necessary, discuss with M.D. possible use of chemotherapy

Since the multimodal therapeutic approach is essentially problem-centered, assessment and the setting of objectives are logically related. A relationship also exists between assessment and treatment, for within a problem-centered approach the aim of diagnosis is always the design of the most effective treatment for each particular problem (Mischel, 1968). The selection of appropriate treatments (techniques) is very likely the most crucial of all decisions made by the therapist. And it is here that a multimodal framework greatly aids such decisions by assisting in the analysis of general complaints into their specific components, which can then be more readily treated by particular techniques. Although it is certainly not always the case that the assignment of a problem to one of the seven modalities per se yields implications for treatment, certain techniques such as those of Ellis' cognitive therapy are clearly appropriate for use with a particular modality. Consistent with a posture of *technical eclecticism*, Lazarus and his coworkers have tended to be more interested in the development and refinement of specific, replicable procedures than in the integration of clinical theory and practice. This deemphasis of deduction from theory and consequent emphasis of induction from clinical phenomena is a viable posture only when clinical phenomena may be organizable on some systematic basis (London, 1972).

Although Lazarus (1973) has indicated that the modality profile of any given client would likely be revised during the course of therapy, it is not clear from his published work what procedures would be used in this process of revision. Clearly assessment, setting of objectives, and selection of treatments are meant to be ongoing throughout therapy, but the role of evaluation within multimodal therapy is yet to be addressed.

The feature of the multimodal approach which renders it conducive throughout to evaluation is its explicitness. For at any given point in therapy, the multimodal system provides precise, highly structured information which can feed back into the system. The same schema which generated the interrelated processes of assessment, setting of objectives, and the treatment itself, can also be used to structure the evaluation of accuracy of assessment, appropriateness of objectives, and efficacy of treatment. Evaluation would occur within each modality and should be of three different varieties: (1) evaluation of implementation is concerned with the adequacy of the application of each therapeutic strategy. It is aimed at determining the extent to which therapeutic techniques are appropriately administered and efficiently adapted. (2) Evaluation of progress involves the inspection of the degree to which therapy is producing the movement in the direction of each stated objective. The progress of therapy is evaluated periodically and systematically relative to diagnosis, objectives, and techniques. Thus, numerous implications for corrective action are generated. (3) Evaluation of outcome occurs at the termination of therapy and provides the answer to the question "To what extent were the therapeutic objectives accomplished?"

The therapist can thus review the cycles of diagnosis, setting of objectives, treatment, and evaluation within each modality and obtain a graphic and highly differentiated picture of what has occurred in therapy. Questions concerning the adequacy of assessments, appropriateness of objectives, and the degree to which interventions were correctly decided upon and applied, can be examined in a fashion which points toward the possibility of real accountability in psychotherapy.

References

Churchman, C. W. *The systems approach*. New York: Dell, 1968.

Kanfer, F. H., & Saslow, G. Behavioral diagnosis. In C. M. Franks (Ed.), *Behavior therapy: appraisal and status*, pp. 417-444. New York: McGraw-Hill, 1969.

Lazarus, A. A. *Behavior therapy and beyond*. New York: McGraw-Hill, 1971.

Lazarus, A. A. Multimodal behavior therapy: Treating the "BASIC-ID." *Journal of Nervous and Mental Disease*, 1973, *156*, 404-411.

London, P. The end of ideology in behavior modification. *American Psychologist*, 1972, *27*, 913-920.

Mischel, W. *Personality and assessment*. New York: Wiley, 1968.

Stufflebeam, D. L., Foley, W. J., Gebhart, W. J., Guba, E. G., Hammond, R. L., Merriman, H. O., & Provus, M. M. *Educational evaluation and decision making*. Ithaca, Ill.: F. E. Peacock, 1971.

Chapter 4

Multimodal Assessment

Arnold A. Lazarus

Introduction

Before describing some specific assessment procedures across the BASIC ID, let us discuss general areas of overlap, as well as a few distinctive points of difference, between multimodal assessment and other diagnostic approaches.

If a therapist is genuinely interested in promoting constructive changes in a client (and here the term ''client'' may refer to an individual, a couple, a family, or a group) it is essential that he or she first obtain a comprehensive understanding of the total context in which the behaviors occur. Cultural and socioeconomic factors provide the overall setting for meaningful intervention. It is not surprising, for example, that assertion training with clients reared in India is often entirely different from assertion training with people reared in New York City. People whose backgrounds have emphasized passive resistance and who regard interpersonal deference as a special virtue do not take readily to the notion that it generally pays to stand up for one's rights. In this connection, I have taught several Indian men who emigrated to the United States to stand up to their American employers without my interfering in any way with the delicate hierarchical structure between father and son, or brother and older brother. In essence, the BASIC ID comes into operation only *after* assessing the broad environmental realities.

The multimodal assessment process begins with the initial interview. In general, the following points are covered:
1. Presenting complaints are obtained.
2. Some understanding of precipitating events is gained.
3. Various antecedent factors are delineated.
4. Maintaining factors are also examined.

5. Some idea is gathered of what the client hopes to derive from therapy.

6. Overt signs of "psychopathology" are carefully noted (e.g., incongruity of affect, word salad, flight of ideas, blocking, etc.).

7. Indications and contraindications for the implementation of various therapeutic styles and techniques are gleaned.

8. Some definite indications emerge as to whether a mutually satisfying relationship can be developed.

The initial phase of multimodal assessment is not too different from that of most broad-spectrum clinicians. Rapport is established and an attempt is made to develop a productive liaison. In history-taking, several distinctive points of emphasis may be apparent (see the Life History Questionnaire in Appendix 1), but the fundamental differences between multimodal assessment and most other forms of psychiatric inquiry usually become clear only after the second or third session.

Excerpts from an edited protocol will illustrate the manner in which assessment and therapy intermingle. The following dialogue was obtained during the third session with a 26-year-old female ex-school teacher who had been married for seven years. The first session had revealed that she suffered from chronic anxiety coupled with insomnia and bouts of depression. Her main reason for seeking therapy was to overcome "problems of communication" in her marriage. There were no signs of any "mental disturbance." Since the client repeatedly alluded to a basic lack of confidence in her intellectual abilities, a formal test was administered during the second session. Her combined WAIS IQ was 128. The many test items afforded the therapist considerable data regarding several significant facets of her *behavior*. She came to the third session in a state of obvious agitation over an argument with her husband.

Client:	I had a big fight with my husband this morning.
Therapist:	What was it all about?
Client:	As always, just over nonsense. I mean it's so stupid. Pete is so goddam stubborn! It all boils down to the fact that I want more children and he doesn't.
Therapist:	I'd like to hear all your *thoughts* and *feelings* about having children.
	(A discussion followed which underscored the fact that she had been an only child and wished for a large family. Her two children, a boy of six and a girl of four, were considered by her husband to be a "balanced number," but she wanted two more children "at least.")
Client:	The fight got started when I mentioned to Pete that my doctor had told me to come off the pill at the end of this month.

Therapist:	Let's try to be very specific. Can you tell me how each of you *behaved*? In other words, I'm asking how you would have looked in the eyes of an observer. Did you discuss the matter quietly, or were voices raised . . . ?
Client:	Pete started yelling almost immediately. He behaved like an animal. I mean. . .
Therapist:	Surely he didn't start yelling as soon as you said you were going off the pill? My guess would be that something else happened beforehand.
Client:	As clearly as I can recall, Pete started in with something like, "Look here! Let's not get into that crap about having more kids." And I got mad.
Therapist:	So you got mad before Pete started yelling?
Client:	Well, I resented the fact that he attacked me right away about the pregnancy idea.
Therapist:	I understand. But could you have handled it differently? You immediately expressed anger and started up a fight. What if you had decided to behave assertively rather than aggressively? (Role-playing then followed during which the therapist modeled assertive responses vis-à-vis husband and wife interaction. This interpersonal focus revealed other dyadic struggles that were subsequently resolved by means of behavior rehearsal.)
Client:	Yes, I guess it does make sense for me to learn "I messages" in place of "You messages."
Therapist:	Getting back to the fight, apart from anger, what other *feelings* did you have?
Client:	(Weeps) I felt so helpless! (Blows her nose)
Therapist:	Helpless?
Client:	Perhaps frightened is a better word.
Therapist:	Helpless and frightened. About what?
Client:	I really don't know.
Therapist:	Let's try a simple *imagery* test. Can you close your eyes and picture yourself ten years from now with your husband and two children?
Client:	(After a pause) Yes.
Therapist:	Can you describe the scene?
Client:	Pete is off to work. . . . The kids are both teenagers. . . . I guess I'd be back at college, or I'd go back to teaching, or maybe do something else.
Therapist:	Such as?
Client:	I don't know.
Therapist:	But if you still had two young children to take care. . . .
Client:	(Laughing) You see right through me, don't you. Yes, I guess I really do lack the confidence to go out into the world.
Therapist:	And I would suggest that this is not the best reason for bringing more children into the world. What do you say to the idea that we concentrate on really increasing your level of self-con-

fidence? After that you can see whether or not you still want to have more children. If your answer is "yes" it will be for entirely different reasons.

Discussion

A lot of progress was made in that third session. By focusing on thoughts, feelings, behaviors, images, and certain interpersonal facets, a central source of anxiety was rapidly identified. Throughout the assessment procedures, immediate therapy was provided when clear-cut difficulties arose. This was not an unusual multimodal session. The foregoing excerpt was not intended to convey something startling or dramatic, but rather to demonstrate the way therapy can be kept "on target" and how important information is elicited by continually monitoring the various modalities.

We have found it extremely useful to keep the BASIC ID formulation in mind as a "compass" or "cognitive map" throughout the course of therapy. After a little practice, it is easy to punctuate a client's discourse with each relevant modality. "I woke up early this morning (*behavior*)* with a tense feeling in my shoulders (*sensory*) and reached for an aspirin and a Valium (*drugs*). Mike was also awake, so we chatted for a while (*interpersonal*) and I recounted an interesting dream (*imagery*). Later, he said something that made me mad (*affect*), so I shared my own expectations (*cognitive*) so as to avoid further misunderstandings." When keeping track mentally of the various modalities that clients refer to while talking, the clinician will often find that by asking a question about a modality that had been omitted, crucial information is likely to emerge. The omission of a significant modality is often a clue to "resistance."

For example, here is a dialogue taken from a subsequent session with the 26-year-old schoolteacher to whom we have already referred:

Therapist: So you were telling me about the party.
Client: Yes, I think we were to the point where Pete and Jerry came in late. Well anyhow, all the people were standing around making small talk (*interpersonal*) and then some of them started to get high (*drugs*) and others were dancing or just listening to the music (*behavior/sensation*). . . . My legs were aching (*sensation*) probably from the tennis, but I managed to dance (*behavior*) and I was having a good time (*affect*), that is until Nora entered the room (*interpersonal*) and then began hitting vodka (*drugs*). But I remembered what you had said and I

---

* As a client speaks, an experienced multimodal therapist makes a mental note to him/herself regarding the particular modality to which the client is referring.

simply told myself that it is her life (*cognitive*) so all in all, I would say that it went off pretty well.

Therapist: That's great. Why allow Nora to mess up things? Now let's try a bit of *imagery*. Will you close your eyes and picture yourself at the party. Just picture it as vividly as you can, and focus on your *feelings* and *emotions*.

Client: (Opens eyes) Gee! I left out the most important part. When I pictured it just now I remembered that Pete got into his old habit of putting me down. I can't help it, but that really makes me mad. . . .

Discussion

During the narrative about the party, the client made no reference to the "imagery modality," and she seemed to gloss over her affective reactions. She was not providing the "full picture." Therefore, before leaving the discussion about the party and proceeding to other issues, the therapist questioned her about affect and imagery. This line of inquiry yielded significant information. Students observing a multimodal therapist in action often inquire, "What made you ask that particular question?" or "How did you know that you would obtain such important information by asking that one?" The answer is that when asking questions within or about modalities that were omitted, important data are often elicited.

Similarly, we have found that when therapy is not proceeding well, it usually pays to ask oneself, "Which modalities have I neglected?" Then, by zeroing in on the neglected modalities, the impasse usually breaks. For example, I treated a highly anxious woman who made excellent progress during the first two months of therapy. Thereafter, her gains became less obvious and we made little headway for two or three sessions. At this juncture I asked myself, "Which modalities have I overlooked or neglected?" After a brief survey, it occurred to me that I had done very little work in the *sensory* modality.

Since the client had frequently referred to herself as "oppressed" and "pressured," I felt that a logical sensory intervention was for me to place my hand on her head while saying, "As I push down on your head, let this action symbolize for you the feelings of pressure and oppression that you mentioned. I want you to resist and fight off this pressure." (Most people tend to straighten up their heads or to push one's hand away when resisting such "oppression.") The client merely began to weep and allowed her head to be pushed down further and further. Since I did not want to reinforce avoidance behavior and passivity, I continued pushing down while saying to her, "Come on, fight back! Resist the oppression!" Finally she exerted some pressure and pushed her head and shoulders upward. I withdrew my hand and said, "Good! Now how does that feel?" This evoked a slew of affective responses. She unleashed a tirade against a maiden aunt whom she vehemently disliked. She also revealed negative feelings about her mother, and spoke about strong disappointments concerning the mother-daughter relationship. These revelations led to assertion training, behavior rehearsal, and other techniques for helping the client cope adaptively with her feelings. Therapy, once more, was proceeding apace.

Exploring Each Modality

When endeavoring to understand another human being, a myriad of questions can be asked. Almost any question can provide some sort of information. "How often do you cut your toenails?" "Do you prefer pineapples to strawberries?" "What brand of toothpaste do you use?" Obviously, some questions will be more "central" than others. "What are your sexual fantasies?" "What is the worst thing you have ever done?" "How do you feel about death?" When trying to to gain a comprehensive picture of their clients, therapists ask many questions. These are often supplemented by personal observation, by information obtained from other people (especially the client's family), from standardized tests and other measuring instruments. Despite this determined effort at thoroughness, many important questions remain unasked and hence unanswered.

From time to time I have asked some of my colleagues the following question: "If you were allowed to ask a client only seven questions, what would they be?" This is a rapid way of determining the overall orientation of almost any clinician. Some people have included the following among their crucial questions: "When were you toilet trained?" "Were you breast-fed or bottle-fed?" "How well did you get along with your siblings?" "Will you tell me what you see in these ink blots?" "How do you express your anger?" "What are your feelings about homosexuality?" "Will you tell me some of your dreams?" It may be interesting for the reader to list his/her seven questions before reading further.

Most multimodal therapists would ask the following types of questions:

1. Which particular behaviors do you wish to increase and which ones do you want to decrease?
2. What negative feelings would you like to reduce or eliminate, and what positive feelings would you like to increase or amplify?

3. Among your five senses, what particular reactions would you care to get rid of, and what kinds of sensations would you like to magnify?
4. What "mental pictures" or images are bothersome to you so that you would like to erase them, and what pleasant images would you care to bring into clearer focus?
5. Which thoughts, values, attitudes, or beliefs get in the way of your happiness?
6. In your dealings with other people, what gets in the way of close, personal, loving, and mutually satisfying interactions?
7. Under what conditions do you use drugs (including alcohol, coffee, and tobacco)?

Obviously, many of these questions are not easily answered. It is often up to the therapist to help the client come to terms with the basic realities tapped by each modality. The cognitive and interpersonal deficits (Numbers 5 and 6) are seldom readily apparent, but if the therapist is searching for answers to these sorts of questions, therapy is likely to remain "on target." Clinical experience has shown that this brief multimodal inquiry can elicit crucial information that frequently escapes more formal testing and routine case histories. The specific questions are aimed at particular behaviors, feelings, sensations, images, etc. the person wishes to increase and decrease. Of course, since the usual multimodal assessment procedures are not limited to seven fundamental questions, the BASIC ID appraisal can extend into a most comprehensive diagnostic work-up.

It may be useful at this point to elaborate upon the sorts of questions that are routinely asked within each modality. Let me stress that a multimodal assessment is not a mechanistic series of questions about behavior, affect, sensation, and so forth. Depending upon the exigencies of each case, it may be necessary first for a therapist simply to listen and do little more than reflect the emotional undertones of the client's narrative in order to develop a therapeutic relationship. Elsewhere, and in some detail, I have spelled out some formative strategies involved in developing rapport (Lazarus, 1971, pp. 31-64). In the present context, let it simply be understood that the multimodal therapist functions as a *clinician* well-versed in the facilitative conditions that engender the client's justified faith and trust. But while some individuals may require no more than the benefits of close rapport, genuine empathy, and nonpossessive warmth, the majority of people who seek our help often need much more. And it is to meet the need of therapeutic thoroughness that the multimodal orientation was conceived. With the forementioned caveats in mind, let us examine the main areas covered within each modality.

Behavior

The mainstay of the behavioral modality is the realization that survival in any society calls for a variety of coping behaviors. Adaptive living among the Hottentots or the Nilotes of Africa calls for different behavioral repertoires than those demanded by Western society. Behavior in this context refers to a continuum of acts ranging from simple motor skills (grooming, walking, eating, smiling) to more complex reactions (playing the guitar, drawing, speaking a foreign language, solving puzzles) all the way to the highly refined nuances of personal perceptiveness and sensitivity (as exemplified perhaps by the best poets and writers) and numerous occupational skills (from surgery to bridge-building). Deficiencies in behaviorial repertoires are most evident in certain regressed patients who need to relearn the elements of basic self-care. But we all undoubtedly lack certain behaviors that may prove useful, or we are burdened by other behaviors that detract from our daily living. And in this connection, relatively simple behaviors such as one's table manners, and somewhat more elaborate responses, such as the way one behaves sexually, may have profound effects on various aspects of one's life.

A multimodal therapist is therefore on the alert for the behavioral excesses and deficits that undermine effective living. Characteristically, one begins the behavioral assessment process by examining presenting complaints in detail. Of particular concern are the actual behaviors themselves, their antecedents, and their consequences. There are some excellent comprehensive accounts of behavioral assessment (e.g., Kanfer and Saslow, 1969; Tharp and Wetzel, 1969) and it is beyond the scope of the present book to deal extensively with any particular modality. The interested reader is referred to a brilliant overview and appraisal of broad-spectrum behavior therapy by O'Leary and Wilson (1975) which has outstanding accounts both of behavioral assessment and intervention.

The major thrust within the behavioral modality is to count, to quantify, to measure almost anything that lends itself to numerical scoring. Not only do *counting, charting,* and *graphing* establish a base rate (often essential for estimating the severity of any problem) but the very act of keeping records often lends some control to the behaviors one wishes to modify. Homework assignments and various self-help procedures underscore the need for clients to monitor their own behaviors if change is to be clearly evident (Lazarus and Fay, 1975). The emphasis is upon frequency, intensity, and duration. The major questions to be asked are when, what, how, who, and where, rather than why. "When did you first behave that way? What was happening at the time? How did you deal with it? Who was with you? Where did you go from there?" Behaviorally, it is also often informative to inquire about *opposites*. "When did you *not* act that way?"

One of the most important behavioral techniques is role-playing, or what I prefer to call *behavior rehearsal* (Lazarus, 1966). As soon as the therapist becomes aware of inappropriate behaviors, he or she can point out the client's errors and can then model a more effective response pattern. Thus, one may deal with appropriate eye-contact, voice projection, posture, gait, or more involved behaviors such as the expression of assertive rather than aggressive feelings, or even the acquisition of sophisticated and subtle elements of high-level negotiations.

As the reader proceeds through the BASIC ID, he or she may well inquire what constitutes "pure" behavior that falls under the "B" category and that can be clearly distinguished from all the other modalities. In a real sense, we can only infer our understanding of other people from their behavior—what they say and don't say, what they do and don't do, how they act, respond, fail to respond, emit nonverbal cues, and so on. We can only presume what goes on in their affective, sensory, cognitive, and imagery modalities by attending to various *behaviors* they emit, both verbal and nonverbal. Since we can see and hear various interpersonal interactions, the interpersonal modality can be viewed as an extension of the behavioral modality. On the other hand, affect, sensation, imagery, and cognition may be considered "internal" as opposed to behavior that is clearly "external" or observable. Most of these internal realities depend upon the client's verbal self-report. "My head hurts." "I feel afraid." "I have this image of my buddy's head being blown off in Vietnam." Often observable concomitants are present (facial grimacing, sweating, trembling, blushing), while appropriate instruments may readily reveal others (tachycardia, rise or fall in blood pressure, temperature changes). We will not belabor the point that therapy remains incomplete until verbal self-reports coupled with objective observations have been carefully scrutinized across each modality of the BASIC ID.

Affect

The affective modality is probably the most "overworked" area in psychotherapy. It is within the domain of "emotional disturbance" that we labor, and we consider our therapeutic interventions successful or worthwhile to the extent that we are able to alleviate suffering while also promoting new adaptive responses. Much confusion has arisen from terms such as "emotional insight," and "emotional maturity," and, despite significant advances in psychophysiology, biofeedback, and biochemistry, the realm of affective responses remains enigmatic. Accordingly, Robert Woolfolk, who has kept abreast of key developments in the affective sphere, was asked to contribute a chapter on the subject. In this section, I merely want to touch on the major issues involved in the assessment of affective disorders from a multimodal perspective.

Recognizing clear-cut aberrations in affective reactions (e.g., the violent rage of a paranoid schizophrenic, the morbid melancholia of a stupefied depressive, the wild and fanciful flight of ideas of a manic reactor) hardly requires any clinical perspicacity. In our daily practices, as well as in our daily lives, the stimuli (both exogenous and endogenous) that elicit anger, anxiety, and various degress of subjective misery demand careful identification. The relevant components concern those feelings and emotions with which we are in touch, as well as those which may exist beyond our level of awareness. And when we talk of people "not being in touch with their feelings," I submit that the feeling most often involved is *anger*. It is often easy to deny, displace, conceal, and suppress anger. It is less easy to conceal anxiety or misery, especially from oneself.* Nevertheless, the point at issue is that in the search for affective responses that require modification, it is advisable to be on the alert for hidden and distorted feelings, and aware that people are indeed capable of concealing certain feelings even from themselves.

Often, it is useful to start by inquiring about specific feelings the client may have concerning the various behavioral excesses and deficits that were revealed during the preliminary discussion. "So when you eat compulsively, what do you actually feel at the time?" "When you let your husband put you down without trying to defend yourself, what is the main feeling you get right after the incident?" The therapist attempts to obtain a profile of the situations that engender anxiety, depression, anger, and other "negative feelings." Also of interest are the stimuli that produce pleasant affective states—joy, love, amusement, and pride. There is no better way of obtaining crucial information from some clients than by asking direct questions. "What makes you cry?" "What makes you glad?" "What makes you scared?" "What makes you mad?" And, as before, opposites are tapped. "When would that event not upset you?" "Can you recall any

---

* In the latter connection, I once received a call from a colleague who informed me that a mutual friend was deeply depressed. When I remarked that our friend's appetite was not affected, that he seemed to sleep soundly, that he was working well, that he seemed enthusiastic about a new sex relationship, and he even told me that he was "very happy," my colleague retorted, "He's so depressed he doesn't even realize he's depressed—and that's the worst type of depression!" Now I am well aware that some "smiling depressives" conceal their true feelings behind an elaborately cheery facade. However, when pressed for their real feelings, it usually takes very little for them to drop their act. Though they may try to hide their basic misery from others, they know how they feel. It is true that some people complain only of somatic discomfort which may be secondary to an unrecognized depression. But nevertheless they are in touch with *discomfort*, despite their inability or unwillingness to articulate their depressive affect.

time when you did not cry when Tom attacked you?'' This approach may provide clues to certain chronic and situational patterns of response.

In case it is not self-evident, let me reiterate that *each modality interacts with every modality*. Thus, while exploring affective responses, the therapist will undoubtedly tap cognitive material and elicit imagery, sensory reactions, and so on.

Sensation

In recent years, sensory reactions have gained attention. This is clearly indicated by the burgeoning treatment of sexual dysfunction where most of the interest has centered around tactile responses. From our present perspective, however, we are interested not only in tactile responses but in every aspect of sensation. Learning to develop our senses—to appreciate and enjoy visual stimuli, auditory responses, olfactory and gustatory delights, tactile pleasures—is an integral part of personal fulfillment and development.

The multimodal clinician learns a good deal by inquiring about the client's specific sensations. Which sounds are pleasant and which are unpleasant? What sights appeal to you and what visual scenes do you dislike? What are your special tastes—likes and dislikes—in food?

Some individuals are almost truncated at the sensory level. They seem to be ''switched off'' below the head. Such people may regard food as simply an antidote to hunger, never appreciating its subtleties of flavor or the nuances of taste. And so it is with all their other senses: the pleasures of a warm bath, a cool breeze, a gentle massage, a vigorous exercise, are all negligible.

Then we have those people who are preoccupied with their sensations, who exaggerate every twitch, every flutter into a major episode. Often they are hypochondriacs who must learn to divert their attention from the sensory modality to other avenues of discourse. To generalize, the aim of multimodal therapy is to achieve a balance both within modalities and between modalities.

It is not uncommon for presenting complaints to be raised in the sensory modality—headaches, dizziness, stomach distress, miscellaneous aches and pains. As always, in delineating the specific focus of sensory complaints, or lack of sensory awareness, the therapist must trace the interactive effects within other related modalities. The following dialogue will clarify this point:

Client:	Well, I've had every medical and neurological test in the book but my headaches still come and go.
Therapist:	Let's get very specific. Can you describe these headaches as accurately as possible? Can you tell me, or show me where your head hurts, and describe exactly how it feels?
Client:	Here (points to right occipital area). It's like a clamp. Tight and throbbing. And the pain will then spread to here and here (points to right temple and jaw).
Therapist:	Does it feel painful when you press there?
Client:	Yes.
Therapist:	That's usually due to spasm.
Client:	I'm aware of the tightness.
Therapist:	Do you notice any times when there is no tightness?
Client:	(Thinks) Not really. Maybe after a hot shower.
Therapist:	Well, for one thing I think we might do some specific relaxation training. I have a cassette tape which I will lend you. But, tell me, what do you usually do for these headaches?
Client:	Well, at the office I take aspirins. At home I go and lie down.
Therapist:	Does that help?
Client:	Temporarily.
Therapist:	Does anything in particular bring on these headaches? For instance, do you notice them more at certain times or in certain places?
Client:	(Pause) I can't say I do. No, not really.
Therapist:	Well, will you keep tabs on these headaches? What I want you to do is make a note each and every time you have a headache. Will you record the time of day, where you are, and more or less what you were doing just before the headache came on. Jot down exactly what you were doing, feeling and thinking. I'd like you to do this very thoroughly. Will you do it?
Client:	Sure. You want to see if there's some pattern?
Therapist:	Right. Also, let's get a base line. Let's see exactly how many times you have a headache over a period of two weeks. Could you also make a notation as to the severity of each attack?
Client:	Like "mild," "moderate," or "severe"?
Therapist:	Right. And would you keep track of how many aspirins you take? By the way, can you tell me what the consequences are when you have a headache?
Client:	How do you mean?
Therapist:	I mean does it spoil your fun? For instance, do you cancel appointments, or not go out?
Client:	Well, my wife was mad at me only last night because we had tickets for a show and my head was splitting and I opted out.
Therapist:	Do you like shows? Especially the one you missed last night. Were you honestly looking forward to it?
Client:	(Laughs) Well, I'll put it to you this way. If it had been a poker game I just might have made it.

Therapist: So these headaches seem to come in handy some of the time.
Client: I wasn't lying. I mean I really did have a headache. . . .

Comment: A brief focus on *sensory* elements led rapidly to several *behavioral* prescriptions, immediately followed by a seemingly critical *interpersonal* process. It is important for therapists to avoid leaping to conclusions or reading too much into situations, but all possible cause-effect sequences are worth exploring. Since behavior is multiply determined, we urge all therapists not to seize on a pet explanation. Much more information would need to be gathered before the therapist could justifiably conclude that the "sensory complaint" (tension headaches) was largely attributable to interactions within another modality, "interpersonal relationships" (or more specifically, the marriage dyad). But one would certainly be entitled to hypothesize that some of the basic tensions *per se* could stem from problems within the marriage.

It is worth pointing out once more that during a multimodal assessment, the therapist deliberately searches for interactive facets across each modality. Thus, one might have begun with "marriage problems," which, in turn, could have led to a detailed exploration of sensory deficits. The effective clinician follows various leads to where the greatest payoffs seem likely.

Imagery

Entire books could be written on the multimodal treatment of each separate modality. The clinician who feels overwhelmed by the myriad complexities within and between modalities may be reassured that effective intervention does not necessarily demand deep and profound familiarity with the information explosion on behavior, affect, sensation, and the rest. We contend that even cursory attention paid to *each* modality in therapy will yield more durable results than treatments that ignore one or more modalities.

In the multimodal context, *imagery* refers to various "mental pictures" that exert an influence upon our lives. For example, I treated a female client who reported: "During sex I always picture my mother's disapproving face and this adds more impetus to my feelings of guilt." In multimodal assessment, I usually employ the following three images:

1. Please picture your childhood home. You might have lived in several places as a child, but nearly everyone thinks of one particular place as his or her "childhood home." Will you concentrate on that image? Close your eyes if that helps. Try to *see* your childhood home. (Pause of

about ten seconds.) Now tell me, where is your mother in that scene? What is she doing? And where is your father, and what is he doing?

2. Now will you take a tour in imagination from room to room in your childhood home? As you go from room to room, look around carefully. See the furnishings. Try to get the atmosphere. Do you notice any special odors? (Note how the "sensory modality" is deliberately introduced into this image.)

3. I want you to picture a special safe place. Any place, real or imagined, in which you feel completely safe. (Pause of about ten seconds.) Go to that specific place. Picture it vividly. (Pause of about ten seconds.) Would you care to describe it to me?

We have selected these particular images out of hundreds at our disposal because trial and error has shown that they often yield important clinical material. The three basic images are discussed in detail, and the various cognitive and affective elements they evoke are clearly delineated. Some people (but very few in our experience) are unwilling or unable to comply with these instructions. When this occurs, it is profitable for the therapist to discuss the "resistance" in considerable detail.

In most instances, each image elicits from the client a host of associated recollections and scenes that reveal a cluster of additional problems requiring therapeutic attention. (The therapeutic use of associated imagery is outlined in Chapter 12.) Here is a rather dramatic example:

Therapist: Now will you take a tour in imagination from room to room in your childhood home?

Client: (Begins sobbing) I'm sorry.

Therapist: No need to apologize. Can you tell me what's happening?

Client: (Still sobbing) It just brought back awful memories. . . . After my mother died, dad sold the house. . . . They moved all our furniture out, room by room. (Breaks down and cries even more) Then the van arrived for the people who had bought the house. As they took our furniture out of the house, the other men were moving the other people's stuff in.

Therapist: There is obviously a lot of sadness tied up with that image, but can you picture that scene even more vividly and tell me what other feelings you have?

Client: (Eyes closed for about 20 seconds) Well, my mind keeps jumping to what happened afterwards. I went to live with my aunt. Boy, I have clear pictures of that scene! I think most of my problems started around that time. . . .

In assessment, the imagery modality is particularly valuable with people who use the cognitive modality to overintellectualize. Elaborate rationalizations are easily punctured when clients are asked to dwell on a particular image and to report their associated feelings. A fairly detailed account of the therapeutic and diagnostic use of imagery in a behavioral context was described by Ahsen and Lazarus (1972). The basic images outlined above were adapted from Ahsen (1968; 1972).

Cognition

Since it is the complexity of his cerebral cortex that sets man apart from the rest of the animal kingdom, the bulk of therapeutic endeavors often centers around the correction of misconceptions. Lazarus and Fay (1975) have listed what they regard to be the 20 most common mistaken beliefs that lead to "emotional disturbance." Several of these common mistakes overlap with the list of 12 major illogical ideas first outlined by Ellis (1958). When assessing the cognitive modality, we are interested in noting which of these "common mistakes" the client usually makes and to which of the "illogical philosophies" he or she subscribes.

Almost any personal interview is bound to elicit a host of faulty cognitions. Thinking back over three clients seen recently, I can furnish some typical examples. A 40-year-old woman told me: "I think I'm too old to change." The same client stated: "I think a woman loses her feminity and becomes like a man when she behaves assertively." A 32-year-old accountant proclaimed: "Any form of oral sex is a perversion." A 22-year-old student remarked: "I believe that silence is golden. . . . I let very few people know what's really on my mind." Since people may labor under all sorts of misconceptions regarding love and sex, failure and success, worthwhile and worthless traits, the meaning and quality of life, or the destiny of mankind, cognitive explorations may continue almost *ad infinitum*. However, we have found it most profitable to examine three fundamental faulty assumptions as basic cognitive lead-ins.

The first lead-in involves what Karen Horney (1950) called *the tyranny of the should*. She pointed out that the "neurotic" often says to him/herself: "Forget about the disgraceful creature you actually *are; this is how you *should* be; and to be this idealized self is all that matters. You should be able to endure everything, to understand everything, to like everybody, to be always productive, etc." (pp. 64-65.) These categorical imperatives—the shoulds, oughts, and musts that people impose on themselves and on others—require close scrutiny. When searching for "shoulds," the therapist does not ordinarily ask the client, "What are your shoulds?" but readily infers them from specific actions. Thus, the hardworking, driving, overambitious, achievement-oriented person is most likely responding to numerous *shoulds* concerning the work ethic, productiveness, and personal fulfillment. The clinician can help the client articulate these shoulds explicitly. "I should succeed at everything I do." "I should constantly strive to be better than others." A discussion of these particular shoulds usually leads into more general issues regarding the specific expectations the client may have for him/herself and for significant others.

The therapeutic goal is to educate clients to eliminate shoulds by replacing them with personal preferences. Successfully treated clients will no longer tell other people what they should and shouldn't do; they will not permit others to tell them what they should and should not do; and they will not impose shoulds and shouldn'ts on themselves. From an assessment standpoint, the therapist cannot claim to have begun to understand someone until he or she is fairly familiar with that person's shoulds and shouldn'ts.

The next cognitive lead-in concerns perfectionistic standards and the way in which many people refuse to accept fallibility. There is a common tendency to forget or deny that since infallibility does not exist, it is inevitably self-defeating to strive for perfectionistic ideals. The most obvious clues in this regard come from statements of self-hatred and self-abnegation. Effective therapy enables people to emerge with a full acceptance of their basic fallibilities. They strive to become less fallible, but never infallible. A thorough cognitive assessment requires a clear understanding of the client's self-downing behaviors.

Our third crucial cognitive input concerns the widespread myth that we are victims of circumstance, and that our miseries derive predominantly from the external events that impinge upon our lives. During assessment interviews, the multimodal clinician pays close attention to the client's attributions. "I blame my unhappiness on the way my wife treats me." "It makes me very depressed when my son doesn't obey me." These faulty cognitions are pointed out to the client at the first judicious opportunity. "Your wife probably treats you as she does because you allow her to, and because you have not enabled her to behave differently towards you." "You upset yourself when your son doesn't obey you, and you probably depress yourself over the mistaken idea that a good son is an obedient son, and if your son is not obedient it means that you have failed him as a parent." These sorts of provocative remarks usually open up other areas for discussion, and many attitudes, values, and beliefs are thus available for exploration. Whenever possible, these therapeutic insights are then translated into *new behaviors* that clients can practice. "So instead of withdrawing and going into a sad sulk the next time your son disobeys you, what are you going to *do* instead?"

Our intention in this section is simply to underscore the value of three specific cognitive lead-ins—shoulds, perfectionism, and external circumstances. Of course, a good deal of time is spent in the cognitive modality with psychologically-minded clients. Numerous plans, decisions, viewpoints, strategies, insights, opinions, outlooks, schemes, expectations, and intentions are discussed in detail throughout the course of therapy. I should like to urge any reader interested in a broader and deeper appreciation of the diagnostic and therapeutic implications of cognition (and its relation to other modalities) to consult Ellis (1962; 1971; 1973). Experimentally minded clinicians may wish to consult Meichenbaum (1973). And for a scholarly and thought-provoking presentation of cognition and behavior modification, Mahoney's (1974) book is unequaled.

Interpersonal Relationships

It is easy to isolate any one modality and argue that it is the "key" area of assessment and therapy. The interpersonal modality is considered to be "the most basic and crucial area of human functioning" by many different theorists, especially Sullivan, Horney, Fromm, and other "dynamic culturalists." From a multimodal perspective, however, it is therapeutically deleterious to aggrandize any particular modality—they are *all* important. Interpersonal communication is certainly a dominant human function, and many of our problems stem from our concerns over the way we relate to other people, and the manner in which they respond to us. In assessment and therapy, the client-therapist dyad is often crucial. These interpersonal communications involve not only overt acts and statements, but also a range of unspoken, nonverbal, covert, and connotative elements. In person-to-person interactions, both words and silence contain a variety of messages. It is easy to become extremely analytical about the numerous relationship messages that pass overtly and covertly from moment to moment. Several communications theorists have spelled out complex chains of interpersonal and intrapersonal communication and metacommunication, including "paralinguistic cues," but their heuristic value for improved therapeutic effectiveness has yet to be demonstrated.

In the assessment of any one dimension, important aspects of every other modality may be introduced. Thus, while working in the interpersonal zone, the multimodal clinician inquires about specific images, feelings, thoughts, and so on that may play a role with regard to significant others. And the manner in which one acts, reacts, or *behaves* interpersonally is often crucial.

Interpersonal assessment begins with two levels of discourse: First, the therapist *listens* to the client's self-reports about the way in which he/she responds to others and vice versa. "I really gave him a piece of my mind!'' ''So I turned to her and pointed out how completely dumb and stupid she is.'' ''I just walked away and said nothing.'' ''I punched him in the mouth.'' ''So I laughed in his face.'' ''She ignored me.'' ''He said that to me in front of all those other people.'' ''I've told him that my breasts are tender but he always hurts me.'' Second, one *observes* the client's actual interpersonal responses. In a group one can see how clients react to other group members and to the therapist. In individual therapy, the client-therapist relationship itself often contains significant clues to the client's general response patterns. However, it is a serious mistake to insist that the client-therapist dyad is necessarily pivotal, or that the client's feelings towards the therapist are identical to those elicited in other important relationships. They may or may not be, and it is incumbent upon the therapist to determine which facets are unique or specific to the ongoing dyad, and which reveal the client's general interpersonal dealings.

It is naive to assume that clients' self-reports are necessarily accurate, but it is misleading to assume that they are necessarily inaccurate. However, it is important to carry out various validity checks. In addition to being on the alert for possible contradictions and inconsistencies, the therapist usually finds it helpful to interview (with the client's prior knowledge and consent) family members, friends, and even employers. When a client resists the notion that ''another point of view may prove useful in helping me understand you more fully,'' this in and of itself is significant interpersonal behavior worthy of exploration.

It is well-known that clients inadvertently and/or deliberately evade certain key issues, obfuscate others, and tend to sabotage various ongoing processes. Power struggles and various role conflicts arise only too often. Logical and common-sense approaches in these instances often backfire, and it is advisable for therapists to be equipped with several paradoxical procedures for cutting through ''resistances'' of this kind. To cite a simple example, a young woman was answering most questions during an assessment interview with ''I don't know.'' I began to frame my questions to her somewhat differently. Instead of a straightforward inquiry such as, ''How did you react when Charlie put you down?'' or ''What did you say when your mother opened your mail?'' I phrased my questions as follows: ''I suppose you don't know how you reacted when Charlie put you down?'' and ''I guess you don't remember what you said when your mother opened your mail?'' In response to this type of inquiry, she gave very complete answers. Two interesting books that deal with paradoxical and strategic techniques are Haley (1973) and Watzlawick, Weakland, and Fisch (1974). (See also Chapter 15 by Allen Fay in the present volume for a more extended discussion of paradoxical procedures.)

An important psychological dictum is that behavior is frequently a function of its consequences. In other words, our actions are generally strengthened or weakened by the rewards or punishments that immediately follow. It is worth remembering that maintaining factors are most frequently found in the interpersonal modality. And in therapy, certain persistent problems can only be overcome by altering the (often subtle) communication patterns that reinforce them. Many of these general allusions will become clearer in the intervention sections that follow.

Drugs

It will be recalled that we use the label "Drugs" to denote much more than the chemical substances that a person ingests. In this modality, the first assessment consideration concerns the person's overall physical appearance, mode of attire, signs of intoxication, noticeable skin disorders, speech disturbances, tics, or psychomotor disorders. The client is asked about physiological complaints—backaches, cramps, headaches, asthma, tachycardia, dizziness, shortness of breath, and so forth. Consultation with a physician is often essential. Chemotherapy is usually required when clients appear to be suffering from physiological depression, or when mood swings from high to low occur for no apparent reason, or when very irrational thoughts and feelings seem to be racing out of control. The multimodal therapist does not see drug treatment as both necessary and sufficient, but when florid symptoms are medically well-controlled, all the other modalities need to be carefully assessed and any problems that emerge must receive specific treatment.

The "D" modality also examines physical fitness, exercise, diet, and general well-being. The client is asked about avocational interests, leisure activities, recreational pursuits, sports, hobbies, and so forth. Slight changes in a sedentary existence such as taking regular evening walks plus the consumption of fewer calories can have almost immediate positive psychological effects.

The following chart summarizes the main aspects of multimodal assessment and might serve as a handy reminder.

B	A	S	I	C	I	D
Increase or Decrease	Feelings about behavior	Vision	Childhood home	Lead-ins	A) Self-reports	Overall appearance
What?	Pleasant/ Unpleasant	Touch	Tour of rooms	1) Shoulds	B) Observation	Physiological complaints
When?	Content Anxiety	Taste	Special safe place	2) Perfectionism	Paradoxical techniques	General well-being
How?	Joy	Sight		3) External attributions	Express feelings/ Receive feelings	
Where?	Anger	Hearing				
Who?	Depression	Pleasant/ Unpleasant				
Frequency	Absence/ Presence	Aware				
Intensity	Hidden affect	Not aware				
Duration	Distorted affect	Overaware				
Opposites						
(The questions in this modality are basic to all other modalities.)						

QUANTIFY WHEREVER POSSIBLE

Multimodal Analysis and Treatment of Compulsive Disorders: A Brief Note

After treating twelve people with compulsive disorders over the past four years, I conducted an analysis of their individual BASIC ID profiles. Strikingly similar patterns emerged. Despite wide variations in background and problem content, a common cluster of identical tendencies across each modality was readily discerned.

Behavior

The most obvious difficulties in this modality centered around several intrusive compulsions. These differed from case to case. One man would fold and unfold each pair of socks in his dresser 96 times before going to bed. One woman had a similar bedtime ritual that was much more elaborate and demanding. Another woman was almost incapacitated by a network of rituals—centering on bathroom activities, eating, walking, talking—that encrusted most of her waking activities.

Affect

The most obvious affective component was focused on anxiety, but in each case, it soon became clear that *anger* was no less a factor in contributing to numerous compulsive rituals.

Sensation

Each case was unduly concerned with bodily processes. There was a clear tendency to notice minute changes in sensory reactions. A slight muscle twinge would be worthy of comment; a heightened awareness of pulse-rate, respiration, and other autonomic functions was evident. This predisposed the 12 individuals towards hypochondriasis.

Imagery

The anger component emerged most clearly in this modality. Most of the clients reported images involving attack, death, and mutilation. Paranoid themes were not uncommon ("I have this picture of my boss finding out about my compulsions and firing me, and then I see everybody turning against me").

Cognition

The predominant cognitive theme involved perfectionistic demands from self and from others. Closely allied to these impossible standards was a high degree of self-abnegation.

Interpersonal

Interpersonal relationships were characterized by combative, competitive, and manipulative behaviors, all within a passive-aggressive context. Many of the clients presented a reasonable, rational facade that belied their basic rigidity and refusal to compromise.

Drugs

In many instances, antidepressant and antianxiety medication was of considerable help in rendering clients more receptive to change across the other modalities.

Implications for Treatment

While it is imprudent to generalize from only 12 cases, it is nonetheless evident that a ''personality profile'' may emerge in which specific therapeutic indications can be discerned. In treating a person with compulsive behaviors, a multimodal therapist would make certain to: (1) devise strategies to prevent or decrease the compulsive behaviors *per se,* while (2) endeavoring to extinguish the client's anxiety and also modifying the anger into adaptive assertion, (3) defusing the preoccupation with minute bodily processes, (4) introducing images involving the client's competency and subjective security, (5) disputing perfectionistic ideals and challenging self-downing ideas, (6) teaching cooperative interpersonal styles and the virtues of flexibility and authenticity, and (7) considering the possible value of certain medication when anxiety and/or depression tend to undermine one's therapeutic endeavors.

At the time of writing, several investigations of multimodal assessment and therapy are in progress. One colleague, in a large hospital setting, is feeding BASIC ID information into a computer for each patient. Interesting trends have already emerged. There are at least eight multimodal studies underway. In one pilot experiment at Princeton University, a student found multimodal procedures significantly more effective than more circumscribed techniques such as desensitization for overcoming test anxiety. Several indications suggest that within the next few years, the value of a multimodal orientation will receive experimental and clinical verification.

References

Ahsen, A. *Basic concepts in eidetic psychotherapy*. New York: Eidetic Publishing House, 1968.

Ahsen, A. *Eidetic parents test and analysis*. New York: Brandon House, Inc., 1972.

Ahsen, A., & Lazarus, A. A. Eidetics: An internal behavior approach. In A. A. Lazarus (Ed.) *Clinical behavior therapy*. New York: Brunner/Mazel, 1972.

Ellis, A. Rational psychotherapy. *Journal of General Psychology*, 1958, *59*, 35-49.

Ellis, A. *Reason and emotion in psychotherapy*. New York: Lyle Stuart, 1962.

Ellis, A. *Growth through reason*. Palo Alto, California: Science and Behavior Books, 1971.

Ellis, A. *Humanistic psychotherapy: The rational-emotive approach*. New York: Julian Press, 1973.

Haley, J. *Uncommon therapy: The psychiatric techniques of Milton H. Erickson, M.D.* New York: W. W. Norton, 1973.

Horney, K. *Neurosis and human growth: The struggle toward self-realization*. New York: W. W. Norton, 1950.

Kanfer, F. H., & Saslow, G. Behavioral diagnosis. In C. M. Franks (Ed.) *Behavior therapy: Appraisal and status*, pp. 417-444. New York: McGraw-Hill, 1969.

Lazarus, A. A. Behavior rehearsal vs. non-directive therapy vs. advice in effecting behavior change. *Behaviour Research and Therapy*, 1966, *4*, 209-212.

Lazarus, A. A. *Behavior therapy and beyond*. New York: McGraw-Hill, 1971.

Lazarus, A. A. & Fay, A. *I can if I want to*. New York: Morrow, 1975.

Mahoney, M. J. *Cognition and behavior modification*. Cambridge, Mass.: Ballinger, 1974.

Meichenbaum, D. H. Cognitive factors in behavior modification: Modifying what clients say to themselves. In C. M. Franks and G. T. Wilson (Eds.) *Annual review of behavior therapy: Theory and practice*, pp. 415-431. New York: Brunner-Mazel, 1973.

O'Leary, K. D., & Wilson, G. T. *Behavior therapy: Application and outcome*. New York: Prentice-Hall, 1975.

Tharp, R. G., & Wetzel, R. J. *Behavior modification in the natural environment*. New York: Academic Press, 1969.

Watzlawick, P., Weakland, J., & Fisch, R. *Change: Principles of problem formation and problem resolution*. New York: W. W. Norton, 1974.

Chapter 5

A Multimodal Perspective on Emotion

Robert L. Woolfolk

With the exception of those individuals who have already acquired considerable familiarity with the concepts of psychotherapy, the therapist rarely interviews people who wish to achieve a reconstruction of their unconscious processes, to become self-actualized, to learn to replace their irrational sentences with rational statements, or to be counter-conditioned. Clients typically seek therapy because they "feel bad": they are anxious, depressed, demoralized, uptight, uncertain, strange, dissatisfied, confused. Hebb's (1949) definition of neurosis emphasized the primary role of emotion: "Neurosis is in practice an undesirable emotional condition which is generalized and persistent." Save for the reification of "neurosis," this definition describes the complaint of most clients, who come to therapy mainly to eliminate or alter these unpleasant feelings.

What happens in therapy after the client describes these unpleasant emotions is in large part a function of the therapist's conceptualization of emotion, which is, in turn, a function of his therapeutic orientation. This is significant for the client, since the way in which the therapist understands statements about feelings will dictate the particular subset of the client's past and present activities that will be considered relevant to assessment and to subsequent intervention.

Current theory and the latest empirical evidence suggest that emotional phenomena result from complex interactions among several systems of the organism. Behavioral, cognitive, phenomenological, perceptual, neurophysiological, and biochemical variables are all involved. Yet most therapists tend to conceptualize emotion in a somewhat rudimentary fashion—as explainable in terms of one or perhaps two of the aforementioned systems. Consequently, these are the systems in which they intervene. For example, Wolpe's understanding of anxiety dictated that he produce parasympathetic dominance by deep muscle relaxation, eating responses, or sexual arousal in the presence of feared stimuli in order to "reciprocally inhibit" anxiety. Assertive training and other behavioral methods were also utilized as counterconditioning agents (Wolpe, 1958), but cognitive factors were considered secondary, if not irrelevant, to the understanding and treatment of anxiety.

An examination of the various schools of therapy reveals how emotion is conceptualized within different technical and theoretical structures. By and large one finds that the kinds of techniques employed in each approach to therapy are quite consistent with its theory of affect. Similarly, the technical narrowness of each school can be viewed as reflecting a corresponding limited understanding of emotion.

In Client-Centered Therapy, verbal reports of affective states are accepted at face value as reflective of unitary experiential processes. Within this framework therapists work for increased recognition, differentiation, acceptance, and expression of feelings (Rogers, 1961). Emotions are "experienced" much as one experiences symphony music or a massage. In reference to putative changes within clients resulting from Client-Centered Therapy, Rogers writes:

> . . . those feelings which have been denied to awareness, bubble through into awareness, are experienced, and increasingly owned. At the upper end of the continuum, living in the process of experiencing a continually changing flow of feelings becomes characteristic of the individual (1961, p. 156).

The metaphorical language of this passage is striking. Feelings can be "denied," or "owned," and can "bubble" and "flow." Emotions are implied to be "in" the organism much as the unextended substance of the soul was thought by Descartes to reside within the boundaries of the skin. Although Client-Centered Therapy greatly emphasizes affect, Rogers would not dispute that behavioral and cognitive factors (especially negative self-appraisals) contribute to the genesis of unpleasant emotions. However, once spawned, emotions tend to be viewed in this system as self-maintaining phenomenological entities or processes with occasional sensory concomitants, rather than as the complex interactions of behavioral, physiological, and cognitive systems. Emotions are viewed from a molar perspective and described in terms of a unitary affective process. Thus the major task of therapy lies in the "exploration" of the client's affective experience within an environment of empathy, genuineness, and unconditional positive regard.

The Rational-Emotive Therapy (RET) of Ellis (1962) stands in extreme contrast to Client-Centered Therapy in many respects, not the least of which is its conceptualization of emotion. Ellis often uses the dictum of

Epictetus—that men are not disturbed by events but rather by their views of events—to summarize his cognitive theory of emotion. The contention here is that thought and emotion are inextricably intertwined—that thinking is the *sine qua non* of feeling states.

Ellis would not deny that affect has a biochemical and physiological substrate or that innate response patterns may account for some small, clinically irrelevant fraction of all human emotionality (Ellis and Harper, 1961). However, virtually all emoting is seen as resulting from the individual's internal monologue of his ideas and beliefs: ". . . much of our emoting takes the form of self-talk or internalized sentences . . . then for all practical purposes the phrases and sentences that we keep telling ourselves frequently *are* or *become* our thoughts and emotions" (Ellis, 1962, p. 50). Negative emotions such as anxiety and depression are assumed to be associated with and to result in general from irrational beliefs, and in particular from self-statements such as "This situation I am in is terrible." The focus of the therapist who believes that "human emotions are largely a form of thinking or result from thinking" (Ellis, 1962, p. 52) is necessarily upon the cognitive modality. Irrational beliefs assumed to be at the root of emotional distress are vigorously challenged and disputed by the therapist, whose goal is to effect the client's adoption of a rational set of personal beliefs. The assumption is always: where thought travels so shall feeling follow.

A somewhat more rigorous and empirical, yet highly simplistic conceptualization of emotion has been put forth by traditional S-R theory (Eysenck and Beech, 1971; Wolpe, 1958). Under this formulation, the model for the acquisition of emotional responses is that of Pavlovian conditioning. The majority of emotional behaviors are seen as conditioned responses to conditioned stimuli which have assumed emotion-eliciting properties following successive pairings with various unconditioned stimuli. For example, fear or anxiety is viewed as an innately determined autonomic response to noxious stimuli. Individuals learn their neurotic fears much as little Albert (Watson and Rayner, 1920) learned to fear furry objects—through presentations of aversive stimuli in contiguity with previously neutral stimuli.

For Wolpe, fear is the cornerstone of "unadaptive behavior." Thus the task of the therapist is largely to ferret out the stimuli to which fear (sympathetic arousal) has been conditioned, and subsequently to break the stimulus-response connection by means of "reciprocal inhibition" or counterconditioning. As was noted earlier, various behavioral methods are employed to produce a physiological base to be paired with the conditioned stimulus or its image. The counterconditioning presumably occurs as a physiological substrate incompatible with fear becomes conditioned to the fear-producing stimulus, finally supplanting fear as the conditioned response. A putative "reciprocal inhibition" occurring at the level of the autonomic nervous system is assumed to account for any resulting anxiety diminution and lessened avoidance behavior.

If it is correct that no one class of factors is both necessary and sufficient to account for all emotionality in all human beings, and this is my contention, then treatments which limit their focus to a restricted range of these classes are likely to be of limited applicability and effectiveness. Lazarus (1973), after conducting follow-up studies of his clinical cases has hypothesized that a consideration of a broad range of modalities in therapy is necessary to produce durable results. If only multiple-factor theories of emotion can account for the research data across situations and individuals, it would seem that optimal effectiveness in the treatment of emotional disorders would require assessment and intervention within all relevant systems.

If the theory of emotion held by a school of therapy places limits both upon its range of techniques and upon its effectiveness, then therapists should attempt to ensure that their views of emotion are neither contradicted nor shown to be overly simplistic by contemporary research and theory. They can do so only by examining scientific inquiry into the nature of emotion.

Theories of Emotion

The James-Lange theory (James, 1890) identified emotion with the activity of the autonomic nervous system. Transposing the conventional presumption that physiological changes occur as a consequence of psychological feeling states, James wrote that, "bodily changes follow directly from the perception of the exciting fact, and our feeling of the same changes as they occur *is* the emotion" (1890). He believed that perception of stimuli could directly produce distinctive sets of visceral and behavioral activity, which in turn were fed back into the central nervous system. Feedback from these somatic reaction patterns, experienced at cortical levels, was held to constitute the phenomenology of emotion.

A necessary assumption of the James-Lange theory or of any peripheralist theory identifying emotion with bodily changes and visceral feelings is that the peripheral response systems are capable *in themselves* of producing all of the highly differentiated patterns of human emotionality. If the peripheralist position is correct, all variations in emotion should be accompanied by distinguishable variations in bodily activity.

The peripheralist contention that autonomic events *are* emotions has had wide influence, particularly upon behaviorally oriented psychologists.

Mowrer's (1950) theory of avoidance was based upon the assumption of equivalence between fear responses and autonomic activity. As we have seen, Wolpe also saw anxiety as an exclusively autonomic response pattern.

Cannon's (1927) investigations led him to conclude that autonomic activity could not represent a sufficient cause of subjective feeling states. He presented the following evidence in support of his argument:

1. The viscera are relatively insensitive structures.

2. Sympathectomies performed on animals do not alter emotional behavior.

3. Changes in the autonomic nervous system do not in many cases occur rapidly enough to be the single cause of experienced affect.

4. Changes in the viscera found during emotional states also occur in the absence of experienced affect.

In terms of Cannon's centralist theory of emotion, autonomic patterns associated with such emotions as fear and anger are in fact indistinguishable. Sympathetic excitation—the "flight or fight" reaction—is seen as the response to all emergency situations. The more placid emotions are similarly uniform at the visceral level and are characterized by inhibition of the sympathetic nervous system and disinhibition of the parasympathetic nervous system. Innervation of the autonomic nervous system as well as the production of emotional experience are controlled by subcortical centers which respond directly to sensory and cortical input. When stimulated, "these neurons (of the thalamus) discharge in a particular combination, they not only innervate muscles and viscera but also excite afferent paths to the cortex by direct connection. . . . The peculiar quality of the emotion is added to the simple sensation when the thalamic processes are roused" (1927, p. 120).

Cannon's work was important for behavior theory because in addition to suggesting that specific autonomic response patterns cannot be the sole source of emotionality, it postulated that the peripheral physiological substrate of emotion can be explained in terms of the undifferentiated activities of the sympathetic and parasympathetic nervous systems. Cannon argued that autonomic activity can vary only along the continuum of arousal and that the autonomic accompaniments of any given emotional response represent no more than the degree of arousal associated with that response.

The assumption that physiological accompaniments of emotion lack complexity and are distinguishable only in terms of magnitude prompted the work of Schachter and Singer (1962). If visceral sensations could not be the sole cause of emotion, then emotionality must involve at least one other response system of the organism. These investigators set out to investigate the hypothesis that emotions result from an interaction of cognitive and physiological factors. More specifically, Schachter and Singer attempted to test the assumption that (1) perceived physiological arousal is necessary for emotion; (2) the cognitive evaluation and labeling of physiological arousal is the source of emotional content.

In their now-classic study, autonomic arousal was manipulated by injecting half of the subjects with epinephrine and half with a placebo. The experimenters gave accurate information to some epinephrine subjects about what drug effects they would experience, misled others, and left the remainder uninformed. Subjects were then placed in either an anger-inducing or a euphoria-inducing situation. An analysis of self-report and behavioral data seemingly indicated that emotional responsiveness was far greater for subjects in the epinephrine-uninformed and epinephrine-misinformed conditions then for those in the other conditions. At first glance the results of the study do seem to be consistent with the investigators' hypotheses. Subjects who were not physiologically aroused remained relatively unemotional. Those with a nonemotional explanation for their arousal were also unemotional. However, the subjects who were given no explanation for their arousal presumably labeled it as emotion and were consequently more emotional. The authors therefore concluded that emotions result from cognitive explanations of exteroceptively perceived arousal.

The Schachter and Singer study and the two-factor theory of emotion (Schachter, 1964) have had substantial influence both upon the scientific study of emotion and upon research in psychotherapy. However, the original research is open to severe criticisms both in terms of its methodology and the conceptual appropriateness of its authors' assumption that they studied true emotional analogues (Lang, 1971; R.S. Lazarus, 1968; Plutchik and Ax, 1967). The critique of this study presented below serves not only to illustrate problems endemic to the particular research but also to underscore the complexity of emotional phenomena.

A very basic methodological problem with the study centers around the use of an internal post hoc analysis of findings. Initial analyses of behavioral data in the "euphoria" condition and subjective reports in both the "euphoria" and "anger" conditions did not show significant differences between placebo and epinephrine uninformed groups. This would weigh against the authors' hypothesis that varied arousal in the face of constant eliciting conditions produces varied emotionality. In a further analysis of these same data, which did yield significant results on these comparisons, those epinephrine-uninformed subjects who stated in response to a postexperimental questionnaire that they believed some aspect of their bodily reactions had been drug-produced were excluded. The elimination of these "self-informing" subjects is questionable because the post hoc assessment did not determine *when* the subjects' correct attribution took place—during or after the emotion-provoking situation. In any case, all that can be demonstrated post hoc is a *correlational* and not a *causal* relationship between self-informing and emotionality. In testing their hypothesis, the authors exclude from the data analysis subjects who are *assumed* to have demonstrated lessened emotionality *because* they reported attribution of bodily state to drug effects. They beg the question by assuming their hypothesis in testing their hypothesis.

A recent doctoral dissertation (Marshall, 1974) attempted to replicate the Schachter and Singer experiment using only the "euphoria" condition. No differences were found between a placebo group and an epinephrine-misinformed group on either behavioral or self-report measures. Once again these findings fail to support the hypotheses concerning one set of interactions between cognitive and physiological variables.

The authors' assumption that subcutaneous injection of epinephrine produced a true experimental analogue of "emotional arousal" is also subject to question. Glandular secretion of adrenalin is a gradual infusion which produces cardiovascular effects dissimilar to that of rapid injection (Keefe and Neil, 1965). Schachter and Singer did not take multiple physiological measures during the presentation of situational cues. The authors used pulse rates (as counted by experimenters) as an independent measure of arousal. Pulse rate is highly variable following administration of epinephrine (Goodman and Gillman, 1960), and, in any case, cannot be assumed to be a valid index of sympathetic arousal in view of the great proportion of variance in other measures (e.g., GSR, blood pressure) left unaccounted for.

Despite the aforementioned methodological problems with the original research, the Schachterian theory of emotion has been embraced by some in the clinical community. If emotional behavior commonly occurs in the manner described by Schachter and Singer, then the implications for psychotherapy would be most significant. Since perceived arousal and certain cognitions (cf. Ellis) are both considered necessary for emotion, modifications in either of these areas should produce a concomitant altera-tion in experienced affect. A number of investigators have gone so far as to assume that emotional patterns of long standing become quite malleable when subjects are either given false feedback about their levels of arousal or are induced to attribute the source of their arousal to emotionally uncharged stimuli. A study (Valins and Ray, 1967) that sought to reduce avoidance behavior in "snake phobics" through use of a misattribution manipulation has been cited as having demonstrated that the selfperceptive process is the crucial mechanism underlying systematic densensitization (Murray and Jacobson, 1971). In an influential paper, Wilkins (1971) has conceptualized systematic densensitization as a primarily cognitive pro-cess in which individuals reduce anxiety by observing themselves failing to signal anxiety in response to hierarchy items, and consequently inferring that they are not afraid. The logical and empirical difficulties inherent in this kind of purely cognitive explanation of systematic densensitization have been pointed out by Davison and Wilson (1973).

The Valins and Ray study itself has been severely criticized on methodological grounds (Bandura, 1969; Davison and Wilson, 1973). Several attempts to replicate the study failed to show the false feedback manipulation effective in reducing fear or behavioral avoidance (Gaupp, Stern, and Galbraith, 1972; Kent, Wilson, and Nelson, 1972; Sushinsky and Bootzin, 1970). However, each of these replication attempts constituted a more conservative test of the effects of false feedback than did the research of Valins and Ray. In the replications, subjects were either pretested to insure selection of truly fearful individuals or posttested without using the monetary incentive employed by Valins and Ray. Speculating that these procedural variations may have obscured the effects of false feedback, Borkovec and Glasgow (1973) found that snake phobics exposed to an actual snake during pretesting manifested higher levels of physiological arousal during the experiment than did subjects who were not pretested. Of subjects receiving false feedback, only those who were not pretested showed significantly less avoidance than controls following feedback. In yet another study (Borkovec, Wall, and Stone, 1974) false feedback of heart rate was found to be ineffective in reducing reported anxiety or behavioral manifestations of fear.

Studies which have attempted to alter persistent emotional patterns by inducing misattribution of arousal have achieved little success. Cognitive manipulations would seem to be relatively ineffectual in altering emotions associated with high levels of physiological arousal. Clearly, even if Schachter's theory is partially correct, emotional states of long standing cannot be easily modified. The phobic individual with a lengthy history of labeling arousal in the presence of the feared stimulus is quite unlikely to change his opinion about what that arousal signifies. However, a more reasonable explanation for the shortcomings in research studies that attempt to verify the two-factor theory of Schachter is that the theory provides an incomplete and inaccurately simplistic explanation of emotional functioning.

Recent reformulations of the concept of arousal (Lacey, 1967; Routtenberg, 1968) suggest that theories of emotion which subscribe to the notion of arousal as a simple, undifferentiated process underlying all emotion are on less than firm footing. Lacey (1958; 1967) has demonstrated a fractionation of sympathetic subsystems in response to arousing stimuli. A single stimulus may produce some responses in a sympathetic direction while others may show a parasympathetic pattern. The notion of arousal as the undifferentiated substrate of all emotion is further weakened by the substantial body of evidence indicating that some emotions are physiologically distinguishable.

Provided with a unique opportunity for direct observation of a stomach through an abdominal fistula, Wolf and Wolff (1947) found different patterns of gastric activity associated with fear and anger. During angry periods, motility, blood flow, and secretion of acid were increased. Reports of fear were associated with inhibition of these functions. In a study which examined 14 physiological indicators of subjects exposed to fear- and anger-inducing situations (Ax, 1953), subjects' reports indicated that the experimental manipulations were successful in producing "genuine" emotions. Half of the dependent measures showed significant differences in the extent to which they were present in fear and anger. Ax concluded that a fear reaction corresponded to the pattern produced by the action of epinephrine, whereas the responses associated with anger were similar to the pattern produced by a combination of ephinephrine and norepinephrine. A replication of the Ax (1953) study also examined physiological accompaniments of a cold pressor test (J. Schachter, 1957). This research substantiated Ax's conclusions with respect to fear and anger while finding still a third norepinephrine-like pattern associated with the cold pressor test. Further evidence supporting the physiological differences between fear and anger is found in studies of infrahuman species. Examination of the adrenal medullas of animals whose survival is dependent on fearful responses (e.g., rabbits) reveal a preponderance of epinephrine, while predators whose aggressive behavior is anger-like show much higher ratios of norepinephrine (Funkenstein, 1955).

However, although it has been shown that physiological differences do exist, research also indicates a considerable physiological overlap among emotions. While Ax (1953) found differences between fear and anger on seven measures, the differences on the remaining seven were nonsignificant. At the present level of technology one can make discriminations only among some emotional states, but one cannot with psychophysiological indices account for a satisfactory portion of the variance in self-reports of emotion. Some of the failure to find more differences and differences of greater magnitude may result from investigators seeking stable response patterns to particular stimuli across subjects. Studies employing this format could not identify consistent intrasubject patterns of physiological differentiation in the presence of high intersubject variability and intrasubject consistency in response to stressful stimulation. In a study which examined the physiological accompaniments of task performance under varying levels of motivational arousal, Schnore (1959) also found consistency within subjects and differences across subjects.

The rather compelling evidence demonstrating some physiological differentiation of emotions indicates that variation in autonomic response patterns could conceivably be an important but insufficient factor in the production of emotion. Although Cannon demonstrated that loss of interoceptive feedback from the autonomic nervous system did not eliminate emotional *behavior* in animals, he did not demonstrate maintenance of emotional *experience* as his subjects were unable to report on their effective levels. Studies of patients with spinal cord injuries indicate that loss of autonomic neural feedback is associated with a lessened capacity to experience emotion and that specific emotions may be attenuated by certain localized injuries (Hohmann, 1966). A large body of research and theory argues for the existence of feedback mechanisms which bypass the associative cortex to directly mediate the influence of peripheral response systems upon awareness.

Such feedback loops could allow behavior and autonomic activity to influence emotional states directly. Thus it would not be necessary for peripheral activity to be perceived exteroceptively and evaluated in order to actuate emotional experience. For example, it has been shown that distension of the sinus of the cartoid artery has an effect on electrocortical activity (Bonvallet, Dell, and Heibel, 1954). Lacey (1967) has argued that this provides evidence of a mechanism whereby changes in blood pressure could affect cortical activity. Gellhorn (1970), theorizing from an impressive data base, has proposed that proprioception arising from autonomic and muscular activity directly influences hypothalamic centers to produce emotionality.

The manner in which emotion is expressed behaviorally may have important implications both for the quality of emotional experience and for the underlying physiology. Tompkins (1962; 1970) has attributed an important role to the effects of facial expressions upon subcortical centers. Owing to the great number and density of receptors in the facial musculature, alterations in facial expression, are seen as a source of direct influence upon the central nervous system. A recent study (Laird, 1974) offers strong support for this theory. Subjects' facial expressions first were molded into "smiles" or "frowns" without their being aware of the nature of these expressions. Subjects were then exposed to a variety of stimuli. They reported feeling happier when smiling than when frowning. Smiling subjects also rated a series of cartoons as more humorous than did frowning subjects. In a series of studies (Funkenstein, King, and Drolette, 1957), the biochemical correlates of emotion were found to vary as a function of style of emotional expression. The outward expression of anger was found to be associated with the secretion of norephinephrine, while unexpressed anger directed inward was associated with secretion of epinephrine.

It should be clear from the preceding discussion that any adequate theory of emotion must take into account the potential effects of peripheral systems (autonomic and overt-motor) on affect. Mechanisms exist which can allow autonomic events to directly influence emotionality. Behavior can also affect the quality of emotional experience. There is much evidence that peripheral events are more complicated and subtle than once thought by various proponents of undimensional arousal. It is likely that these peripheral response systems interact with neocortical-cognitive activity in a highly complex fashion.

With the exception of Schachter's tow-factor theory, many researchers, until recently, have neglected the role of cognitive factors in emotion. Arnold (1960; 1970) and R.S. Lazarus (1968) have conceptualized emotion as intimately connected to a cognitive process of situational *appraisal:* an emotion is defined as "a felt tendency toward anything appraised as good (enhancing) and away from anything appraised as bad (harmful)" (Arnold, 1970, p. 176). This view of emotion sees affects as integral features of the information processing and coping capabilities of the organism (R.S. Lazarus, 1968; Pribram, 1967). According to this formulation, emotions are generated in the organism by evaluations of consequences to it implied by sensory input or retrieval of stored input in the form of images or cognitions. Both felt emotions and physiological accompaniments are generated as a result of a cognitive process of appraisal. It should be noted that the assumptions of cognitive-appraisal theory are quite similar to those of Ellis' Rational-Emotive Therapy. Emotions are seen to follow from cognizing—as implying some belief or evaluation.

There is much evidence to support cognitive-appraisal theory. In R.S. Lazarus' laboratory it has been demonstrated that the process of appraisal directly influences emotionality. In a series of studies (Lazarus and Opton, 1966; Lazarus, Speisman, Mordkoff, and Davison, 1962) physiological measures were recorded while subjects viewed a highly stressful film. Autonomic reactivity was reduced in those subjects who were instructed to deny or intellectualize the emotionally charged aspects of the film. A number of clinical studies have shown that modifying cognitions in the form of self-verbalizations can lead to changes in emotional responding (Meichenbaum, 1972; Meichenbaum, Gilmore, and Fedoravicius, 1971).

The cognitive-appraisal theory of emotion can be contrasted with that of Schachter. The former views emotions as resulting from the perception and appraisal of the autonomic arousal occasioned by the stimulus properties of a given situation. In this sense a Schachterian schema may be regarded as a special case of cognitive-appraisal theory—particularly viable when situational cues are vague and ill-defined or when the individual's social learning history does not readily provide categories or constructions to place upon a situation, thus making rapid evaluation difficult.

In summary, if any one conclusion is warranted from the discussion of emotion presented here, it is that at this juncture in history no one conceptualization can satisfactorily account for all human emotion. The response systems of the organism which influence experienced affect are numerous and their interactions complex. Increasing sophistication on the part of therapists should lead to an abandonment of the attempt to conceive of all emotion in terms of any one response system of the organism. To deal adequately with the complexities of emotionality, the therapist must bring to bear a variety of perspectives upon the clinical situation.

Multisystem Perspectives

Lang (1968) has pointed out that although early desensitization research was directed toward the elimination of phobic anxiety, this "phobic anxiety" was typically measured in terms of three partially independent response systems: behavioral, phenomenological, and physiological. Even so-called monosymptomatic phobias are complex events involving avoidance responses, self-reports of fear, and autonomic innervation. Low correlations among these variables indicate that they vary independently of one another. In the case of the more global complaints usually observed in the clinical situation, the complexity of system interactions is increased. For example, take the case of the man who is anxious in confrontations with his wife. Behavioral deficits may interact with pre-existing dysfunctional social roles to produce cognitions leading to emotion-generating self-verbalizations. Emotionality generated via this route may combine synergystically with autonomic arousal classically conditioned to certain verbal and nonverbal cues. This entire process may be amplified by immediate situational appraisal or self-labeling of perceived bodily changes. The individual who seems to be a likely candidate for desensitization or assertion training—or cognitive restructuring or relationship therapy—may be a candidate for all four. Therapies have, for reasons of ignorance or dogma, failed to produce multisystem approaches to the modification of aversive affects.

Lazarus' advocacy of broad-spectrum behavioral treatment (1967) was an early attempt to address systematically in therapy an expanded range of factors which might influence emotional adjustment. Lang (1971) called for systematic intervention across a range of modalities when he proposed a therapy for anxiety that involved (a) shaping of verbal sets (cognitions), (b) teaching of coping behaviors, and (c) attenuation of autonomic arousal. He saw psychotherapy as ideally consisting of "a vigorous multisystem training program, tailored to the unique behavioral topography presented by the patient" (p. 109). Based on an extensive review of the psychophysiological literature, he argued that because of our poor understanding of the nature of interaction between response systems, it cannot be expected that changes in one response system resulting from narrow therapeutic programs will automatically generalize to other systems. He speculated that the achievement of durable therapeutic results may necessitate the separate treatment of each response system involved. Lazarus (1973) reached a similar conclusion through an examination of clinical data.

In earlier chapters of this volume Lazarus provided an outline of Multimodal Therapy and described the BASIC ID mnemonic. Through long-term follow-up evaluations of his clinical cases, Lazarus (1973) reports that relapse rates are lessened when the processes of assessment and treatment occur across all of these modalities. Intriguing as this finding may be, the usefulness of this system to one clinician hardly constitutes acceptable scientific evidence either for its effectiveness, or for the existence of the modalities as anything more than potentially important clinical abstractions.

Only controlled outcome studies can conclusively demonstrate the clinical efficacy of a multimodal approach. However, independent of outcome research, an important question can still be asked: is there some scientific basis for supposing that these modalities have a special place in the topography of the emotional response? The answer is unequivocally yes. In fact, it can be argued that each of the five intrapersonal psychological modalities (behavior, affect, sensation, imagery, and cognition) corresponds to a particular response system in the organism that has been documented by basic scientific research.

Behavior forms the basis of observation in psychology. The effects of behavior on emotion have been reported in the preceding review. This represented one of the dimensions of the emotional response which emerged from Lang's analysis of the desensitization literature.

Affect can be viewed as the manifestation of interactions among the other systems. It must be considered as a separate response system, however. Self-report of affect does not correlate highly with measures of other systems and was another significant dimension to emerge from Lang's (1969) review of the desensitization literature. This system is also a uniquely sensitive and varied component of the information processing capacity of the organism. The emotional "tuning" of an individual, or the availability of affect under varying stimulus conditions, has great implications for the way he deals with the environment. The individual who responds with little or no affect to potentially damaging or stressful events may not react with appropriate coping. The individual who is "out of touch" with affect must place total reliance on his cognitive processing systems. This person may not only find himself to be socially undesirable, but also cut off from a potentially useful source of feedback and evaluation.

Sensation, as Lazarus notes, subsumes the sympathetic and parasympathetic nervous systems. Autonomic responses constituted another independent dimension of emotional responding according to Lang's (1969) laboratory findings. The importance of this system and its effects on emotion have been documented in the preceding review.

Cognition is unquestionably a fundamental contributor to emotion, if not its primary basis. Attribution theorists (Schachter) and appraisal theorists (R. S. Lazarus, M. Arnold) and much research have attested to the role of cognition in emotion. Recent research has demonstrated that cognition is not a unitary phenomenon; there are at least two distinguishable modes of cognizing (see Bogen, 1969; and Kimura, 1973, for reviews). These investigations have shown that the right and left cerebral hemispheres represent a dichotomy in consciousness. Verbal cognitions are mediated by the left hemisphere while visual-spatial cognitions are mediated by the right hemisphere. The fact that each cerebral hemisphere is specialized to function in one of two distinct modes of information processing provides further corroboration of the validity of Lazarus' schema. Lazarus' modalities of cognition and imagery directly correspond to the verbal processing mode (left-side) and visual-spatial processing mode (right-side), respectively.

The role of biochemical factors in emotion, particularly the actions of the catecholamines, has been established by extensive research (Kety, 1967). An examination of this literature is beyond the scope of this review.

The interpersonal modality represents a different level of analysis than do the other modalities and obviously cannot correspond to any intraorganismic response system.

Rather than emerging as mere clinical abstractions, Lazarus' modalities achieve support as basic constructs of psychophysiology. The questions a multimodal therapist asks a client during the assessment of emotional disturbance are quite similar to the questions an investigator asks of subjects in the psychophysiology laboratory (Schwartz, 1974). Questions about feelings, thoughts, and images as well as behavioral and autonomic measurements, often supply the basic data in this kind of research. The commonality is not adventitious. The fullest understanding of the emotional aspects of human existence requires a comprehensive study of the modalities of the BASIC ID.

References

Arnold, M. B. Perennial problems in the field of emotion. In M. B. Arnold (Ed.), *Feelings and emotions*. New York: Academic Press, 1970.

Arnold, M. B. *Emotion and personality*. Columbia University Press: New York, 1960.

Ax, A. F. The physiological differentiation between fear and anger in humans. *Psychosomatic Medicine*, 1953, *15*, 433-442.

Bandura, A. *Principles of behavior modification*. New York: Holt, Rinehart and Winston, 1969.

Bogen, J. E. The other side of the brain II: An oppositional mind. *Bulletin of the Los Angeles Neurological Societies*, 1969, *34*, 135-162.

Bonvallet, M., Dell, P., & Heibel, G. Tonus sympathique et activité electrique corticale. *Electroencephalography and Clinical Neurophysiology*, 1954, *6*, 119-144.

Borkovec, T. D., & Glasgow, R. E. Boundary conditions of false heart-rate feedback effects on avoidance behavior: A resolution of discrepant results. *Behavior Research and Therapy*, 1973, *11*, 171-177.

Borkevec, T. D., Wall, R. L., & Stone, N. M. False physiological feedback and the maintenance of speech anxiety. *Journal of Abnormal Psychology*, 1974, *83*, 164-168.

Cannon, W. B. The James-Lange theory of emotions: A critical examination and an alternative theory. *American Journal of Psychology*, 1927, *39*, 106-124.

Davison, G. C., and Wilson, G. T. Processes of fear reduction in systematic desensitization: Cognitive and social reinforcement factors in humans. *Behavior Therapy*, 1973, *4*, 1-21.

Ellis, A. *Reason and emotion in psychotherapy*. New York: Lyle Stuart, 1962.

Ellis, A., & Harper, R. *A guide to rational living*. No. Hollywood, Calif.: Wilshire, 1961.

Eysenck, H. J., & Beech, H. R. Counter conditioning and related methods. In A. E. Bergin & S. L. Garfield (Eds.), *Handbook of psychotherapy and behavior change*. New York: Wiley, 1971.

Funkenstein, D. H. The physiology of fear and anger. *Scientific American*, 1955, *192*, 74-80.

Funkenstein, D. H., King, S. H., & Drolette, M. E. *Mastery of stress*. Cambridge, Mass.: Harvard University Press, 1957.

Gaupp, L. A., Stern, R. M., & Galbraith, G. G. False heart-rate feedback and reciprocal inhibition by aversive relief in the treatment of snake avoidance behavior. *Behavior Therapy*, 1972, *3*, 7-20.

Gellhorn, E. The emotions and the ergotropic and trophotropic systems. *Psychologische Forschung*, 1970, *34*, 48-94.

Goodman, L. S., & Gillman, A. *The pharmacological basis of therapeutics*. New York: Macmillan, 1965.

Hebb, D. O. Spontaneous neurosis in champanzees: Theoretical relations with clinical and experimental phenomena. *Psychosomatic Medicine*, 1947, *9*, 3-16.

Hohmann, G. W. Some effects of spinal cord lessions on experienced emotional feelings. *Psychophysiology,* 1966, *3,* 143-156.

James, W. *Principles of psychology.* New York: Holt, 1890.

Keefe, C., & Neil, E. *Samson Wright's applied physiology.* New York: Oxford University Press, 1965.

Kent, R. N., Wilson, G. T., & Nelson, R. Effects of false heart-rate feedback on avoidance behavior: An investigation of "cognitive desensitization." *Behavior Therapy,* 1972, *3,* 1-6.

Kety, S. S. Psychoendocrine systems and emotion: Biological aspects. In D. C. Glass (Ed.), *Neurophysiology and emotion.* New York: Rockefeller University Press, 1967.

Kimura, D. The asymmetry of the human brain. *Scientific American,* 1973, *228,* 70-78.

Lacey, J. I. Somatic response patterning and stress: Some revisions of activation theory. In M. H. Appley & R. Trumbull (Eds.), *Psychological stress: Issues in research.* New York: Appleton-Century-Crofts, 1967.

Lacey, J. I., & Lacey, B. C. Verification and extention of the principle of autonomic response stereotypy. *American Journal of Physiology,* 1958, *71,* 50-73.

Laird, J. D. Self-attribution of emotion: The effects of expressive behavior on the quality of emotional experience. *Journal of Personality and Social Psychology,* 1974, *29,* 475-486.

Lang, P. J. The mechanics of desensitization and the laboratory study of human fear. In C. M. Franks (Ed.), *Behavior therapy: Appraisal and status.* New York: McGraw-Hill, 1969.

Lang, P. J. The application of psychophysiological methods. In A. E. Bergin & S. L. Garfield (Eds.), *Handbook of psychotherapy and behavior change.* New York: Wiley, 1971.

Lazarus, A. A. In support of technical eclecticism. *Psychological Reports,* 1967, *21,* 415-416.

Lazarus, A. A. Multimodal behavior therapy: Treating the "BASIC ID." *Journal of Nervous and Mental Disease,* 1973, *156,* 404-411.

Lazarus, R. S. Emotions and adaptation: Conceptual and empirical relations. In W. J. Arnold (Ed.) *Nebraska symposium on motivation.* Lincoln: University of Nebraska Press, 1968.

Lazarus, R. S., & Opton, E. M. The study of psychological stress: A summary of theoretical formulations and experimental findings. In C. D. Spielberger (Ed.), *Anxiety and behavior.* New York: Academic Press, 1966.

Lazarus, R. S., Speisman, J. D., Mordkoff, A. M., & Davison, L. A. A laboratory study of psychological stress produced by a motion picture film. *Psychological Monographs,* 1962, *76* (Whole No. 553).

Marshall, G. *Cognitive social and physiological determinants of emotional states: A replication and extension.* Unpublished dissertation, Stanford University, 1974.

Meichenbaum, D. Cognitive modification of test anxious college students. *Journal of Consulting and Clinical Psychology,* 1972, *39,* 370-380.

Meichenbaum, D., Gilmore, J., & Fedoravicius, A. Group insight vs. group desensitization in treating speech anxiety. *Journal of Consulting and Clinical Psychology,* 1971, *36,* 410-421.

Mowrer, O. H. *Learning theory and personality dynamics.* New York: Ronald Press, 1950.

Murray, E. J., & Jacobson, L. I. The nature of learning in traditional and behavioral psychotherapy. In A. E. Bergin & S. L. Garfield (Eds.), *Handbook of psychotherapy and behavior change.* New York: Wiley, 1971.

Plutchik, R., & Ax, A. F. A critique of determinants of emotional state by Schachter and Singer (1962). *Psychophysiology,* 1967, *4,* 78-82.

Pribram, K. H. The new neurology and the biology of emotion: A structural approach. *American Psychologist,* 1967, *22,* 830-838.

Rogers, C. R. *On becoming a person.* Boston: Houghton Mifflin, 1961.

Routtenberg, A. The two-arousal hypothesis: Recticular formulation and limbic system. *Psychological Review,* 1968, *75,* 51-80.

Schachter, J. Pain, fear, and anger in hypertensives and normotensives. *Psychosomatic Medicine,* 1957, *19,* 17-29.

Schachter, S. The interaction of cognitive and physiological determinants of emotional state. In L. Berkowitz (Ed.), *Advance in experimental social psychology.* Vol. 1. New York: Academic Press, 1964.

Schachter, S., & Singer, J. E. Cognitive, social, and physiological determinants of emotional state. *Psychological Review,* 1962, *69,* 379-399.

Schnore, M. M. Individual patterns of physiological activity as a function of task differences and degree of arousal. *Journal of Experimental Psychology.* 1959, *58,* 117-128.

Schwartz, G. Personal communication, 1974.

Sushinsky, L. W., & Bootzin, R. R. Cognitive desensitization as a model of systematic desensitization. *Behavior Research and Therapy,* 1970, *8,* 29-34.

Tompkins, S. S. *Affect, imagery and consciousness:* Vol. 1. The positive affects. New York: Springer, 1962.

Tompkins, S. S. Affect as the primary motivational system. In M. B. Arnold (Ed.), *Feelings and emotions.* New York: Academic Press, 1970.

Valins, S., & Ray, A. A. Effects of cognitive desensitization on avoidance behavior. *Journal of Personality and Social Psychology,* 1967, *7,* 345-350.

Watson, J. B., & Rayner, R. Conditioned emotional reactions. *Journal of Experimental Psychology,* 1920, *3,* 1-14.

Wilkins, W. Desensitization: Social and cognitive factors underlying the effectiveness of Wolpe's procedure. *Psychological Bulletin,* 1971, *76,* 311-317.

Wolf, S., & Wolff, H. G. *Human gastric function.* Oxford, England: Oxford University Press, 1947.

Wolpe, J. *Psychotherapy by reciprocal inhibition.* Palo Alto, Calif.: Stanford University Press, 1958.

Chapter 6

The Drug Modality

Allen Fay

If therapists were asked to choose the one modality of the BASIC ID which they considered to be least related to the other six, most would undoubtedly select the D modality (drugs or biological factors). Their choice would result partly from their acceptance of the dichotomization of mind and body—an unfortunate and inaccurate notion that has far-reaching consequences in assessment, therapy, and the training of therapists. The purpose of this chapter is to help therapists integrate the drug modality into their conceptualization of problems and their repertoire of therapeutic techniques. I have presented a brief, nontechnical clinical review of some of the principles and issues in drug therapy, but would further recommend several basic and lucid review books (Appleton and Davis, 1973; Hollister, 1973; and Honigfeld and Howard, 1973). One may readily keep abreast of the newest developments in the field by consulting the International Drug Therapy Newsletter (Ayd).

The discussion that follows will be confined to drugs rather than to other biological or somatic interventions (ECT, insulin, electrosleep, psychosurgery, etc.). Medications considered to be dangerous, of little therapeutic value, or not sufficiently specific in their action will be omitted, as will pharmacological agents not currently available in the United States. Drug therapy for the various organic brain syndromes will likewise not be covered.

Despite its apparent uniqueness, the drug modality interacts substantially with the other areas of the BASIC ID. For example, because the actual taking of drugs is a *behavior* related to the suggestions of the prescriber, it is in part dependent on the relationship between the patient and the prescriber *(interpersonal)*. Various beliefs are associated with taking medication, e.g., "If I take medication it means I'm sick; if I don't take it, it means

Appreciation is expressed to Dr. Richard Schaeffer of Scottsdale, Arizona for sharing many of his invaluable ideas and clinical experiences about psychotropic drug therapy.

I'm not sick''; or "Nothing can help me" *(cognition)*. Or, one may hear "My friend took Thorazine and walked around like a zombie. I picture it vividly *(imagery)* and it terrifies me *(affect)*''; or "When I take Stelazine, I feel as if I'm jumping out of my skin and my mouth gets very dry *(sensory)*.'' Therefore, it is clear that the taking of drugs is affected by the six other modalities and in turn produces results which affect the other modalities, e.g., by eliminating hallucinations and delusions,, relieving depression, reducing assaultive behavior, allaying anxiety, and thereby facilitating interpersonal contact.

Despite the unequivocal value of drugs in the treatment of psychological (biopsychological) dysfunctions, many practitioners—both medical and nonmedical—regard them as ancillary, employ them as a last resort, or eschew their use altogether. These tendencies persist, even in the face of considerable evidence which supports the idea of a primary biological disturbance in schizophrenia and manic depressive "illness" (possibly in other affective disturbances as well). The often stated view that schizophrenia is not a viable concept obscures the issue. If we, as clinicians, recognize that many people's lives are seriously disrupted by grossly maladaptive cognitions, behaviors, images, affects, sensations, and interpersonal styles, which do not respond to nonpharmacological interventions but are substantially relieved by psychotropic drugs, then the particular term we use to denote this phenomenon becomes irrelevant. Our interest lies in relieving the distress of such individuals through appropriate medication, thus enabling them to feel better and to benefit from a variety of useful techniques encompassed by the other modalities. People with major biological deficits usually lag behind their peers in the acquisition of adaptive responses; yet for some individuals, appropriate intervention in the D modality will effect prompt and dramatic relief of a long-standing disturbance where years of prior therapy have been to no avail. In fact, drugs represent the only modality that has been consistently proven effective in schizophrenia and manic-depressive disorders. In such cases, medication can be considered as a necessary though not always sufficient condition for the satisfactory resolution of the difficulty.

Therapists with limited training or experience in the use of psychiatric drugs often regard pharmacotherapy as awesome and highly complex even though the major "prescriber" of drugs in this country is the "layman" who is constantly acquiring and using a dazzling array of over-the-counter and even restricted medicinal substances. Most of the major original psychotropic drugs were serendipitously discovered, and, despite numerous experimental studies supporting the value of antischizophrenic drugs in particular, the use of psychopharmacological agents by the clinician still tends to be largely empirical. There is little reason to believe that nonmedical therapists, even clients themselves, cannot be trained in the principles of medication use. In fact, many patients have become quite expert at practical psychopharmacy. It seems likely that the dearth of physicians and their relative unavailability to the majority of people who could benefit from medication, as well as the growing trend in medicine to train paraprofessionals, will lead ultimately and inexorably to the wider dissemination of information about the drug modality. Even now, it is not infrequent for patients to have access to the *Physician's Desk Reference,* an annual compendium of information issued by drug manufacturers about indications, dose forms, dose ranges, and side effects and precautions for all drugs. In a few countries, notably Japan, most drugs (including the psychotropic agents) are freely available without prescription.

If the material which follows is to have practical clinical value for the reader, at least one of the following two propositions must be accepted:

1. A substantial primary biological element is operative in some of the mental dysfunctions of unknown origin (schizophrenia and some primary affective disorders).

2. Regardless of any substantial primary biological aberration that may or may not be operative, symptomatic relief may be achieved in a significant number of clients (patients, consultees, helpees, etc.) through the use of drugs. The benefit here may be predominately pharmacological or nonpharmacological (placebo) (Rickels, 1968).

The basic principles are quite simple, and psychiatric drugs may be divided along clinical lines into three compartments: (I) antischizophrenia drugs, (II) antiaffective disorders drugs, and (III) antianxiety drugs. These compartments will later be subdivided on the basis of chemical and clinical considerations. However, an attempt at rigorous definition or a more explicit separation of these entities will not be made, since it is understood that there are widely differing definitions, particularly of schizophrenia. In this regard the concept of "schizophrenic spectrum" is useful in that it includes some persons considered "borderline" or schizoid who may benefit from drug therapy. Not infrequently it may prove difficult to differentiate schizophrenia from primary affective disorders. (For an excellent review of diagnosis see Woodruff et al., 1974.) In addition, drugs used in one group of disorders may be effective at times in another, e.g., Mellaril (thioridazine) and other antischizophrenia agents are often useful in the treatment of "agitated depression." Likewise, Sinequan or Adipin (doxepin), an antidepressant (Compartment II), may also be useful as an antianxiety agent. Similarly, Tofranil (imipramine) and other antidepressants (Compartment II) are effective in stopping panic attacks in the "phobic-anxiety syndrome." Mild depressions, especially when accompanied by anxiety, sometimes respond to Compartment III drugs (e.g., Serax or Tranxene) (although work in the nondrug modalities tends to be more productive in the treatment of milder depressions).

The case for therapeutic efficacy is most persuasive for the anti-schizophrenia drugs, somewhat less compelling for the antiaffective disorders drugs (except lithium)and least convincing (at least experimentally) for the antianxiety drugs. For example, a major problem with the antidepressant drugs is the long latency period (ten days to three weeks) before the clinical effects become evident. This lag is a major reason for the continuing popularity of shock treatment (ECT). Also militating against the rigorous demonstration of drug efficacy is the high spontaneous remission rates for many disorders as well as the enormous influence of placebo effects. Noncompliance (the failure to take a prescribed drug in the dose recommended or even at all) in both extramural and intramural settings is also a major problem, with up to 70 percent of patients either not taking the prescribed drugs or taking them in a manner other than prescribed. Further difficulties are created by individual (genetic and nongenetic) differences, which result in variations, often marked, in the responses of different people to identical doses of the same drug.

Despite these problems and limitations, the enlightened use of drugs involves straightforward rather than arcane procedures. It is simply a matter of:

1. Forming an hypothesis about which compartment is the most relevant one.
2. Knowing which drugs are in each compartment.
3. Mastering a few basic rules of prescribing.
4. Being aware of potential side effects or other problems that may result from the use of drugs and knowing what precautions to take. This is the major area where expert knowledge is important, especially where medical problems and other (nonpsychiatric) drugs are involved.

Once a working hypothesis about the appropriate diagnostic compartment is proposed by a therapist who knows which drugs belong in each compartment, the basis for a rational drug choice has been established. Note that the term diagnosis is used here operationally—patients are not labeled. Drugs are recommended largely because it has been observed that people with particular symptoms and dysfunctions are most apt to feel better and to function more to their satisfaction under the influence of certain medications. Although the efficacy of certain drugs has been established, there are no absolute criteria for defining the "conditions" or "illnesses" which the drugs are "treating." Chemical parameters are now beginning to be identified which will enable more precise diagnostic statements to be made in the future.

The Drugs Themselves

There are about 40 psychotropic agents currently available. The three major compartments of psychiatric drugs presented above may be divided into subcompartments, and, in some cases, sub-subcompartments. The various groups are generally designated by technical names relating to their chemical structures. However, it is less crucial to learn the technical names of the subcompartments (although this would be well worth the effort), than it is to know which drugs belong to the various compartments and subcompartments. The names are provided in Table 1, which despite its complex appearance, is basically simple if one keeps in mind the tricompartmental concept.*

Note that Compartment I is the largest, containing five groups of drugs in current active use. The first three groups (phenothiazines, thioxanthenes, and butyrophenones) are widely prescribed and have been available for many years; the latter two are very new, and insufficient data have been accumulated about them. Subcompartments C, D, and E of Compartment I currently have one member each and Subcompartment B has two. Subcompartment A, the phenothiazines, has three groups, Group 2 (the piperazines) containing by far the largest number of drugs. As can be seen in Table 1, Compartments II and III contain three groups each.

There has been some controversy about the practical necessity of knowing all the drugs in each compartment and subcompartment, with some therapists believing it sufficient to know only a few key drugs in each. The present author disagrees with the latter group. For reasons yet unknown, some patients who do not respond to one or more drugs in a particular compartment do respond to other drugs in that compartment which may be closely related chemically, i.e., in the same subcompartments. Often there are subtle differences in side effects even within the same sub-subcompartment. For example, many patients feel uncomfortably sedated by the aliphatic phenothiazines. But Vesprin is much less apt to make them feel "zombie-like" than Thorazine. The piperazine phenothiazines are apt to cause extrapyramidal side effects (Parkinson effects or various abnormal movements), yet among these drugs Trilafon is less likely to cause them than Prolixin, and Proketazine may be still less likely to do so.

Generally, individual drugs are named in three ways. The most scientific (but least used) is the *chemical* name, a cumbersome technical

---

* Anyone who is deterred by the grotesque or chimerical qualities of this table could possibly profit from some work in the cognitive modality, so that the cognition "This is impossible, who can learn this ridiculous nonsense?" through transmogrification becomes "What some fools can learn, any fool can learn."

Table 1

I. Antischizophrenia	II. Antiaffective Disorders	III. Antianxiety

A. Phenothiazines
  1. aliphatic group
    a. Thorazine* (chlorpromazine)
    b. Vesprin* (triflupromazine)
  2. piperazine group
    a. Trilafon (perphenazine)
    b. Compazine (prochlorperazine)
    c. Prolixin (fluphenazine)
      Permitil (fluphenazine)
    d. Stelazine (trifluoperazine)
    e. Tindal (acetophenazine)
    f. Proketazine (carphenazine)
    g. Repoise (butaperazine)
  3. piperidine group
    a. Mellaril* (thioridazine)
    b. Serentil (mesoridazine)
    c. Quide (piperacetazine)
 	
B. Thioxanthenes
  1. aliphatic group
    Taractan* (chlorprothixene)
  2. piperazine group
    Navane (thiothixene)
 	
C. Butyrophenones
    Haldol (haloperidol)
 	
D. Dihydroindolones
    Moban (molindone)
 	
E. Dibenzoxazepines
    Loxitane (loxapine)
	A. Tricyclics
	  1. Tofranil (imipramine)
	  2. Pertofrane (desipramine)
	    Norpramin (desipramine)
	  3. Elavil* (amitriptyline)
	  4. Aventyl (nortriptyline)
	  5. Vivactil (protriptyline)
	  6. Sinequan* (doxepin)
	    Adipin* (doxepin)
	
	B. MAO Inhibitors
	  1. Parnate (tranylcypromine)
	  2. Nardil (phenelzine)
	  3. Marplan (isocarboxazid)
	
	C. Lithane (lithium)
	    Lithonate (lithium)
	    Eskalith (lithium)
		A. Benzodiazepines
		  1. Librium (chlordiazepoxide)
		  2. Valium* (diazepam)
		  3. Serax (oxazepam)
		  4. Dalmane* (flurazepam)
		  5. Tranxene (clorazepate)
		
		B. Propanediols
		  1. Miltown (meprobamate)
		    Equanil (meprobamate)
		  2. Tybatran (tybamate)
		
		C. Diphenylmethanes
		  1. Atarax (hydroxazine)
		    Vistaril (hydroxazine)
		  2. Benadryl* (diphenhydramine)

* More sedative drugs—note that virtually all of the drugs may be sedating in some individuals whereas other patients are sedated by none.

characterization of the drug, which describes its chemical structure. *Generic* names are shorter scientific designations which often provide clues about the structure, and serve as the accepted standard names for drugs regardless of the manufacturer. The *proprietary* or brand name bears the least resemblance to the chemical structure, often being merely a catchy fabrication. By convention, brand names are capitalized and generic names are not. Thus, if five companies manufacture the same drug, a practitioner must learn five different brand names. As the number of effective agents proliferates, as patents lapse and as patent holders lease manufacturing rights to other companies, a veritable Tower of Babel is in the making. In light of this situation, we would urge practitioners to learn generic names. They are more scientific as well as ultimately less costly for the consumer, partly because of the lower advertising expenses.

All of the drugs listed in Compartment I are effective against schizophrenia. The doses vary, the piperazine drugs (A2 and B2) and the butyrophenones (C) (haloperidol) having the highest milligram potency.* The relative milligram strengths of the antischizophrenic drugs are listed in Table 2. Thus, 1 mg. of Stelazine (trifluoperazine) equals 20 mgs. of Thorazine (chlorpromazine). Acutely psychotic patients generally respond to about 600-1000 mgs. of Thorazine a day and can often be maintained at a preventive dose of 200-400 mgs. Patients suffering from chronic schizophrenia may require any amount of medication, 300-600 mgs. a day being an average requirement. Sometimes the equivalent of 3000 mgs. or more of Thorazine may be required. Since Thorazine (chlorpromazine) was the first antischizophrenia drug, it is used as the standard with which the newer ones are compared.

Comparable figures are not available for the drugs in Compartments II and III, but the recommended dose ranges are given in Table 2. All of the Tricyclics are comparable in their antidepressant effect, although doxepin is slightly weaker than the others. Elavil (amitriptyline) and Tofranil (imipramine) are used in the same dose. Their respective relatives Aventyl (nortriptyline) and Pertofrane (desipramine) are prescribed in somewhat lower doses. Ten mg. of Vivactil (protriptyline) is roughly the equivalent of 50 mg. of Tofranil or Elavil. Among the MAO inhibitor group of antidepressants, Parnate (tranylcypromine) is the most effective, and Nardil (phenelzine) only slightly less so. Marplan (isocarboxazid) is a bit less effective still, although in specific cases it may be of great benefit.

---

* Note the difference between milligram potency and efficacy. Since all of the antischizophrenic drugs listed are equally effective in schizophrenia, one must establish a table of comparably effective doses. However, when dealing with the drugs used to treat affective disorders, we find that Marplan is not as effective as Elavil: i.e., the number of depressed patients responding to each will not be the same no matter what the dose. This may be related to the probable existence of distinct chemical subtypes of depression.

Table 2

Name of Drug	Relative mg. Potency (to Thorazine):	Daily Dose Range mg. /day	Tablet (T) and /or Capsule (C) Preparations Commonly Used (mgs.)
Compartment I: Antischizophrenia			
Thorazine (chlorpromazine)	1:1	30-2000	(T 10, 25, 50, 100, 200)
Vesprin (triflupromazine)	4:1		(S* 30, 75, 150, 200, 300)
Trilafon (perphenazine)	10:1		T 10, 25, 50
Compazine (prochlorperazine)	7:1		T 2, 4, 8
Prolixin, Permitil (fluphenazine)	70:1		T 5, 10, 25
Stelazine (trifluoperazine)	20:1		T 1, 2.5, 5; T .25, 1, 2.5, 5, 10
Tindal (acetophenazine)	5:1		T 1, 2, 5, 10
Proketazine (carphenazine)	4:1		T 20
Repoise (butaperazine)	7:1		T 12.5, 25, 50
Mellaril (thioridazine)	1:1		T 5, 10, 25
Serentil (mesoridazine)	2:1		T 10, 15, 25, 50, 100, 150, 200
Quide (piperacetazine)	4:1		T 10, 25, 50, 100
Taractan (chlorprothixene)	1:1		T 10, 25
Navane (thiothixene)	20:1		T 25, 50, 100
Haldol (haloperidol)	100:1		C 1, 2, 5, 10, 20
Moban (molindone)	8:1		T ½, 1, 2, 5, 10
Loxitane (loxapine)	10:1		T 5, 10, 25
			C 10, 25, 50

Name of Drug	Relative mg. Potency (to Thorazine):	Daily Dose Range mg./day	Tablet (T) and/or Capsule (C) Preparations Commonly Used (mgs.)
Compartment II: Antiaffective Disorders			
Tofranil (imipramine)		30-300	T 10, 25, 50; PM**C 75, 100, 125, 150
Pertofrane, Norpramin (desipramine)		25-200	C 25, 50; T 25, 50
Elavil (amitriptyline)		50-300	T 10, 25, 50, 75, 100
Aventyl (nortriptyline)		30-100	C 10, 25
Vivactil (protriptyline)		15-60	T 5, 10
Sinequan, Adipin (doxepin)		25-300	C 10, 25, 50, 100; T 10, 25, 50
Parnate (tranylcypromine)		20-730	T 10
Nardil (phenelzine)		45-75	T 15
Marplan (isocarboxazid)		10-30	T 10
Lithane (lithium)			T 300
Lithonate (lithium)		600-2400	C 300, T 300
Eskalith (lithium)			C 300
Compartment III: Antianxiety			
Librium (chlordiazepoxide)		15-200	T 5, 10, 25; C 5, 10, 25
Valium (diazepam)		2-40	T 2, 5, 10
Serax (oxazepam)		30-120	C 10, 15, 30
Dalmane (flurazepam)		15-60	T 15, 30
Tranxene (clorazepate)		7.5-60	C 3.75, 7.5, 15, T 22.5
Miltown, Equanil (meprobamate)		1200-2400	T 200, 400, 600; T 200, 400; C 400
Tybatran (tybamate)		750-3000	C 125, 250, 350
Atarax, Vistaril (hydroxazine)		75-400	T 10, 25, 50, 100; C 25, 50, 100
Benadryl (diphenhydramine)		25-200	C 25, 50

* Spansules
** Tofranil PM long-acting

Of the drugs listed in Compartment III, the benzodiazepines are the most useful. Among these, Valium (diazepam), Dalmane (flurazepam) and Tranxene (chlorazepate) may be more effective than Librium (chlordiazepoxide) and Serax (oxazepam). The other antianxiety agents are generally less valuable, but in selected instances may be worth trying. For example, Tybatran (tybamate) sometimes proves helpful when somatic complaints are prominent.

How to Choose a Drug

The following is a list of questions and considerations which may prove useful to the reader in selecting a particular drug regimen:

1. *Which compartment is most appropriate?*

a. Are major disruptions in cognitive functions present, as well as markedly impoverished or chaotic interpersonal relationships and/or hallucinations or delusions, which were evident in the patient's twenties, teens, or earlier (schizophrenia)?

b. Are signs of a classical biological depression noted: loss of appetite, severe insomnia (especially early morning awakening), feelings of worthlessness and guilt, suicidal ideations in a middle-aged individual? These classical depressions are somewhat more likely to respond to the Elavil-Tofranil group of antidepressants (see Table 2), whereas atypical depressions are more apt to remit with the MAO inhibitors. On the other hand, are we dealing with mania (sustained hyperactivity, euphoria, severe insomnia, irritability, pressured speech, grandiosity) in the absence of a history consistent with schizophrenia or chronic drug abuse?

c. Is the disturbance manifested primarily by anxiety? Do the symptoms fall generally within the range of "neurotic" disturbances, without producing incapacitation or profound disruptions in daily functioning? Let us reiterate: gray areas exist between compartments, but a tentative hypothesis can be made about the most relevant one.

2. *Is the difficulty acute (lasting a few hours, days, or weeks) or chronic (continuous over a period of years)?* Acute disorders, especially schizophrenia, have a tendency to respond very quickly to drugs, and, by definition, have a high spontaneous remission rate. With proper medication, acute schizophrenia may remit in a matter of hours or less. In such cases, drugs can often be decreased and sometimes even eliminated after several weeks of therapy. A considerable degree of symptom relief in chronic schizophrenia or chronic anxiety states may also be achieved fairly promptly, although several weeks may be required in some cases.

3. *If acute, has the problem occurred on several previous occasions?*

If so, it is important to consider preventive medication after recovery from the acute episode. For example, if a person has had several schizophrenic decompensations, a small maintenance dose of antischizophrenic medication will generally be helpful on an ongoing basis. Many patients find the notion of medication for life terrifying. But if taking one or two tablets a day can prevent the agonies that usually accompany acute psychosis, does it make sense not to suggest this course to a patient? (Of course, no one is bound by such a suggestion.) The "revolving door syndrome" refers to the repeated rehospitalization of persons for recurring acute schizophrenic episodes. Each acute attack is successfully treated with drugs in the hospital and the patient is discharged. After leaving the hospital, he (she) stops taking the medication for any one of a variety of reasons, among which are the following:

a. Insufficient information about prevention made available to the patient.

b. Poor follow-up or lack of relationship between prescriber and patient.

c. Patient's mistrust of the hospital, which is seen as an instrument of coercion.

d. Prescriber's own ambivalence about the usefulness of medication.

e. Faulty patient cognition—"I feel better, so there is no point" rather than "I probably feel better because of the drug, and if it can prevent a recurrence, I will continue to use it."

f. Patient's shame about "being defective" or viewing medication as a "crutch."

g. Family, peer, or community pressure not to take the drugs.

h. Unpleasant side effects, especially if unexpected.

i. Dissatisfaction with the so-called "therapeutic" effects, e.g., many "patients" enjoy mania even though some of its consequences may be highly aversive.

The discovery of the effectiveness of lithium in preventing cyclical (recurrent) affective disorders—bipolar* or unipolar (depressive only)—is one of pharmacology's monumental achievements, the full implications of which have yet to be realized. Lithium is also the specific treatment for mania, although usually a lag period of two days to a week occurs before effects are evident. If the mania is severe, an antischizophrenia drug may be prescribed until the lithium takes effect. Lithium may also provide relief for some depressive episodes, especially if the acute episode is part of a cyclical disorder or if there is a family history of affective illness, but at the present time it is recommended that other antidepressants be used first.

---

* This term is used when there is a history of episodes of depression and mania, but it is often used even if one episode of mania occurs (isolated mania is rare).

4. *Which drugs have been taken by the patient before and with what results?* Drugs which have worked before are likely to work again in the same individual, and drugs which have not worked before are not likely to work in the future. If the individual has not had medication previously, it is useful to know that there are similar response patterns between first degree blood relatives. It is important, also, to be aware of previous untoward reactions, since patients may be deterred from taking a particular drug, or any drug at all, by earlier experiences with serious or unpleasant side effects. Certain chemically related drugs tend to have similar side effects, so that someone experiencing refractory Parkinson type side effects from Prolixin (antischizophrenia compartment-phenothiazine subcompartment-*piperazine group*) might fare better with Vesprin (antischizophrenia compartment-phenothiazine subcompartment-*aliphatic group*). Many people have no idea what drugs they have taken in the past. Yet the prescriber has the legal and ethical obligation to inform the "prescribee" of the name of the drug, the dose, the reason it is being recommended, and at least the most commonly occurring side effects. (An invaluable part of an individual's repertoire of assertive responses is the ability to ask any expert consultant not only to perform the desired function, but to answer questions and educate the client as well. As therapists, we can reinforce this sort of behavior by supplying our clients with complete and accurate information.) One can generally ascertain the drug taken by showing the patient pictures of the tablets and capsules, and requesting that he or she identify the medication in question. For this purpose, a drug identification guide is invaluable. (See bibliography.)

5. *In what dose has the drug been used before?* The appropriate drugs may have been used but in inadequate doses. This is one of the most common causes of drug failure. Side effects may occur in some people who initially receive full doses rather than minimal ones with gradual increases. On the other hand, various side effects (Parkinson-related) may be obliterated with larger doses.

6. *Is insomnia a prominent feature of the symptomatology?* Insomnia is a frequent accompaniment of many biopsychological dysfunctions. In nonpsychotic disorders, it is probably best managed with such nonpharmacological interventions as relaxation training, autosuggestion, and various stimulus control techniques. If these prove ineffective, sedative drugs in Compartment III or doxepin (Compartment II) would be recommended. For treatment of insomnia, it is suggested that sedative drugs be administered shortly before bedtime. We are recommending here drugs whose primary effect is antischizophrenic, antidepressive, and antianxiety, but which also have sedative properties. Sedative and nonsedative drugs are found in each compartment (Table 1). The use of standard hypnotics ("sleeping pills") such as barbiturates, Doriden, Placidyl, Noludar is

strongly discouraged because of the addictive potential, the lack of specificity in terms of anxiety relief, and the narrow margin of safety and potential lethality for suicidal patients. However, among these hypnotics, chloral hydrate is relatively benign.

7. *Is there a history of drug abuse?* Most of the drugs in the various compartments are not susceptible to abuse. However, a few in Compartment III have been misused and in general would not be prescribed for people with addictive tendencies. Meprobamate (Miltown, Equanil) clearly has addictive potential. Some individuals will abuse other members of Compartment III (e.g., Valium). The other compartments are safe in this regard, although on rare occasions a patient has abused the antidepressant Parnate, which is very similar in chemical structure to amphetamine.

8. *Are strong suicidal tendencies present?* Although one may commit suicide with a host of readily available remedies and toxins, many people are prone to take pills either impulsively or by design, with or without suicidal intent, and it is important for the prescribing clinician to know which drugs are safe and which are not in this regard. Drugs in Compartment II are the most hazardous in terms of suicidal potential. Although some people have committed suicide by taking three times the maximum recommended dose of Elavil, one would find it very difficult to kill oneself by taking an overdose of Thorazine (Compartment I) or Librium (Compartment III) unless these agents were combined with substantial quantities of alcohol or other drugs.

9. *Is there a history of noncompliance?* Even the best and most appropriate medications will not produce the changes for which they are designed if they are not taken by the patient. It is recommended that the therapist be truly noncoercive, i.e., an expert or consultant who makes recommendations rather than a person who dictates "treatment." It is particularly important that he or she make available to the patient what is known about the symptoms in question, and the efficacy of the drugs, as well as freely discussing any potential side effects. Experience has shown that the greater the trust, the higher the compliance, although a number of other factors are involved as well. The level of noncompliance is truly appalling (Blackwell, 1973). Long-acting injectable preparations of an antischizophrenic drug (Prolixin) are available for patients who are receptive to the idea of taking medication but who are forgetful or who find the oral schedule bothersome. The effects of one injection generally last two weeks (in some instances, up to four weeks).

10. *What is the age of the patient and the general level of health, especially with regard to heart, blood pressure, kidney, and liver as well as the presence of prostate enlargement, glaucoma, or drug allergies?* It is important that the organs which metabolize and excrete drugs are intact (liver, kidney). A relatively healthy individual will have a higher tolerance

of the many side effects than would someone with a multiplicity of medical problems. It is a medical truism that children and elderly patients do not tolerate drugs as well as young or middle-aged adults, and tolerance should be tested with small doses. In a geriatric population, weaker drugs or those with fewer side effects would be tried first, e.g., doxepin (Sinequan, Adipin) instead of amitriptyline (Elavil). Mild drugs of Compartment III which are relatively free from side effects (Serax-oxazepam) may also prove useful in the nonpsychotic depressions of older persons.

How to Prescribe a Drug

1. Select a drug based on the considerations mentioned above, e.g., matching the drug with the appropriate diagnostic compartment.

2. Select a route of administration (oral or injection). Medication will almost always be taken by mouth. Intramuscular injections of these medications tend to be uncomfortable for the patient and are reserved for emergencies. However, as an exception to this policy, injection of a long-acting antischizophrenia drug, Prolixin (fluphenazine), may be given every two to four weeks as a convenience to the patient who otherwise would be taking pills one, two, or three times a day. Intravenous medication is available for some drugs, but is used extremely rarely. A few drugs may be administered in suppository form for people who are vomiting or who abhor "pills."

3. Start with a small dose and gradually increase it until a therapeutic effect is noted; poorly tolerated side effects occur; or the dose far exceeds the level at which positive effects may reasonably be expected. Note that many drugs are effective in some individuals only when administered in quantities much larger than the maximum dose recommended by the manufacturer. However, legal problems may arise here unless the patient is apprised of all the facts. Some clinicians have prescribed as much as 100 times the usual recommended dose in particular situations. The principle of increasing doses applies mainly to Compartments I and III, since the margin of safety is much lower for the drugs in Compartment II.

4. If a drug is not effective even after large doses have been taken by the patient it is generally advisable to turn to a drug in another subcompartment. If a particular agent is to be discontinued because of very unpleasant side effects, a drug may be chosen which is less likely to produce those side effects. For example, if an antischizophrenia drug is used from sub-subcompartment A2 (phenothiazine-piperazine), e.g., Trilafon (perphenazine), where the side effects are most likely to be Parkinson-related (restlessness, tremor, rigidity, abnormal movements) and these cannot be

adequately controlled by the usual anti-Parkinson medications, then the clinician would switch his patient to a drug in A1 or A3 or B1, which would then be more apt to cause sedation as a side effect. Drugs from different subcompartments may also be prescribed in combination to produce different effects. For example, a sedative drug might be used at bedtime and a nonsedative drug might be used during the daytime, e.g. Thorazine (chlorpromazine) at bedtime and Stelazine (trifluoperazine) during waking hours. It is also feasible to combine drugs from different compartments. In fact, at times it is justified to try almost anything to relieve intolerable symptoms.* However, when using antidepressants in a "depressed" individual who, in fact, has a more schizophrenic configuration, one may precipitate an acute psychosis. In general, if schizophrenia is suspected in a depressed patient, it is better to start with a drug from Compartment I, and often the "depression" will lift. If an antidepressant (Compartment II) is used in such patients, it is crucial to counter that drug with an antischizophrenia agent to prevent the activation of a latent schizophrenia. This situation provides one of the few justifications for the use of single preparation drug combinations such as Triavil and Etrafon, which are fixed dose combinations of Trilafon (a phenothiazine) and Elavil (a tricyclic antidepressant). Another justified use would occur in the treatment of noncompliant patients who might find one pill more acceptable than two. As of this writing, the FDA still interdicts the combined use of tricyclics and MAO inhibitors because of earlier adverse reports. There should be at least a one-week hiatus between the stopping of one and the starting of the other. However, a number of clinicians have noted considerable benefit from the combination in otherwise refractory depressions with no increase in side effects. It is important to be aware of the many drug and diet incompatabilities of MAO inhibitors (see *Physician's Desk Reference*). Some female patients whose depressions do not seem to respond to the tricyclic group benefit from the addition of small doses of thyroid hormones even if their thyroid tests are normal. Lithium may enhance the antidepressant effects of the Tricyclics or the MAO inhibitors as well as having an antidepressant effect itself in some patients.

5. Over the years practitioners have tended to use a dose schedule of two to four times a day. While such a schedule is usually desirable in the initial phases of treatment, it has been demonstrated that for a majority of patients the entire day's medication can be given at one time. Generally the best time is in the evening so that the problem of sedation is minimized. This once-a-day routine facilitates compliance and lowers the cost for the patient (one 200 mg. Thorazine tablet costs less than half the cost of four 50 mg. tablets). Once a regular drug regimen is being maintained, especially

---

* Keeping in mind the dictum "primum non nocere"—above all, do not harm.

when a protracted course is planned, "drug holidays" (prescribed drug-free periods) are very useful. Most people who take long-term maintenance medication can manage very well without it for one or two days, or even for a week or two at a time every few months. Often, omitting drugs on alternate days or on weekends proves workable. The drug holiday is a practice which has been used more and more of late and is highly recommended for those who can tolerate it because of the decreased likelihood of long-range toxicity. However, complex scheduling may lead to reduced compliance.

6. How long does one continue to prescribe drugs for the patient? If there has been an acute schizophrenic episode and it was the first, it is generally a good idea to continue recommending medication for at least a couple of months following the episode. For a second episode, it is best to continue for a year or more, and if three episodes have occurred, indefinitely. This is merely a rule of thumb, however. Some people who have recovered from a third episode have been able to manage very nicely without medication, but the risk is considerable. For a large majority of people who experienced acute schizophrenic episodes, maintenance medication is absolutely protective against a recurrence. Of course, chronic conditions would call for ongoing medication. If anti-Parkinson drugs are used, it is usually possible to stop them after a month or two (while continuing the phenothiazines, butyrophenones, etc.) without recurrence of the neurological side effects. For acute depressions which have lifted following the use of antidepressant medication, it is advisable to continue the medication for six weeks to three months after the depression has completely lifted. If several depressions have occurred (with or without attacks of mania), lithium should be considered for its preventive effects. However, the preventive value of lithium is greater for the bipolar affective disorders. In recurrent depressions, prolonged use of Tricyclics or MAO inhibitors would also be justified, but at a lower dose than that administered during the acute episode. Patients whose recurring depressions are treated with ECT have a far lower relapse rate when maintenance antidepressant medication is employed.

Unwanted Effects

It is imperative to have an understanding of the various potential side effects, and to know how to avoid them or deal with them when they occur. A detailed review of side effects is not feasible here, but an excellent, authoritative, and comprehensive treatment of the subject is available (Shader, and Di Mascio, 1970). It is a good idea to be aware of the medical history of the patient (including previous untoward drug reactions) and of the results of a recent physical examination as well as current medications, before prescribing any psychotropic drug, especially those in Compartment I and II. In addition, a number of drug incompatabilities have been discovered (Hansten, 1975), but the major problems exist with Compartment II drugs, especially the MAO inhibitors. It is important for the patient to avoid stimulants, nasal decongestants, narcotics, and antihypertensives (among others) as well as a variety of foods (especially aged cheese) when MAO inhibitors have been prescribed (see listings in *Physician's Desk Reference* under the individual drugs). Also, tricyclic antidepressants will interfere with the action of some antihypertensive medications. When specific medical problems are present, contact with the treating internist or general practitioner should be maintained.

Unfortunately, dozens of undesirable effects accompany the use of psychotropic drugs. Therefore, it is necessary for the therapist to be convinced of the efficacy of these agents, to have a keen appreciation of the various response patterns associated with these medications, and to establish a good rapport with the patient for whom the drugs are prescribed. Although the vast majority of the side effects are not serious and are completely reversible, a few are severe and potentially dangerous. It must also be mentioned that some drug reactions are manifestations of the "negative placebo effect" (undesirable effects totally unrelated to the pharmacological properties of the particular drug involved). Undesirable effects can be classified according to their frequency, to their seriousness, to the body organ or system they affect, or to the time of onset (whether very early in the course of medication or after many months or years). The most common unwanted effects for Compartments I and II are:

1. Sedation.
2. Autonomic disturbances (dry mouth, constipation, delayed urination, blurred vision, dizziness with sudden changes of position).
3. Neurological effects related to Parkinson's syndrome, mainly with piperazine drugs and haloperidol.

Most patients quickly accommodate to sedation and postural hypotension so that within a few days to two weeks these problems are no longer troublesome. Administering the entire daily dose of medication at night or switching to minimally sedative drugs (e.g., a change from Thorazine [chlorpromazine] to Prolixin [fluphenazine]) is usually helpful. It is essential to warn patients about any sedative effects, particularly when their daily activities require a high degree of alertness—driving, using dangerous power tools, working at heights, etc. Postural hypotension is more apt to occur with the more sedative drugs. It can be minimized by suggesting that the patient avoid standing up or getting out of bed suddenly. Other autonomic disturbances generally are dealt with by reduction of dosage, although constipation may be overcome by diet modification or a mild laxative (Colace—100 mg./day). When administered to persons suffering from one type of glaucoma, the drugs may precipitate an acute attack, and they may also cause urinary retention, necessitating catheterization in individuals with prostate enlargement. The range of Parkinson and related symptoms (abnormal movements, restlessness, tremor, rigidity) may be prevented by starting the patient with small doses of medication and gradually increasing them. On the other hand, these effects usually are obliterated at much higher dosages. Anti-Parkinson drugs (Artane, Cogentin, Kemadrin, and Akineton) will relieve the unwanted effects in most instances. These agents are usually given by mouth, roughly 4-15 mgs. per day. Benadryl is also very useful, 25-100 mgs. a day, and occasionally is administered intramuscularly or even intravenously for acute dystonias (painful, severe, and sudden muscle spasms). These drugs block the parasympathetic nervous system (anticholinergic effect) as do the antischizophrenic and tricyclic antidepressant drugs, and therefore may accentuate any autonomic effects already present. In rare instances large doses of antischizophrenic, antidepressant, and anti-Parkinson drugs may produce severe anticholinergic poisoning with paralysis of the intestines, delerium, and high fever. In such cases intravenous administration of physostigmine is generally life-saving.

The common effects occur early in the course of therapy, usually within one hour to a few days after the drugs are taken. A late, serious, and usually irreversible neurological sequel which is not part of the Parkinson-like complex, and is in fact worsened by anti-Parkinson drugs, is called tardive (late) *dyskinesia* (abnormal movements). Unfortunately, it is not rare, and it occurs especially in older persons who have been on anti-schizophrenia medication for at least six months. Other serious complications are agranulocytosis (loss of a type of white blood cell vital in fighting infections), which is extremely rare, and pigmented retinopathy (a cause of permanent damage to the retina of the eye) which may occur with large doses of Mellaril (more than 800 mgs. per day over long periods of time).

Special mention should be made of lithium, which is highly toxic if the therapeutic dose range is exceeded. It is important, particularly at the beginning of treatment, to check the level of lithium in the blood. The usual therapeutic blood level is 0.6-1.5 milliequivalents per liter which usually is achieved with a daily dose of 600-2400 milligrams. However, acute manic patients require the higher doses to achieve this blood level as well as an adequate clinical effect. Toxic effects that may appear include tremor, nausea, vomiting, diarrhea, drowsiness, and other more severe neurological, cardiovascular and gastrointestinal symptoms. About 4 per cent of patients on lithium develop a benign thyroid goiter.

Among other uncommon effects of the drugs listed in Compartments I and II are jaundice—mainly with Thorazine (not serious) and MAO inhibitors (potentially serious)—electrocardiogram changes and abnormal heart rhythms, and skin eruptions (sometimes related to sun exposure). Occasionally, with prolonged use, the patient may develop abnormal skin pigmentations, as well as pigment deposits in the lens of the eye. Women on substantial doses of medication often have delayed or absent menstrual periods and sometimes lactation may occur. Occasional breast enlargement in males may ensue. Decreased libido may occur as well as erectile and ejaculatory disturbances. Weight gain is frequent. Many of the drugs in Compartments I and II lower the convulsive threshold and occasionally a susceptible individual will develop seizures. Of course, the avoidance of all drugs during pregnancy is desirable, but if there are compelling indications, the use of most psychotropic drugs is justified, especially after the third month.

Despite the plethora of potential unwanted effects, some of which are very disturbing, the drugs mentioned here can at times be life-saving, and many persons will not experience untoward effects at all. Often patients will elect to suffer undesirable side effects if the drug relieves intolerable depression or other disruptive symptoms.

The major side effects associated with Compartment III drugs are sedation, and, when large doses are administered, slurred speech and incoordination. The potential for abuse of these drugs by addiction-prone individuals has already been noted. However, Tybatran (tybamate) is a notable exception. Because side effects tend to be comparatively mild with Compartment III drugs, these will not be discussed further here.

Some side effects usually considered undesirable have been used therapeutically, e.g., Mellaril (thiroidazine) in small doses slows ejaculation and has been prescribed occasionally for premature ejaculation. The urinary retaining properties of Tofranil (imipramine) may be a factor in its usefulness for the control of enuresis.

Some of the psychotropic drugs have other therapeutic uses as well. Valium (diazepam) and Miltown or Equanil (meprobamate) are good muscle relaxants. In that capacity, as well as for their specific antianxiety properties, they may be of value in desensitization procedures. Valium is also effective in treating seizure disorders, and, when administered intravenously, is effective in controlling unremitting convulsions (status epilepticus). Compazine (prochlorperazine) and many other phenothiazines serve as good antiemetics. MAO inhibitors are helpful in the treatment of narcolepsy. Haldol is used in the uncommon neurological syndrome of Gilles de la Tourette.

Some drugs which are not discussed specifically in this chapter may have salutary effects as well, e.g., Dilantin (diphenylhydantoin) may occasionally have dramatic effects in persons prone to episodic outbursts of uncontrollable anger (neurological consultation advised here). Amphetamines, in addition to their widespread and at times unjustified use in treating minimal brain dysfunction, sometimes relieve depersonalization phenomena in nonschizophrenic individuals. In general, however, to use amphetamines is to court disaster because of their marked addictiveness and their tendency to produce severe psychosis. Nevertheless, they may be effective in a few selective cases. Cylert (pemoline), a stimulant, recently marketed for minimal brain dysfunction, may also be useful for mild depressions.

Conclusion

The biological modality has experienced an explosive growth phase in the past 20 years, which we urge therapists of every persuasion to heed. It is conceivable that monolithic practitioners will become troglodytes, whereas multimodal therapists and their clients may well reap the benefits of an enlightened psychobiological perspective. One need not, indeed probably cannot, become expert or equally facile with all modalities; but it is to be hoped that a basic understanding of some of the principles of drug therapy will be attained by all practitioners.

References

Appleton, W. S., & Davis, J. M. *Practical clinical psychopharmacology.* New York: Medcom Press, 1973.

Ayd, F. J. *International drug therapy newsletter.*

Blackwell, B. Patient compliance. *New England Journal of Medicine,* 1973, *289,* 249.

Drug identification guide. Oradell, New Jersey: Medical Economics Company, 1975.

Hansten, P. D. *Drug interactions.* (3rd edition.) Philadelphia: Lea and Febiger, 1975.

Hollister, L. *Clinical use of psychotherapeutic drugs.* Springfield, Illinois: Charles C Thomas, 1973.

Honigfeld, G., & Howard, A. *Psychiatric drugs.* New York: Academic Press, 1973.

Physicians desk reference. Oradell, New Jersey: Medical Economics Company.

Rickels, K. *Non-specific factors in drug therapy*. Springfield, Illinois: Charles C Thomas, 1968.

Shader, R. I., & Di Mascio, A. *Psychotropic drug side effects*. Baltimore: The Williams and Wilkins Company, 1970.

Woodruff, R. A., Jr., Goodwin, D. W., & Guze, S. B. *Psychiatric diagnosis*. New York: Oxford University Press, 1974.

Chapter 7

Wanted: A Multimodal Theory of Personality

Arnold A. Lazarus

Why do people behave as they do? The answer to this question depends upon having a clinical understanding of personality—what it is, how it is formed, and so on. Yet it is an unfortunate fact that the field of psychology has no generally accepted theory of personality. There is even widespread controversy over an acceptable definition of personality. As far back as 1937, Gordon Allport listed 50 different definitions; and even today, the term has different abstract meanings such as one's popular appeal, one's outward appearance (as distinct from how one really is), one's style of life, one's characteristic adjustment to environmental conditions, and so forth. As P. Holzman points out, "personality never *is,* it is always *becoming*."[1] The essence of personality is that people are continuously changing, but they also have characteristics that make them recognizable and relatively stable.

It is my intent in this article to outline some problems that the psychological community faces in developing such a theory, and then to suggest an approach which I believe could prove more fruitful than many others that have been taken.

Most of the relationships we pursue—especially our more intimate interactions such as friendship and marriage—are based upon certain regularities of behavior. While the tight controls of laboratory interaction provide little evidence for the assumption that behavior is consistent in different situations, our everyday experiences point to the fact that we can usually predict certain significant behavior patterns with considerable accuracy. It is somewhat of a cliché, but nonetheless true, to remark that past behavior often tends to be the best predictor of future behavior.

From *Fields Within Fields,* 1974, *13,* 67-72. Reprinted by permission of the World Institute Council.

It would actually be simple to make a strong case for the essential predictability of human behavior, or to argue equally strongly for the basic unpredictability of human behavior—especially under specified conditions. Our selectivity of perception would permit us to choose our subjects, tasks, criteria, etc., so as to win either or both arguments. Indeed, it would seem that many of our personal interactions are predicated on the assumption that people are consistently inconsistent and yet fundamentally predictable. We automatically employ a stochastic process whereby we assign probabilities to our own behavior and to the behavior of others. "There is a 50 percent probability that the boss will fire me if I don't complete my report." "It seems to be about 80 percent certain that I'm going to take that job in California." "If we can convince Mrs. Smith to stop reinforcing Johnny's verbal outbursts, it is almost certain that they will diminish in frequency and in intensity."

In a broad sense, although environmental conditions maintain behavior, clinicians who endeavor to modify behavior are often dismayed to discover how stubborn and persistent various behaviors remain even in the face of gross environmental manipulations. A case in point is that of a 34-year-old man who had developed an elaborate series of rituals which interfered with his daily functioning and had become disruptive for all the members of his household. He was hospitalized, and apart from the times when he was actively coerced to participate in occupational therapy or encouraged to take part in ward activities, his rituals showed no decrement (despite the fact that his wife was no longer reinforcing his behavior by means of attention, and in spite of the fact that his day-to-day demands and living conditions had altered significantly). It is easy to "explain" such persistent behavior by means of a label such as "obsessive-compulsive-personality-type." The reification of this label can all too readily serve as a prediction, a diagnosis, an explanation, and offer a host of descriptions (e.g., obsessional types are rigid, anal, stubborn, stingy, passive-aggressive, introverted, and picayune). The foregoing labels and global dispositions tend to obfuscate our understanding of human behavior. Yet, it remains the task of anyone interested in the study of "personality" to account for the existence of various stable and persistent behavior patterns. Conceivably, this might then throw light on the matter for those interested in "personality change."

Numerous constructs have been offered to account for the vagaries and similarities of human behavior—possession by good or evil spirits, a host of instincts, and, more recently, traits, states, styles, types, and various stages have been invoked, replete with habits, attitudes, dispositions, factors, and intrapsychic dynamics. The foregoing variables tend to categorize people on the basis of relatively small amounts of information. The obverse position is exemplified by an insistence and emphasis upon behavioral and situational specificity.[2] Laboratory studies have shown that in order to predict various responses, we must know precise details concerning the subject's sex, age, immediate prior experiences, previous models, the exact rewards being offered, etc., plus a host of "moderator variables" such as the experimenter's sex, age, physical appearance, voice quality, etc.

But it is also pointed out that "the discriminativeness found in behavior is *not* so great that we cannot recognize continuity in people. It is also not so great that we have to treat each new behavior from a person as if we never saw anything like it from him before."[3] Thus, we must emphasize again that despite the fundamental faults in those theories that postulate immutable traits, enduring dispositions, and global tendencies that consistently and predictably cut across virtually all environmental conditions, we are nevertheless left with undeniable regularities and continuities of behavior. The term "personality" is employed as an abstraction to express these regularities and continuities of behavior.

Clinical Success as a Key to "Personality"

The question then becomes "What sorts of data regarding these regularities should we be collecting?" One may venture to suggest that many of the foremost personality theorists have been asking the wrong sorts of questions, and have been gathering immaculate data that prove quite useless for the prediction and control of behavior—let alone for meaningful descriptions and explanations of behavior. In the areas of "personality" and "psychotherapy," a penchant for researchers to find fascination with a few favored constructs or modalities has given rise to a plethora of fragmentary and contradictory theories. Thus, in "personality" research, hedonism as a guiding principle, or the need for "self-actualization," or the all-consuming nature of sex and aggression are typical of the unitary constructs that allegedly account for all sorts of human complexities. It seems that many hours of computer time have been wasted in churning out innumerable correlations between test scores and "traits" such as dogmatism, rigidity, anxiety, personal space, defensiveness, etc. The hopeful assumption is that these correlation coefficients can and will provide relevant information about more basic dimensions of human functioning.[4] Hopeful and wishful thoughts have not fared too well in most scientific arenas!

Nonetheless, trait language can convey an arithmetical penchant for an individual to respond in a predictable manner. A statement such as "That child is shy," gives us general clues as to the probable frequency of his approach and avoidance behaviors across several conditions. But it is always useful to ask, "Under what conditions is he *not* shy?" The foregoing implies that situation-free traits made up of enduring global dispositions are speculative fictions. Unfortunately, however, there is still a highly prevalent tendency to ascribe causative properties to these shorthand descriptive terms we call "traits." To say that a child's low frequency of communication with his peers is *caused* by his shyness represents a most inaccurate notion that continues to hinder the understanding of human behavior. Indeed, the circular and vertiginous notion that shy behaviors are caused by "shyness traits" is a view held by many laymen and unfortunately by certain professionals as well.

Practicing therapists may find an extreme paucity of consistent, well-integrated, and parsimonious theories of "personality" that can guide them in their professional endeavors. Yet many existing modes and systems of therapeutic practice have been inferred from numerous theories of "personality." It has long seemed logical to develop a theory of "personality" from which therapeutic techniques for "personality change" are then derived to strengthen the underlying propositions. Freud and the neo-Freudians traverse the aforementioned path of endeavor. Leaving aside that it is a logical error to assume that the efficacy of one's techniques necessarily confirm the theories that spawned them, it might prove most productive to examine matters quite differently, and in fact to proceed the other way around. If we abstract some salient facts from successful clinical practice, what light might they shed upon personality theory? For example, if a therapist amassed considerable data to show that a regimen of relaxation plus meditation produced an exacerbation of symptomatology in most persons labeling themselves as "depressed," whereas people labeling themselves "anxious" tended to respond positively, what implications would this finding have for the study of "personality"? More generally, if therapy outcome studies revealed a tendency for clients to relapse unless treatments x, y, and z were administered, what could one then infer about "personality"?

Developing a Multimodal Approach

I have argued that successful therapy is predicated upon a combination of cognitive, social learning, and personalistic variables.[5] W. Mischel postulates essentially the same variables as vital for the development of a viable psychology of personality. But whereas Mischel's schema rests upon a range of cognitive, affective, motoric, and interpersonal processes, clinical evidence has been presented to show that at least two additional modalities require careful scrutiny, viz., imagery and sensation.[6]

It must be stressed that image formation is a crucial component of thinking. In other words, cognitive processes involve various levels of construct formation, abstract reasoning, intentions, plans, decisions, expectancies, values, belief systems, internalized rules, and mental imagery—innumerable events, scenes, people, and places drawn from past experience. Any cognitive schema that ignores imagery is bound to be incomplete. It is curious that Mischel's cognitive social learning reconceptualization of personality pays relatively little attention to the importance of imagery, even though some of his experiments attest to its critical importance. For example, in determining under what conditions children would wait for an extended period for reward objects, Mischel and B. Moore found that children can readily, through instruction, transform the real objects in front of them into color pictures in their heads.[7] Children could thus picture marshmallows, for example, as cotton balls and thereby remain willing to delay gratification for long periods of time. M. Horowitz succinctly expresses the importance of imagery by pointing out that "a man chased by a lion will retain an image of the lion rather than looking over his shoulder to remind himself why he is running."[8] A. Ellis has also come to appreciate that image formation is essential for comprehensive therapy, and now uses what he terms "rational emotive imagery."[9]

It is also surprising that sensory experience has played a minor role in most therapeutic systems. While many individuals have adopted Masters and Johnson's "sensate focus" methods for treating sexual inadequacy, they tend to overlook the fact that sensory experience is highly important in other realms of life as well. For example, many hypochondriacs seem to have overacute kinesthetic perceptions, so that they attend to very minor levels of discomfort and are thereby distracted from focusing upon more important, nonsensory, stimuli. Conversely, the vague "existential alienation" of some individuals often proves to be a function of insufficient sensory awareness. It is worth noting that critical distinctions between sensory and emotive aspects of experience are often overlooked. In our everyday language, we often subsume sensory and affective modes under single labels such as "feeling," "tension," "fear," "warmth," "sensitivity," etc.

In other words, we should not ignore the fact that our behavior is governed by our self-images, plus the way we perceive others, and by the visual, auditory, tactile, olfactory, and gustatory stimuli we avoid, and those to which we attend. The present orientation holds that information about a person's salient behaviors, affective processes, sensory reactions, imagery, cognitions, and interpersonal relationships provides a most cogent and composite integration of the relevant dimensions of human experience that may be said to constitute "personality."

The point at issue is that to develop an overall theory of personality we must take cognizance of a wider range of overt and covert processes than most theorists have considered. The latter would commence with the interplay between "thoughts," "sensations," "emotions," and "images." Just as general psychology has been concerned with the study of sensations, perceptions, cognitions, and emotions—in addition to a wide range of motor responses—the psychology of "personality" would seem to call for the detailed study of each modality (and their interactions) in order to gain a comprehensive understanding of the individual.

The foregoing assertions come from the fact that durable clinical results appear to follow a therapeutic regimen that deliberately and specifically focuses upon a client's overt behaviors, affective processes, sensations, images, cognitions, and interpersonal relationships.[6,10] Clinical follow-ups suggest that unless each modality is specifically and directly investigated and, if necessary, modified, the "cure" is likely to be somewhat ephemeral—as measured by a higher relapse rate. And yet several well-known systems of therapy overlook or ignore many of these basic modalities. For example whereas the proponents of "bioenergetic analysis" employ several neo-Reichian techniques for reducing surplus tensions and for stirring up dormant sensory and affective reactions, they pay little heed to cognitive processes, or to the specific modification of intrusive images.[11] Furthermore they ignore the correction of specific interpersonal and behavioral deficits by omitting any systematic modeling or reshaping procedures from their therapeutic armamentarium. Similarly, classical psychoanalysts are often averse to the direct modification of overt behaviors, and they often avoid offering advice and guidance, let alone administering sensory exercises such as relaxation training, deep breathing exercises, or other specific antianxiety techniques.

There is an understandable penchant to seek for unitary "cures" and unitary explanations of behavior and "personality." In the area of psychotherapy we find supporters of pristine insights arguing with pundits of primal therapy, plus some three or four dozen other points of view. Relaxation therapy has been put forward as a virtual panacea by some. Others see an exclusive therapeutic virtue in the processes of disinhibition or "excitation." Similarly, personality theorists have made far-reaching predictions regarding the ramifications of being predominantly introverted, and/or having an internal locus of control, and/or embracing a narcissistic lifestyle, etc. On the other hand, the tendency to measure small units of behavior—e.g., for how long and under what conditions will an individual continue to squeeze a hand dynamometer?—is rampant in the field of "personality measurement" and merely serves to generate fragmented and molecular pieces of information about human functioning. I am arguing for a different kind of specificity as well as a closer examination of broader categories of behavior as contained across the multimodal areas alluded to above.

The Smoking "Habit"

A simple illustration may clarify the basic thrust of this position. People addicted to cigarettes are often said to have a "bad habit." This seemingly unitary notion—habit—is shown to consist of critical interactions within each of the basic modalities. A group of smokers will display individual differences in *behavior*. Apart from different ways of lighting and actually smoking their cigarettes (box tapping, fiddling, sucking, inhaling, ring blowing, etc.), some people prefer to smoke when eating, others only smoke when drinking, others chain-smoke, and so forth. The *affective* components, upon inquiry, are shown to include anxiety ("I smoke when I'm anxious or nervous!"), anger ("When I feel mad a cigarette calms me down!"), sadness or depression ("When I'm unhappy cigarettes seem to cheer me up!"), and even joy ("When I feel really happy a cigarette tops things off!"). Similarly, sensory elements range from tension release to a host of oral and olfactory satisfactions (e.g., "If I eat something too sweet, only a cigarette seems to get the taste out of my mouth!"). In terms of *imagery*, heavy smokers whom we have questioned reported a variety of reactions such as, "Looking cool and sophisticated," "Seeing myself as an adult," plus scenes that feature in films and advertisements such as, "Being tough like Bogart," or "Looking elegant." An inquiry into cognitive processes revealed numerous rationalizations. "Cigarettes clear out my sinuses." "They give me something to do with my hands." "I find that I get fewer colds because the smoke kills off germs." "They help my digestion." *Interpersonal* factors include "being sociable," "making contact more readily," "feeling at ease," etc.

Of course a generalized addiction to nicotine may override most other considerations, but clinically, we have found that people who wish to stop smoking are more readily and long-lastingly helped if attention is paid to each modality, rather than when a single method (e.g., hypnosis or aversion therapy) is employed. For instance, one alters the behavioral conditions under which smoking is to occur (e.g., "Begin by limiting your smoking to the first 15 minutes of any hour."), and one simultaneously attends to the affective elements ("When you feel anxious try to employ the differential relaxation you have just learned instead of reaching for a cigarette."). In addition, a simple sensory exercise is often helpful, viz., inhaling an ammonia compound while smoking so as to develop a distinctly negative sensory association. Imagery is effective in two distinct ways.

First, one modifies the individual's positive imagery ("Instead of identifying with Bogart, picture yourself telling him that in the light of recent medical evidence, anyone who smokes is asking for trouble."), and then one also introduces aversive imagery ("Whenever you light up a cigarette try to think of scenes that literally nauseate you."). Not to labor the point any further, we are stressing the fact that apart from generating several intervention strategies, a multimodal *assessment* brings to light a significant network of fundamental intrapersonal and interpersonal processes that may be said to constitute one's "personality."

Multimodal Assessments and Personality Theory

The value of the BASIC ID schema for clinical assessment or problem identification has been presented elsewhere, but for present purposes we are proposing these separate yet interactive modalities with a view to *personality assessment*. The construction of a BASIC ID personality profile should pose few problems for someone skilled in testing and scaling methods. And it is my contention that it would provide an elegant and parsimonious range of dimensions for the meaningful investigation of those significant continuities of behavior we term "personality." What is called for is a personality theory which explicitly examines and integrates what is known about each of these separate yet interactive modalities.

Nevertheless, a range of dimensions, however parsimonious and elegant, is not yet a theory. We need a framework for explaining and justifying these clinical observations. But the statement that every experience has a tendency to influence the way we behave, feel, sense, imagine, think, relate interpersonally, and respond biologically, probably says as much about "human personality" as anything else to date.

Notes

Special thanks are expressed to Gordon F. Boals for his assistance with the first draft of the manuscript.

1. P. Holzman, "Personality," *Annual Review of Psychology, 25,* 1974, p. 247.
2. W. Mischel, *Personality and assessment,* (New York: Wiley, 1968).
3. W. Mischel, "Towards a cognitive social learning reconceptualization of personality," *Psychological Review, 80,* 1973, p. 252.
4. A. Edwards and R. Abbot, "Measurement of personality traits: Theory and technique," *Annual Review of Psychology, 24,* 1973, p. 241.

5. A. Lazarus, *Behavior therapy and beyond*, (New York: McGraw-Hill, 1971).
6. A. Lazarus, "Multimodial behavior therapy: Treating the BASIC ID," *Journal of Nervous and Mental Disease, 156,* 1973, p. 404.
7. W. Mischel and B. Moore, "Cognitive transformations of the stimulus in delay of gratification," unpublished manuscript, Stanford U., 1973.
8. M. Horowitz, *Image formation and cognition,* (New York: Appleton-Century-Crofts, 1970).
9. A. Ellis, *Growth through reason,* (Palo Alto, Calif: Science and Behavior Books, 1971).
10. A. Lazarus, "Multimodial behavior therapy in groups," In G. Gazda (Ed.), *Basic approaches to group psychotherapy and group counseling,* rev. ed. (Springfield, Ill.: Charles C Thomas, 1975).
11. A. Lowen, *The betrayal of the body,* (New York: Macmillan, 1967).

Part Two

Clinical Reports and Case Studies

Chapter 8 is included to underscore how a basic clinical syndrome such as "depression" is perceived as an interactive process through the viewpiece of each modality of the BASIC ID.

Frank Richardson describes a multimodal approach to anxiety management training in Chapter 9. He emphasizes acquiring self-management skills for coping with stress and anxiety. This chapter describes the AMT program in sufficient detail for the reader to acquire a repertoire of ingenious and effective techniques for overcoming anxiety.

Donald Keat (Chapter 10) shows how a sensitive clinician can adapt the multimodal approach to the treatment of children. His two case studies capture the essence of multimodal therapy—its potential for specificity, thoroughness, and personalistic diversity.

The multimodal therapist requires a wide range of techniques among which hypnosis can serve an extremely useful function. Robert Karlin and Patricia McKeon (Chapter 11) provide precise ways in which hypnotic techniques can fit into and amplify the multimodal behavior therapy orientation. Two case histories provide some inventive treatment strategies.

In Chapter 12 I discuss certain polemical issues concerning multimodal therapy with special reference to group therapy. This chapter outlines in some detail the technique of *associated imagery*.

In Chapter 13 Dan Bridell and Sandra Leiblum describe the successful treatment of a case that was considered intractable by previous therapists. They demonstrate how a multimodal approach enables the therapist to monitor each modality and discover neglected areas of concern.

William Mulligan (Chapter 14) shows how seemingly unitary problems may, in fact, consist of interactive difficulties that are unraveled and resolved during the course of multimodal therapy. While focusing primarily on treating his client's obesity, Mulligan attempts to ferret out the active ingredients of the observed behavioral changes.

Although Chapter 15 by Allen Fay is not explicitly directed at multimodal therapy, it is important for *all* therapists to be familiar with paradoxical techniques. From a multimodal standpoint, paradoxical interventions are primarily concerned with interpersonal and cognitive procedures for helping "resistant clients." Indeed, regardless of one's theoretical orientation, therapists require extraordinary techniques when confronted by patients who, despite their stated desire to change, prove extremely refractory even in the face of the most skillfully applied multimodal interventions.

The value of a therapeutic orientation cannot be ascertained on the basis of one person's experience; the approach must be put to the test by others. It is significant that Carole Pearl and Vito Guarnaccia (Chapter 16) have been able to apply multimodal behavior therapy to the field of mental retardation.

I decided to include my article from *Psychology Today* (Chapter 17) in order to demonstrate how the multimodal approach is uniquely suited to the comprehensive treatment of sexual inadequacies.

Chapter 8

Multimodal Behavioral Treatment of Depression

Arnold A. Lazarus

From a strict behavioral point of view, "depression" is a hypothetical construct, and, to avoid the snares of subjectivity, depression would be defined as a general weakening of one's behavioral repertoire (Skinner, 1953). But this leaves the practicing clinician empty-handed if not empty-headed. For as Ferster (1965) points out: "Whether a man who moves and acts slowly is 'depressed' or merely moving slowly is not easily or reliably determined by observing his behavior alone."

In "depression" a catalogue of overt responses could cover a variety of reactions such as decreased food intake, psychomotor retardation, insomnia, or a fitful sleep pattern, and we might establish a base rate of frequent weeping, statements of dejection, pessimism, and self-reproach, general apathy, withdrawal, impaired concentration, somatic complaints, and perhaps suicidal attempts. However, as Ferster's (1973) functional analysis of depression failed to note, there are also "smiling depressives" who deny their pervasive gloom and still pose a constant suicidal threat. There is no need to belabor the fact that the term "depression" encompasses too much, remains ill-defined, and has been attributed to a variety of antecedent factors. However, in our daily practices we are all consulted by many persons who say they feel "depressed."

The present paper describes a multimodal behavior therapy approach employed with chronically depressed patients for whom drugs and/or ECT seem to have had limited utility. Seven interactive modalities are continuously monitored: overt behavior, affective processes, sensory reactions,

From *Behavior Therapy*. 5, 549-554. Copyright 1974 by Academic Press, Inc. Reprinted by permission.

emotive imagery, cognitive components, interpersonal relationships, and a "medical modality" especially characterized by indications and contraindications for the use of drugs or medication.

In the majority of cases, depression appears to be engendered by inadequate or insufficient reinforcers. Positive reinforcers have diminished and/or have lost their effectiveness. Above all, depressed persons seem to have little hope for future positive reinforcement. Many factors can contribute to the aforementioned state of affairs. Obvious contingencies include any abrupt environmental shift—loss of money, health, friendship, status, loves ones—and less obvious factors may involve loss of youth, loss of striving, loss of pride. It is important to try and pinpoint the specific reinforcement deficits. Careful history-taking and various psychodiagnostic tests may prove helpful in so doing. The essence of a successful treatment process is one in which people are enabled to recognize and utilize various reinforcers at their disposal.

When positive reinforcers are weakened or removed, the net result is usually a diminished behavioral repertoire—leading to response extinction. Severe depression results when the absent or missing reinforcer happens to be a discriminative stimulus, a pivotal link in the person's reinforcement repertoire, e.g., the demise of a beloved spouse. In such a case, even though alternative reinforcers are made available, the person yearns for the reestablishment of the exact reinforcement pattern that he/she had enjoyed. In these instances, treatment often amounts to a concerted effort to discover ways and means of reducing the patient's counterproductive tendencies. Realistically, one may have to rely on the truism "time heals," because the passage of time permits new and competing responses to emerge.

When "anxiety" is a prominent feature interspersed within the depressive reaction, the usual behavioral standbys such as assertive training, systematic desensitization, and deep muscle relaxation may play a useful role. Dengrove (1966) reported on the successful use of desensitization in overcoming grief reactions, whether stemming from the death of a loved one, separation, or desertion. He commenced by having the patient visualize the person or the "lost object" in a series of formerly happy and pleasant contexts. Then, under conditions of deep muscle relaxation, he slowly moved forward in time, progressing gradually to the traumatic event. If personal fear of death or reactions of guilt were present, these were included in the "anxiety hierarchy." The foregoing stands in marked contrast to Freud's (1925) admonition that any interference with the so-called "normal emotion of grief" is "inadvisable or even harmful."

But let us review the multimodal (BASIC ID) approach to those patients whose inner dejection, despair, misery, despondency, futility, gloom and nuclear unworthiness have characterized their daily experiences for months or perhaps years. In the behavioral modality, an activity chart is constructed. Where feasible, an observer tallies and graphs base rates of the depressed person's daily activities over three or four days. Some patients prefer to keep their own activity charts. The obvious inference is that there is a correlation between a high activity level and a diminution of depressive affect. However, this is not a one-to-one relationship, for people can busy themselves with meaningless drudgery and remain depressed (or become even more depressed) despite an increase in activity per se. Thus, the emphasis is upon a catalogue of rewarding activities.

Of course, the severely depressed patient will insist that he is not worthy of pleasure or rewards. One proceeds to find out what activities had been rewarding in the past. One may use any available "reinforcement schedule" or "pleasant events schedule" or draw up one's own checklist. The endeavor is to establish numerous behaviors, sensations, images, ideas, people, and places that the person had found reinforcing. We try to obtain at least 50 items from which to work; e.g., playing tennis, buying clothes, reading comics, playing cards, telling jokes, taking a warm shower, making love, reliving pleasant scenes, listening to music, having a massage, eating in a good restaurant, talking on the telephone, discussing religion, visiting friends, winning an argument, going to auctions, playing with pets. Having a list of activities which were, and probably still could be, rewarding enables the clinician to start "prescribing" a graded series of potentially reinforcing responses.

Some depressed patients take to this reinforcement melange very readily; others remain unmotivated and quite recalcitrant. In the latter instances, it is necessary for the therapist to commence treatment by expending more time and effort than usual. It is important to make home visits and home observations (described as "our most powerful procedure" by Lewinsohn, 1974). By offering and displaying therapeutic interest and concern, we do not reinforce depressive reactions but "reverse the downhill cycle within which the depressed patient finds himself at the point where he asks for help" (Lewinsohn, 1974). I have had many depressed patients "shadowing" me—i.e., attending classes with me, performing routine chores around the office, meeting with my students, and thus avoiding patterns of social isolation and inertia.

In one instance, the patient would just lie in bed each day. In this case, the therapist would drive over to his house, get him out of bed, and, if necessary, take him by the hand into several potentially reinforcing activities. Initial dependency was clearly fostered, but within about a month the positive reinforcers themselves began to take effect and the patient began to generate independent activities for the first time in years. This man needed to know that, for whatever reasons, there were people in the world who cared sufficiently for him to get him mobilized. It became obvious that he was testing us to see whether we would let go of him unless he "shaped up" rapidly and readily.

The foregoing vignette indicates that, even in a task-oriented approach, many cognitive, affective, and interpersonal processes contaminate or facilitate the treatment outcomes. This is what many therapists seem to imply when they state that they automatically employ a multimodal treatment regimen. But I am referring to the deliberate and specific modification of negative elements within each modality. Thus, in the affective modality, apart from obvious misery and gloom, we often find "anxiety" (which is then countered by specific behavior therapy techniques) as well as "anger." Certain psychodynamic formulations of depression stress a deflection where the anger is turned inward. However, in examining the source of various anger responses, many of these appear to be secondary to the depression. What seems to happen is that significant others are inevitably placed in a difficult double-bind when dealing with depressed persons. If they show warmth and sympathy, they tend to reinforce the depressive behavior; if they withdraw, they increase the general reinforcement deprivation, incur the depressed person's (usually unexpressed) wrath, and often arouse guilt feelings within themselves. Training the depressed person to emit assertive responses is probably the single most effective strategy in these instances.

When dealing with the sensory modality, one not only compiles a list of pleasant visual, auditory, tactile, olfactory, and gustatory stimuli to add to the "reinforcement or pleasant events schedule," but one also employs several exercises typically advocated by "bioenergetic analysis" to promote muscle tone, and to elicit sensory-affective reactions (e.g., by pounding or pushing or yelling). Within a social learning theory framework, the rationale for these procedures is to produce sufficient arousal for subsequent assertive training to have personal significance.

Imagery is especially useful for purposes of desensitization, for mentally rehearsing the depressed individual to take heed of reinforcing events, and for using "time projection" techniques, with or without hypnosis, where the depressed individual actually pictures himself engaging in future rewarding activities (Lazarus, 1968).

The principal cognitive intervention is aimed at eliminating the non sequitur "therefore I am worthless" (Beck, 1967). Using many of the rational-emotive techniques advocated by Ellis (1962; 1973), one parses irrational self-talk, challenges impossibly high standards that some depressives try to maintain, and employs "thought blocking" to disrupt certain obsessional ruminations. Patients are also explicitly rewarded for making positive and self-approving statements.

At the interpersonal level, new social skills are deliberately taught. The use of role-playing and behavior rehearsal is often extremely effective in overcoming social and interpersonal deficits. In essence, the patient is taught four specific skills: saying "no!" to unreasonable requests; asking for favors from others; expressing positive feelings; and volunteering criticism and disapproval.

Drugs are often extremely important; however, a multimodal orientation argues against the use of a single modality for the treatment of any case (Lazarus, 1973). Even when drugs have lightened and stabilized the patient's mood, it is necessary to examine and remedy any residual problems involving behavior, affect, sensation, imagery, cognition, and interpersonal relationships. The multimodal approach is predicated on the assumption that the durability of treatment outcomes will be in direct proportion to the extent to which problem identification (diagnosis) systematically explores each of the modalities, whereupon therapeutic intervention remedies whatever deficits and maladaptive patterns emerge.*

References

Beck, A. T. *Depression: Clinical, experimental and theoretical aspects.* New York: Hoeber-Harper, 1967.

Dengrove, E. *Treatment of nonphobic disorders by behavior therapy.* Lecture to the Association for Advancement of Behavior Therapy, New York, December 17, 1966.

Ellis, A. *Reason and emotion in psychotherapy.* New York: Stuart, 1962.

Ellis, A. *Humanistic psychotherapy: The rational-emotive approach.* New York: Julian Press, 1973.

Ferster, C. B. Classification of behavioral pathology. In L. Krasner and L. P. Ullmann (Eds.), *Research in behavior modification,* pp. 6-26. New York: Holt, Rinehart and Winston, 1965.

Ferster, C. B. A functional analysis of depression. *American Psychologist,* 1973, *28,* 857-870.

Freud, S. Mourning and melancholia. In *Collected papers,* Vol. IV. London: Hogarth, 1925.

Lazarus, A. A. Learning theory and the treatment of depression. *Behaviour Research and Therapy,* 1968, *6,* 83-89.

* My trainees and I have consistently found that the multimodal orientation has enabled us to help individuals whose prognostic outlooks appeared to be anything but favorable. Our statistics over the past year show that 22 of 26 individuals in whom chronic depression had persisted for months and for years in some instances (despite traditional psychiatric intervention) responded to multimodal therapy by making significant gains in a mean of three months—usually consisting of one individual and one group meeting per week. Follow-up to date underscores the durability of our results.

Lazarus, A. A. Multimodal behavior therapy: Treating the "BASIC ID." *Journal of Nervous and Mental Disease,* 1973, *156,* 404-411.

Lewinsohn, P. M. Clinical and theoretical aspects of depression. In K. S. Calhoun, H. E. Adams, K. M. Mitchell (Eds.), *Innovative treatment methods in psychopathology.* New York: Wiley, 1974.

Skinner, B. F. *Science and human behavior.* New York: Macmillan, 1953.

Chapter 9

Anxiety Management Training: A Multimodal Approach

Frank C. Richardson

This chapter describes a multimodal training program, designed to teach a wide range of self-management skills for coping with stress and anxiety. In addition to helping clients eliminate specific, anxiety-based problems in functioning, such as phobias and some psychosomatic disorders, the program should help individuals gain control over general, trait, or "free-floating" anxiety. The format and tenor of the program is distinctly educational in nature, and it employs a number of straightforward didactic techniques. The approach was developed very much in the spirit of a recent description of rational-emotive therapy by Ellis (1973):

> My therapeutic approach is unusually didactic. I continually explain to my clients what the *general* mechanisms of emotional disturbances are, how these usually arise, how they become ingrained, and what can be done to combat them. I therefore . . . teach them many things a good psychology professor would teach them—except that the teaching is usually of an individual nature, and is specifically designed to utilize the facts of the client's current life (p. 155).

Anxiety management training (1) focuses on a broad but delimited area of functioning—namely, coping with stress and maladaptive anxious responding; (2) systematically educates clients in the use of several overt behavioral and cognitive self-control techniques for managing stress and anxiety; and (3) attempts to increase the benefits from training and their durability by dealing explicitly with the different zones or modalities of clients' functioning, such as behavior, affect, sensation, cognition, interpersonal relationships, and imagery. Thus, it follows the approach outlined by Lazarus (1973) in combining techniques, strategies, and modalities in a multimodal program for anxiety control.

Anxiety management training (AMT) was originally developed

within a conditioning framework as a behavior therapy technique intended to correct several deficiencies in systematic desensitization, especially its exclusive focus on current maladaptive behavior (Suinn and Richardson, 1971). It was hoped that this new procedure would effectively eliminate a wider range of maladaptive anxious responses other than those associated with the specific hierarchies used in treatment, so that it would prepare the client for coping with future tensions he or she might encounter.

The original AMT program involves using instructions and cues to arouse anxiety responses and training clients to develop responses that compete with anxiety—typically, relaxation and feelings of competency. Clients are shown how to arouse high levels of anxiety by picturing a frightening scene and by actively generating common physiological symptoms of anxiety. Competing responses are developed through deep muscle relaxation training and the visualization of a "success scene" associated with realistic feelings of competency and mastery. The training proper consists of about four minutes of instructions (which may be tape-recorded) to develop feelings and symptoms of anxiety, followed by about four minutes of instructions to either relax, or, on alternate trials, develop competency feelings. The original program involves about three hours of training, with only one hour devoted to practice in directly counteracting self-generated anxiety. This procedure has been found as effective as systematic desensitization in treating mathematics anxiety (Suinn and Richardson, 1971) and is highly effective in reducing public-speaking anxiety (Nicoletti, 1972) and test anxiety (Richardson and Suinn, 1974). AMT has also been found effective in lowering self-reported general or trait anxiety in two studies (Edie, 1972; Nicoletti, 1972).

Originally AMT was explained in terms of conditioning theory (Suinn, 1975; Suinn and Richardson, 1971). Unlike desensitization, in which a relaxation response was attached to anxiety-provoking stimuli, AMT was thought to attach reciprocally inhibiting relaxation or competency feelings to the onset or increasing levels of the anxiety response itself, that is, to the musculoskeletal or autonomic cues associated with anxiety. Thus, in any situation where maladaptive anxiety was aroused, the arousal itself would trigger strong competing responses in a relatively automatic manner.

There are obvious logical difficulties with this explanation of AMT's effects. At the very least it presupposes a cognitive discrimination between realistic danger situations where fear is rationally justified and those where it is not. Also, it appears to use "conditioning" language in a highly metaphorical manner (London, 1972) in order to describe the learning of several active self-management skills in counteracting anxiety. However, the revised multimodal AMT program that will be described below incorporates (1) techniques designed to make clients aware of (while teaching them to modify) their maladaptive beliefs and patterns of self-verbalizations that cause specific and general anxiety problems and (2) additional behavior therapy techniques designed to help clients realign perceptions, thinking, fantasy, and everyday interpersonal behaviors in accord with more rational and adaptive perspectives. This approach retains the original AMT notion of attacking the root mechanisms of maladaptive anxiety in a manner most likely to generalize to other current and future problems. However, in practice and theory, the emphasis is on rational reevaluation and the learning of a number of active self-management skills rather than on the counterconditioning of relaxation or competency feelings to internal anxiety cues.

In developing such a program, we found it advantageous to borrow and adapt techniques described by other recent writers to equip persons to cope more effectively with anxiety and stress. Sipprelli and his colleagues (Bornstein and Sipprelli, 1973) have applied a procedure termed "induced anxiety" to problems of overeating. The induced anxiety method is, in fact, quite similar to the original AMT program. It employs alternating instructions to self-induce intense anxiety followed by relaxation. Meichenbaum and Cameron (1973) have developed a "stress innoculation" approach to anxiety management which attempts to modify very general patterns of anxiety-arousing self-verbalizations. Like AMT, this technique has been found effective in reducing fears that are not dealt with directly in treatment. Janis and Leventhal (1965) and Janis (1971) discuss the effects of certain educational procedures designed to have an emotionally innoculating effect on persons about to be exposed to severe life stresses.

The revised AMT program utilizes six to eight weekly two-hour small group training sessions, accompanied by a number of homework assignments and exercises. The first three or four sessions are devoted mainly to discussions and exercises designed to promote awareness of common and idiosyncratic maladaptive beliefs and patterns of coping with anxiety-generating stress, especially chronic anxiety and tension. In addition, systematic attempts are made to develop more rational and calming perspectives and approaches to stress management. The remaining sessions consist primarily of direct training in counteracting anxiety and the working of more rational perspectives into one's daily behavior. The sequence of activities, which overlap and do not always occur in exactly the same order, are as follows: (a) an initial discussion of common sources of stress and the nature and symptoms of anxiety and fear; (b) the completion (at home) of a general fear and social anxiety inventory; (c) keeping a diary about experiences with stressful situations, and specific successes and failures in coping with them; (d) the beginning of training in deep muscle relaxation, including practice in differential relaxation, as well as self-control instructions to practice relaxing in everyday stressful situations; (e) the identification and discussion of maladaptive or irrational beliefs and the patterns of anxiety-producing self-verbalizations that cause client's anxiety; (f) the developments (and writing down) of alternative, calming, more rational beliefs and perspectives coupled with alternative, more adaptive patterns of self-talk for stress situations; (g) a session of instructions to self-induce anxiety followed by relaxation or competency scenes; (h) several sessions centered around repeated imaginal rehearsal of coping relatively unanxiously with various commonly disturbing life situations; (i) specific homework assignments to try out some new strategy or behavior during the coming week and to report on it at the next session.

Training for a small group of about six clients begins with a structured discussion in which the leader or therapist presents a series of thought-provoking questions or provocative statements and then attempts socratically to lead clients to discover for themselves a number of basic "truths" about anxiety and tension. Initially the statement is made by the leader that all of us have to cope daily with a number of stressful situations and events that may and often do produce some anxiety. These situations may be difficult, irritating, involve decisions with uncertain outcomes, or in some other way constitute a "problem." The group members are asked to brainstorm about and discuss briefly (for 15 or 20 minutes) as many of these situations as they can. After a few minutes hesitation a lively and involving discussion usually ensues. Clients mention, discuss, complain, and laugh about numerous daily stresses and events that "bug" them. The situations mentioned are often unexpected in that they are everyday occurrences with which most members can identify: deciding what to wear in the morning, shopping in a supermarket, driving on freeways, seeing a very attractive member of the same sex, receiving a phone call from someone you don't wish to talk to, preparing a meal for guests, being called to task by a boss or supervisor, not understanding something you have just read in a textbook, and so on. It is emphasized that these problems and "stress points" are serious and important matters for nearly everyone. The goal is to develop a range of strategies for coping with them. Permission to talk about such daily stresses and attempts to lend dignity to the ongoing struggle usually lead to the expression of frustration, anxiety, and irritation followed by a great deal of humor and relief. This discussion seems to create considerable group rapport very rapidly, perhaps more quickly than the discussion of topics that are ostensibly more "heavy."

At this point the leader may steer the group towards a discussion about other enduring and stressful problems in daily living. Achievement pressures, financial concerns, worries about "what am I going to be when I grow up and will I be any good at it," sexual and relationship concerns, are mentioned as stresses that continue to exert pressure and cause periodic or chronic worry or tension. Next the leader briefly summarizes the discussion and points out that the group seems to have developed a good shared understanding or picture of the range of everyday and major life stresses that confront most people in our society. Following such a successful opening discussion by a skillful leader who adopts a relaxed and matter-of-fact approach, people will candidly share some of their most personal and anguish-causing concerns in living.

The second major focus for discussion is the experience of anxiety, worry, and fear. Clients are asked to describe how, and to what extent, they commonly experience anxiety in response to various forms of stress. Physical tension, other physiological symptoms, headaches, fatigue, a fearful outlook, and cognitive worry are discussed. The centrality of specific worries and general anxieties is pointed out—in a sense, it is suggested that anxiety largely *is* worry about oneself and various outcomes of events. In general, anxious clients are aware that they worry a great deal, and are able to describe the circumstances and dynamics of their worries in detail. The leader may underscore evidence of the fruitless and self-defeating character of most worry. Often clients will have already made these observations for themselves, but see no alternatives. At this point it is useful for the therapist to inquire about and review the manner in which clients have coped with worry and tension to date. Many people only apply vague attempts to "try to relax," or "try not to worry." Group members often wonder whether it is indeed possible to cope more effectively with the many stresses they encounter, although they comment that some individuals seem to be able to do so. However, they may recall a few occasions when they successfully cut through fruitless worry and relaxed, or took action, or enjoyed themselves. It seems useful to allow the group to struggle with the question of how to develop more effective coping techniques for a while, and then to outline how it is possible to learn to perceive and cope with stressful situations and anxiety much more effectively. This is achieved by discussing the main points to be covered in the rest of the program.

Each of the first three or four sessions concludes with 20-25 minutes of deep muscle relaxation training. Relaxation is presented as a self-managment skill which can be useful in helping one relax physically and emotionally in a variety of life situations. Group members are encouraged to practice relaxation at home. They are given a general fear inventory (Tasto, Hickson, and Rubin, 1973) and a social anxiety inventory (Richardson and Tasto, 1975) to complete at home, both of which can be used to identify different classes of fear-evoking events for their own and the therapist's information. Clients are also asked to begin keeping a simple diary in which they will make ongoing notes on matters pertinent to the training.

The next group session attempts to help clients come to view and analyze problems in anxiety and stress management in terms of basic rational-emotive (Ellis, 1962) and behavioral self-control (Thoreson and Mahoney, 1974) principles. Of course, it is important that such a view be developed by clients out of their own experiences and personal reflections, with a minimum of psychological jargon. The therapist begins with the provocative assertion that intense or chronic anxiety and worry serve no useful function in living, and that with some effort every adult man or woman can control if not eliminate them. Such a statement is usually received by highly anxious persons with a mixture of great interest and shocked disbelief. At various points in the didactic portion of the AMT program it seems helpful to encourage clients to speculate and develop alternative perspectives before providing them with further new information or guiding principles. In this case they might be asked temporarily to assume the complete veracity of the proposition and to speculate about how a person might function without anxiety. Often creative suggestions emerge, and we have found it useful to stimulate thinking on the basis of assumptions opposite to those commonly accepted. In any case, the leader's next step is to discuss with group members how the intense fear reactions leading to arousal and mobilization for flight may once have served a useful purpose in dangerous or primitive environments, but are almost entirely disfunctional in contemporary society. The onset of anxiety may usefully signal to a person that he faces some problem or conflict of which he was unaware. Continued or intensified anxiety becomes unnecessary if one chooses to "stop and think," and thus find some solution to the problem at hand, or, if none is possible, to change one's goals or resign oneself to a disappointment that may be cause for temporary regret, but not for continued fear or apprehension. Although most clients find this view attractive, they remark that they cannot picture specifically how to cope with fear and implement such a rational perspective.

At this point the therapists leads clients in a discussion of the basic premise of rational-emotive therapy, e.g., that anxiety and other maladaptive feelings are caused not by external situations, but by what we tell ourselves about them. Clear statements of this premise, together with examples and suggestions concerning its ramifications are available elsewhere (Ellis and Harper, 1975; Meichenbaum, 1974) and need not be reviewed here. In essence, preferably by analysis of examples drawn from the clients' experience, one provides a meaningful glimpse of the surprising degree to which we generally behave and feel as we think—how several arbitrary assumptions and patterns of self-talk literally compel us to feel bad about and cope ineffectively with many problems in living. Usually a few clients will grasp the idea of self-talk with great excitement and clearly verbalize the long, repetitive chains of self-statements that really *are* their anxiety and lead to chronic tension. The therapist then points out that as we begin to grasp the step by step process of anxious thinking and behaving we are enabled to devise or describe and actively practice specific alternative approaches to stress.

The remainder of the first three or four sessions are devoted primarily to identifying anxiety arousing maladaptive beliefs and patterns of self-talk and developing specific alternative beliefs and self-statements that will greatly reduce anxiety in daily living. Many irrational beliefs or assumptions associated with general anxiety fall into the category of superstitious beliefs about the efficacy of cognitive worry. Clients provide abundant examples of trains of thinking and attributions which ascribe successful coping with daily stresses or the avoiding of imagined disasters to the presence of worry, while real or imagined failures are attributed to not worrying quite enough. The example of a horse who notices himself running, assumes he must be fleeing some real danger, runs faster, notices he is running faster, infers that the danger has increased in magnitude or is closer at hand, runs even faster, etc., is useful for underscoring the self-escalating effects of chronic worrying. These beliefs must be examined and discussed in some detail. Many clients are attached to the profoundly superstitious belief that worry alone keeps them alert to possible danger or protects them from committing various moral or social errors. It is important to criticize and even attack the irrationality of assumptions about the causal efficacy of worry but still leave clients the freedom to abandon them on their own initiative. Changes in such beliefs have an impact across many modalities and are often tantamount to basic personality change. One client, with considerable anguish, repeatedly questioned what would happen to her and what she would do if she gave up her chronic worry. She stopped mid-sentence, seemed to relax greatly and said, "I know what I'd do. I would just enjoy a quiet mind, deal with any problems when they came up, and occasionally of my own free will think about things that would do me some good!"

A second important category of anxiety-engendering beliefs is characterized by the close connection of ideas about self-worth and feelings of well-being with social and other performances that may be negatively evaluated by others, leading to chronic feelings of danger and threat. Most generally anxious individuals are perfectionists. It is usually not difficult to rediscover with them how their impossibly high expectations and standards, in an imperfect world, cause them to live in continual fear of disappointing themselves or others. The maximum benefit from critically examining these beliefs occurs when, following Ellis (1973), one immediately attacks the root of the problem by suggesting that the most rational and humane approach may not be merely to replace negative with positive self-evaluations, but to actually break the connection between self-worth and performances altogether. Ellis suggests that one can learn to stop evaluating *oneself* and instead evaluate one's *behavior* and *experiences* in terms of their pleasant or rewarding qualities. There are such eloquently written statements of this point of view (Ellis and Harper, 1975; Rubin, 1975) that in a multifaceted treatment program of this kind it seems wasteful not to prescribe appropriate ''bibliotherapy.'' Discussion of these matters may uncover important aspects of the interpersonal modality, such as excessive reliance upon the opinions of others, fear of rejection, and the like.

A third category of common, anxiety-producing misconceptions involves the client's view of what most other people are really like and how they supposedly react to or evaluate the client—variations on the theme that ''some other people lead smooth and almost painless lives and there must be something wrong with me because I don't.'' A generally anxious outlook usually involves some mistaken belief or image whereby at least some other people either (1) do not experience the stresses, uncertainties, or moments of self-doubt that the client does, or (2) possess some magic coping skill that makes their experience of these stresses qualitatively different from the client's (i.e., less painful). For many clients this image of a qualitatively different state of existence for others serves both as a standard with which they unfavorably compare themselves, and an ideal which they hope somehow, someday to attain. A great deal of worry consists precisely of ruminative, unfavorable comparisons between oneself and others, and by undoing these mistaken assumptions, one removes a significant reason or motive for chronic worry.

These categories of mistaken beliefs have emerged from previous experience with AMT for general anxiety and are offered as a guide to therapists in fostering a comprehensive examination of such assumptions. Actual training, of course, proceeds in a more piecemeal fashion as group members raise their experiences and ideas for discussion. Clients are assigned two related kinds of written homework. First, they are asked to (a) write down personal examples of maladaptive or irrational beliefs which presumably arouse anxiety in them; (b) develop and write down statements of alternative, calming, more realistic beliefs and perspectives; and (c) make notes about the ways in which they would be thinking, feeling, and behaving differently if they replaced the first with the second set of beliefs. Second, they are requested to write down several examples of anxiety-producing self-talk, and to generate alternative, calming patterns of self-verbalization that they could realistically use in stressful life situations. It is essential that their statements of beliefs and self-talk be expressed in colloquial, personally convincing language. Clients are told that they will be using these specific statements in the second half of the program. Many of these statements are reviewed in the group session, and clients seem to learn a great deal vicariously from the remarks and examples of others. As one instance of a maladaptive belief, a 29-year-old male graduate student wrote: "Most people mean well but feel they have to be competitive and critical, so a lot of social and work situations are kind of charged with tension. Things might get nasty at any minute." As an alternative, rational perspective he wrote: "The world is basically a calm, neutral place, no angels or demons in it. There's plenty of room to maneuver, no disasters are likely." Notes he made about how he might behave differently included: "Quit walking on eggshells, hiding out, then trying to come out and be clever every now and then. Think what you think, say what you think. Don't just try to trust more, create trust by taking the initiative and acting like relaxed cooperation is the way things will go. I would quit speculating about others' thought or motives—ask or forget about it." Heavy emphasis is placed on generating precise written statements of these kinds of perspectives. Moving from a vague to a precise, written statement of a belief often involves important additional cognitive clarification and restructuring.

The final three or four sessions of the program are devoted mainly to direct training in counteracting anxiety and working the more rational perspectives into one's daily behavior. Relaxation training in the early sessions moves from an emphasis on the tensing and relaxation of major muscle groups to exercises that focus on developing several related kinds of pleasant feelings and sensations. Pleasant images are also used to deepen relaxation and develop sensitivities and skills in the imagery modality. At the beginning of the direct training sessions the therapist points out that relaxation training has probably increased the clients' awareness and appreciation of a variety of relaxed and pleasant sensations. He suggests that creating such sensations for oneself by managing one's own experience or by changing the environment is an important skill which clients can continue to develop. In a brief discussion, group members are asked to review the kinds of pleasant or rewarding sensations and related experiences they have enjoyed, to brainstorm about specific ways they could be increased or intensified, and to consider specific new experiences in the sensory modality they might wish to develop.

At this point clients are exposed to the original AMT procedure of self-induced anxiety followed by relaxation or competency scenes. In addition, clients are instructed to use their specific and newly acquired beliefs and self-verbalizations to assist them in arousing and counteracting anxiety. They are thus given intensive training in (a) calming themselves physically and emotionally and (b) rationally reevaluating their fears.

Following are some excerpts from the anxiety induction and relaxation-reevaluation instructions used in this training.

> Now, in just a moment you will be experiencing some stress and anxiety. Take just a moment to *stay* very relaxed and prepare for the experience. Keeping relaxed, just tell yourself not to tense up or worry about the stress experience. Tell yourself, remind yourself, that when the time comes you *will* be able to cope effectively with the anxiety, and *eliminate* it. . . . All right, let the relaxation go now and concentrate on letting yourself become *anxious,* let the feelings of anxiety and fearfulness develop *now.* Focus in on the anxious bodily sensations, and *tell* yourself anxious and panicky things to arouse *much* anxiety. . . . Feel your heart starting to pound and your breathing becoming very shallow and irregular . . . actually *tell* yourself over and over some of the fearful and upsetting things that *make* you anxious and dread what's coming, really *say* them. . . . Use some of the irrational and disturbing ideas and outlooks that cause anxiety in you to develop even more fearfulness. *Look* at the world that way. Really *see* things in a panicky way. . . . Let the anxiety *completely* take over. Let it become more and more intense.

> Now, you are *anxious,* but you can *relax.* Right now, take in a very deep breath, let it out slowly, and relax. Good, very good. Notice the really refreshing feelings of relaxation that spread throughout your whole body, from head to toe . . . actually *tell* yourself calming and relaxing things, and notice that you *become* much more relaxed and serene . . . relax yourself even further by specifically recalling some of the calm, rational ideas and outlooks you have worked out for yourself. Right now, really *see* the world in these terms. *Nothing* to be afraid of, things can be handled as they come up. *Nothing* to worry about. Think calm, approach things calmly, and you *become* calm and unanxious. . . . Enjoy this *peaceful* and *rewarding* state that *you* have achieved. Be *pleased* with what you have accomplished, be *proud* of it.

The somewhat paradoxical idea and experience of actively self-generating intense anxiety is often a source of comment and further insight for clients. Individuals often have idiosyncratic (although almost never negative or disturbing) reactions to this training. It provides many with a much deeper understanding of the way in which anxious states are cognitively self-generated. Others are impressed with the seeming arbitrariness of the constrasting assumptions of anxious and calm outlooks, and thereby feel increased control over the choice of assumptions guiding their behavior. Others surprise themselves by coping quickly and effectively with anxious states qualitatively similar to those they experience in everyday life. This kind of training is limited to one session since many clients have reported that additional sessions are unnecessary.

The final two meetings center around "coping imagery" (Meichen-

baum, 1973) or clients' cognitive and imaginal rehearsal of coping relatively unanxiously with various life situations that commonly disturb them.
They are asked to make as varied a list as possible of five or six situations
that they find anxiety-producing. The list should include those situations
that are particularly representative of their chronic difficulties in managing
stress and anxiety. Each client is instructed to select one of these stressful
situations, to visualize himself beginning to get anxious, and then to
imagine himself relaxing, talking to, and instructing himself in an appropriate, calming manner, rationally reevaluating his fear, and then proceeding to cope smoothly and relatively unanxiously with the situation. Imaginal rehearsal of this process is repeated a number of times for each
situation. Each of these last three or four sessions begins with reports of any
successes or noteworthy problems from recent experience, and concludes
by discussing any new strategies suggested during the training session.
Where possible, specific homework assignments are given. Clients are
requested to try out a new behavior or approach during the coming week
and to report on it at the next session.

A final discussion with clients summarizes what they have learned and
emphasizes their specific successes. The therapist points out that they have
not just acquired certain tools for counteracting anxiety, but have learned to
tune into and assess the quality of their experience in its different dimensions or modalities. They are encouraged to approach the future in terms of
ongoing self-assessments and self-modifications in keeping with the basic
skills in anxiety management they have now acquired. What this process
might involve over time is projected for each individual and is discussed as
specifically as possible.

Two initial studies of the multimodal AMT program's feasability and
effectiveness were conducted in the fall of 1974 at the University of Texas.
One study involved a group of eight highly anxious undergraduate education majors who volunteered to pilot what was described as a "mini-course
in coping with stress and anxiety" that might later be offered on a regular
basis to teacher-trainees as part of an "affective curriculum." Thus, they
were probably participating in the program as much for reasons of curiosity
and general educational interest as for therapy. This group and a waiting-
list control group of nine students completed the State-Trait Anxiety
Inventory-Trait Form (Spielberger, Gorsuch, and Lushene, 1970) about
one week before and six weeks after the AMT program. (This program
comprised six sessions conducted over a two-week period.) The results
showed a significant reduction in self-reported general anxiety for the
treatment as compared with the control group.

The task-oriented, educational focus of the AMT program elicited
high levels of participation and appropriate self-disclosure from students.
Following medical checkups between the fourth and fifth sessions, two

students reported that their blood pressure was within normal limits for the first time in several years. Two others reported success in virtually eliminating tension headaches of a chronic, moderately severe nature. One student claimed to have overcome severe test anxiety, and another reported conquering public-speaking anxiety that had prevented her from completing assignments in a speech class and had interfered with student teaching duties.

The second study found the multimodal AMT program as effective as Meichenbaum's (1972) cognitive modification procedure in reducing self-reported test anxiety in new, first semester students at the university, as compared with a waiting-list control group of students. Complete data from this study, including first year grades for treatment and control subjects, have not yet been obtained at the time of writing.

A program of this type may prove useful in treating a variety of specific and general anxiety-related problems. Besides effectively dealing with common phobias and general anxiety, this approach may be useful in treating psychosomatic disorders stemming at least in part from high levels of chronic tension. Suinn (1974) has applied a version of the original AMT program to the rehabilitation of cardiac patients. The present writer is currently using the program described in this chapter, together with social assertiveness training, in a multimodal approach to the emotional retraining of duodenal ulcer patients. Yet, the most important uses for a program of this type may be educational and preventive, rather than remedial. In this connection, anxiety management training may prove to be a powerful means of teaching improved perspectives, coping strategies, and self-management skills to children and young adults who have not yet experienced the full measure of the stresses in which contemporary life abounds. And by deliberately incorporating each modality of the BASIC ID in this program, a more thorough and comprehensive treatment regimen is ensured.

References

Bornstein, P. H., & Sipprelli, C. N. Group treatment of obesity by induced anxiety. *Behaviour Research and Therapy*, 1973, *11*, 339-341.

Edie, C. *Uses of anxiety management training in treating trait anxiety*. Unpublished dissertation, Colorado State University, 1972.

Ellis, A. *Humanistic psychotherapy*. New York: McGraw-Hill, 1973.

Ellis, A., & Harper, R. *A new guide to rational living*. Englewood Cliffs, New Jersey: Prentice-Hall, 1975.

Janis, I. L. *Stress and frustration*. New York: Rand McNally, 1968.

Janis, I. L., & Leventhal, H. Psychological aspects of physical illness and hospital care. In B. Wolman (Ed.), *Handbook of clinical psychology*. New York: McGraw-Hill, 1965.

Lazarus, A. A. *Behavior therapy and beyond*. New York: McGraw-Hill, 1971.

Lazarus, A. A. Multimodal behavior therapy: Treating the "BASIC ID." *Journal of Nervous and Mental Disease*, 1973, *156*, 404-411.

London, P. The end of ideology in behavior modification. *American Psychologist*, 1972, *27*, 913-920.

Meichenbaum, D. Cognitive modification of test anxious college students. *Journal of Consulting and Clinical Psychology*, 1972, *39*, 370-380.

Meichenbaum, D. Cognitive factors in behavior modification: Modifying what clients say to themselves. In C. M. Franks and G. T. Wilson (Eds.), *Annual review of behavior therapy: Theory and practice*, pp. 416-431. Vol. 1. New York: Brunner/Mazel, 1973.

Meichenbaum, D. Self-instructional methods. In F. H. Kanfer and A. P. Goldstein (Eds.), *Helping people change*, pp. 357-392. New York: Pergamon, 1974.

Meichenbaum, D., & Cameron, R. *Stress innoculation: A skills training approach to anxiety management*. Unpublished manuscript, University of Waterloo, 1973.

Nicoletti, J. *Anxiety management training*. Unpublished doctoral dissertation, Colorado State University, 1972.

Richardson, F. C., & Suinn, R. Effects of two short-term desensitization methods in the treatment of test anxiety. *Journal of Counseling Psychology*, 1974, *21*, 457-458.

Richardson, F. C., & Tasto, D. Factor analysis of a social anxiety inventory. *Behavior Therapy*, 1976, in press.

Rubin, T. I. *Compassion and self-hate*. New York: McKay, 1975.

Spielberger, C. D., Gorsuch, R., & Lushene, R. *The State-trait anxiety (STAI) manual for form X*. Palo Alto: Consulting Psychologists Press, 1970.

Suinn, R. Behavior therapy for cardiac patients. *Behavior Therapy*, 1974, *5*, 569-571.

Suinn, R. Anxiety management training for general anxiety. In R. Suinn and R. G. Weigel (Eds.), *The innovative psychological therapies: Critical and creative contributions*. New York: Harper and Row, 1975, in press.

Suinn, R., & Richardson, F. C. Anxiety management training: A non-specific behavior therapy program for anxiety control. *Behavior Therapy*, 1971, *4*, 498-511.

Thoreson, C. E., & Mahoney, M. J. *Behavioral self-control*. New York: Holt, Rinehart and Winston, 1974.

Chapter 10

Multimodal Therapy with Children: Two Case Histories

Donald B. Keat, II

In the search for effective clinical techniques, the most sensible approach involves the therapist's use of whatever procedure promises to be the most potent antidote for the particular problem at hand. The counselor or therapist, therefore, may employ any effective technique drawn from any discipline (Lazarus, 1967). In this "personalistic" approach to therapy, the clinician constantly seeks new and useful techniques capable of achieving constructive therapeutic ends (Lazarus, 1971).

In this chapter the seven modalities of the BASIC ID will be considered and applied to two child cases by the use of (1) problem identification (diagnosis) and (2) specific treatment strategies across each modality.

The Case of Scott

The identified patient was a nine-year-old adopted boy, Scott. He was the oldest child in a family of three children. Both parents were well educated, the father being an internationally known person in his field. The major presenting problems for Scott were the behavioral disorders of cheating and stealing, inhibited expression of feelings, tension, poor reading skills, low self image, severe sibling rivalry, and hyperactivity.

Accurate problem identification (diagnosis) precedes effective therapy. In Scott's case, input data for the BASIC ID were gleaned from an initial interview with the parents as well as three sessions with the child. Once the therapist has assessed the core problems by investigating each of the BASIC ID zones, the next task is to select possible therapeutic approaches for dealing with them during both individual child therapy as well as sessions with the parents. During these hours the therapist must draw upon his armamentarium of techniques in order to treat the various areas of concern effectively. The following Modality Profile (Table 1) is presented as a means of tying together the diagnostic and treatment aspects of the case illustration.

Problems and Treatment Strategies

Behavior. One of the clusters of behaviors that the parents were interested in lessening was cheating-stealing. Toward that end, I read stories to Scott that dealt with the lessons or moral values he needed to internalize in order to gain some self-control (e.g., Gardner, 1972; 1974). Another effective technique was to work bibliotherapeutically with the parents (see later discussion under interpersonal relationships). Finally, behavioral contracting (Keat, 1974c) enabled Scott to perceive more clearly what he had to do (e.g., tasks) in order to obtain certain rewards (e.g., money).

A second behavior that Scott's parents wanted to see alleviated was his hyperactivity. Three main approaches were used: (1) The limits inherent in the games and activities during the session provided the child with practice in the control of activity. (2) The parents learned new ways of handling their child's hyperactivity through discussions with the therapist and through reading (e.g., Patterson and Gullion, 1968). (3) Scott's final major environment, school, was restructured by the use of such aids as a screen and a refrigerator box placed between him and the other children, thereby decreasing extraneous stimulation. He could thus focus his attention on his work without being distracted by classmates.

The final behavioral concern of the parents was to increase Scott's frustration tolerance. This goal was approached in two ways. (1) I placed the child in frustrating "real play" work situations (e.g., model-building) as well as group situations in which he faced stress but received support from the therapist. Gradually he built up a repertoire of coping reactions to these situations. (2) I attempted to retrain the child through a mutual storytelling procedure (Gardner, 1971). After Scott related frustrating situations that were handled maladaptively, the therapist told a similar story but offered a more adaptive coping style (Keat, 1974a, pp. 84-86).

Affect. Three affective areas were presented as concerns: blocked feelings, occasional inappropriate outbursts of anger, and Scott's excessive tension. A useful psychotherapeutic game that enables children to overcome inhibited affects is *The talking, feeling, and doing game* (Gardner, 1973). This game usually allows the therapist to gain inroads to important psychological issues in a child's life (e.g., "What's the thing to do if an adult jumps in line in front of you?"). The child obtains token reinforcements (literally) from attempting to respond to the card drawn after throw-

Table 1. Multimodality Profile for Scott

Modality	Problem	Proposed Treatment
Behavior	Behavioral disorder: cheating-stealing	Reading moral stories to the child Bibliotherapy for parents Behavioral contracting
	Hyperactivity	Games during therapy Bibliotherapy for parents Structured school environment
	Poor frustration tolerance	Real play situations Mutual storytelling
Affect	Blocked feelings	Talking, Feeling, Doing Game Parents as models
	Anger expression	Directed Muscular Activity
	Overly tense	Relaxation training
Sensation-school	Poor reader (visual)	Tutoring in school
	Handwriting quality low (tactile)	Skinner's program
	Auditory sequential memory (auditory)	Aural training practice
	Perceptual-motor problems	Training program
Imagery	Low self-image	Mutual storytelling
	Adopted: fears of being abandoned	Thought stopping
Cognition	Failure syndrome	Rational behavioral corrective self-talk
	Problems making choices	Decision-making practice
Interpersonal relationships	Excessive sibling rivalry	Bibliotherapy for parents "Instant replay"
	Lack of filial relationships	Communication training Big Brother
	Peer interaction poor	Group therapy "Hot seat" technique
Drugs	Hyperactivity Short attention span	Referral postponed a while, then stimulant drug prescribed

ing dice and landing on a color corresponding to the talking, feeling, or doing cards. Scott enjoyed this game and played it during many sessions. In addition to this one-to-one approach, the importance of parents as models in the expression of feelings had to be considered—that is, Scott's parents were encouraged to be more expressive of their feelings so that he could learn how to express his own.

The second area of concern was Scott's occasional outbursts of anger. In our society most children learn that angry feelings should not be expressed, and they experience anxiety because of past punishment and fear of future punishment. A procedure which had therapeutic impact in this situation was "directed muscular activity" (Lazarus, 1971). Directed muscular activity (DMA) affords the child a preprogrammed way of expressing feelings of anger. In this fashion, the child can vent feelings physiologically in such a manner that no one gets hurt (Keat, 1974a). Yet children also need to develop verbal, socially acceptable ways of "letting off steam" so that they get in no further trouble with adults. This could even involve the development of foreign language skills; one child client of the author's learned to vent his anger by swearing in Japanese!

The final concern in the affective zone was Scott's excessive bodily tension. The treatment of choice here was relaxation training (Wolpe and Lazarus, 1966; Lazarus, 1970). My process of teaching breathing and relaxation procedures is delineated elsewhere (Keat, 1974a, pp. 67-68), and relaxation directions are available from a variety of sources (Wolpe and Lazarus, 1966, Appendix 4; Lazarus, 1970 and 1971; Keat, 1974b).

Sensation-School. In the field of child treatment, sensation can take on a rather different focus than it does in an adult BASIC ID profile. The case in point illustrates how some sensory areas (visual, tactile, and auditory) can be in need of attention. Therefore, the author has expanded this mode to accommodate the fact that much of the work with children in this zone has to do with school-related areas of reading (visual), handwriting (tactile), auditory memory, and perceptual motor problems.

It is significant that Scott was a poor reader, owing in part to a bilingual start in school when he was in a foreign non-English speaking country for one year. Two years after his return to America, however, he was still not reading. To investigate this further, the author administered an oral reading test (Gray, 1963). The results showed that he was reading at the level of a second grader-first month, although his grade placement was more than halfway through fourth grade. It should be noted that he was functioning in the average range of intelligence on an individually administered scale (Wechsler, 1949). Initial steps to remediate this deficit (as well as most of the other school areas to be discussed) took place at a school conference attended by the parents, teacher, elementary school counselor, learning disabilities specialist, and the child's therapist. With regard to the reading problem, the recommendation was made that the reading specialist see Scott weekly and prescribe special classroom procedures to be used by the language arts teacher. In addition, language arts was to be approached in a multisensory way (e.g., color cuing, training, and so forth).

Scott's parents also reported that his handwriting was poor. Administration of a motor gestalt test (Bender, 1946) scored on a developmental system (Koppitz, 1964) revealed a drawing age of six-and-a-half (a three-year lag). A significant perceptual-motor lag and a learning disability appeared to be present, and further psychodiagnostic procedures seemed to be indicated. Referral was made to the school district's learning disabilities specialist. Scott's visual mode seemed to be intact. However, on a visual motor integration test (Beery and Buktenica, 1967), Scott experienced difficulty in matching motor with visual data. Thus, pencil-paper tasks proved to be laborious for him. Therefore, it seemed that he could benefit from a handwriting program (Skinner and Krakower, 1968).

Deficiencies seemed to be operating in the auditory mode as well. Although his auditory memory was adequate, he tended to make various errors (i.e., he could repeat digits accurately but would add numbers of his own when recalling some sets). There was also an attention factor; his knowledge of verbal instructions was often imprecise. His auditory sequential memory confusion was helped by structuring his learning environment and by giving him aural training practice. This dual approach was effective in both the attention and skill development areas.

Scott's general perceptual-motor problems were ameliorated by the multisensory approach to tasks, reduction of stimuli during work periods, particular remedial programs (e.g., Frostig, 1966), and a reward system for his accomplishments (Keat, 1974a, Appendix D). In particular, I found Scott's use of a daily report system helpful. At the end of the school day Scott recorded on a tape-recorder what he accomplished, what he didn't get done, how he felt about the day, and what he looked forward to on the next day. This tape was shared on a daily basis with his parents and teachers or school counselor, and on a weekly basis with his therapist. Scott already had experience using the tape machine during weekly therapy sessions with the mutual storytelling procedures.

Imagery. This child's self-image was basically very negative. He thought of himself as a failure and pictured himself as an adopted child with all that this label connotes (Carroll, Cunningham, Keat, Sherman, and Paguaga, 1969). More specifically, he feared being deserted as he once had been by his natural parents.

Problems concerning a poor self-image are central to most children in psychotherapy, and thus every therapist is concerned with building a positive self-concept (Keat, et al., 1974). In this case, the poor self-image was treated by a combination of positive reinforcements when feasible as well as by the mutual storytelling technique (Gardner, 1971).

Scott visualized himself as being different—an adopted child. Although this is a common fantasy even among natural-born children, it was a particularly distressing image for him. Eidetic imagery (Ahsen and Lazarus, 1972) might have been a useful procedure to induce feelings of security, but Scott seemed to have some difficulty with this approach. Therefore, a more direct "thought-stopping" (Lazarus, 1971) technique was utilized, resulting in Scott's rejection of such thoughts whenever they intruded.

Cognition. Scott's failure syndrome was related to his poor self-image. Some "cognitive restructuring" (Lazarus, 1971) or "cognitive ecology" (Mahoney, 1973)—"cleaning up" what one says to oneself—is usually helpful in this connection (Keat, 1972). I reprogrammed Scott with such sentences as "I can do it," "I'm a good talker," and so forth. In this manner, corrective self-talk repetitions, focused on real strengths, can lead to internalization of these beliefs. It is also helpful for the parents to be cued into the self-sentence approach (Ellis, 1962, 1973). When focusing on the child, I use such bibliotherapeutic sources as Ellis, Moseley, and Wolfe (1972), or Hauck (1972). When working with the parents on their own sentences, I supply them with a list of 11 rational points of emphasis from Lazarus (1971, adapted from Ellis, 1962). From this list they are to select the one that they want to work on as "psychological homework." Part of the next session is devoted to parsing the irrational self-talk statements and replacing them with more rational ones.

The second main cognitive area in this case concerned decision-making. My therapeutic strategies here evolved from situations arising during the therapy hours. For example, one day when leaving the building to meet his father, Scott was confronted with the choice of exiting through the front doors or one of two sets of side doors. He would usually look to adults for guidance when faced with this type of decision. Instead, I encouraged him to consider and weigh the alternatives himself.

Interpersonal relationships. The interpersonal modality was marked by deficiencies in three major areas: interactions with siblings, parents (especially father), and peers. The primary presenting difficulty in this zone was his excessive sibling rivalry. He engaged in conflicts with his younger (by three years) brother, although he did get along adequately with his two-year-old brother. A dual approach was used in dealing with excessive sibling rivalry. Child handling strategies and bibliotherapeutic readings (e.g., Dreikurs and Soltz, 1964) were worked through with the parents. *Instant Replay* (Bedford, 1974) was used with both parents and child. This is a counseling procedure in which "rough spots" (situations or events that result in unpleasant feelings) are described, feelings related to the rough spots are delineated, "instant replay" is enacted (description of the setting, time, preliminaries, what happened and the end result), the "psychoscope" is shared (the client's thoughts about the rough spot), alternative plans are developed and the consequences of these options are considered. The *Instant Replay* (Bedford, 1974) book involves a sibling conflict story and thus tied directly into Scott's situation.

There was also some lack of filial relationships, especially between father and son. The father was an extremely successful professional who could eke out little time for his children. The filial relationship difficulty was treated in both a remedial as well as an enhancement fashion. In this connection, some communication training was instituted with the parents. It centered on reflective listening and "I-message" transmission (Gordon, 1970). In addition, arrangements were made to provide a "Buddy" or "Big Brother" for Scott. Accordingly, a young couple met with him on a weekly basis for such events as a trip to the bowling alley.

The final interpersonal area was that of peer relationships. The treatment of choice for this difficulty was group therapy. In a group formed at school the boys talked about their favorite things (e.g., football) as well as some of their concerns. One procedure in particular was useful in helping Scott to cope with verbal assaults from others. This technique was the "hot seat" procedure (Mahoney and Mahoney, 1973) in which Scott was placed in a chair ("hot seat") with the task of "keeping cool" while the other children in the group tried to make him angry. After some initial "coaching" by the counselor who sat beside him and reinforced pacifism, Scott was increasingly able to cope with the verbal harangues of the other boys.

Drugs. Hyperactivity and short attention span are behaviors which are often successfully treated by medication. In this situation, since the therapist differentially diagnosed Scott as *not* having minimal brain dysfunction, the consideration of medication was postponed. These multimodal procedures seemed to be having a beneficial effect on all aspects of functioning except the short attention span. Therefore the therapist (in consultation with a physician) supported a two-month trial of a stimulant drug for the paradoxical calming effect. Teachers were not informed of this but were asked for feedback after the prescribed period of time had elapsed. Both teachers and parents thought that his attention and concentration had been enhanced and therefore his dosage was maintained during school hours.

Discussion

This case presentation illustrates the use of a multimodal approach in the therapy of a nine-year-old child and his family. The BASIC ID profile was applied to the problem analysis and proposed treatment procedures. By examining the zones of behavior, affect, sensation, imagery, cognition, interpersonal relations, and drug treatment, the therapist utilized a comprehensive approach which not only alleviated current concerns but also attempted to anticipate areas of future stress.

In this case, most of the zones have responded favorably to the broad spectrum of approaches described in the treatment section. Over the next several months there will be further contacts with both the child and his family. Scott will remain in a group at school for the rest of the year. Before therapy is terminated, the parents and therapist must determine a more suitable school placement for the next year so that difficulties similar to those encountered this year can be prevented. This placement will involve a more structured "traditional" school situation for Scott. Moreover, the parents' training as behavioral managers as well as Scott's self-control advances should allow the therapeutic gains to be maintained during the ensuing years.

The Case of Percy

This case involves the identified client, Percy (aged seven) and an intact family composed of an older brother (eight-and-a-half) and a younger brother (aged two). Both parents were highly educated—the mother was a school teacher, the father a university professor. The primary presenting problems were nighttime phobias, enuresis, lack of friends, sibling rivalry, and various manipulative behaviors. The multimodal analysis of problems and treatment strategies is presented in Table 2.

Problems and Treatment Strategies

Behavior. The primary initial concern of the parents was their child's phobic reactions at night. He became so fearful that he wanted to sleep only in their bedroom or at least have a passageway cut through the wall separating their rooms so that he could reassure himself that his parents were there and he had easy access to them. After the usual assuagement procedures of a nightlight and transition objects had failed to help the problem, the most effective procedure proved to be a behavioral contract. An example of the contingencies involved in the contract was the stipulation that in return for three nights not in the parent's bedroom, Percy would receive a reward of his choosing (e.g., a visit to the Military Museum, a trip to playland, or a purchase of play cars). An additional useful procedure was to tape calming-reassuring sentences (e.g., "Everything's all right;" "Lie down, relax, and think about watching the tennis ball bounce back and forth, back and forth''; see also sentences under cognition zone) which Percy could play for himself when he awoke. This phobic behavior gradually extinguished over several months.

The second and somewhat related behavioral concern was manipulative behavior. This evidenced itself in therapy by limit testing, especially at the termination of a session. The therapist handled these ploys by consistently reminding Percy that only five minutes were left, by confronting him with his behaviors when it was time to leave, and by insisting that he go on time. (Percy's family also had difficulty with schedules. Typically they would appear for appointments five to ten minutes late, and on some occasions even came for therapy on the wrong day.) To facilitate generalization of the child handling procedures to the home, a series of bibliotherapeutic sources was read by the mother and then discussed by both parents during the sessions (e.g., Dreikurs and Soltz, 1964; Patterson and Gullion, 1968; Patterson, 1971; Madsen and Madsen, 1972; Hauck, 1972; Dinkmeyer and McKay, 1973).

The problem of enuresis was alleviated after several months. This recession in the problem probably resulted from the broad spectrum approaches described above combined with specific procedures in the affective area (to be discussed later). Having treated many cases of enuresis I find that when I deal with the broad range of problems in a therapeutic way, such devices as the wee-alert become unnecessary (Keat, et al., 1974).

Percy's self-control behaviors were primarily dealt with by bibliotherapy during the sessions. With this child (as with his father) the direct introduction of materials was not possible because of his profound resistance to direction. Therefore, it was necessary to place the materials strategically so that he would "discover" them and be interested in reading them. Some of the stories utilized were drawn from Dinkmeyer (1970) and included "The Jogger" (about how to handle tensions), "The Box" (dealing with peer rejection), and "The Outsider" (on fluctuating friendships). An additional story of greater length is by Freed (1973) and deals with the attainment of positive strokes or "warm fuzzies" as well as negative encounters or "cold pricklies." These are terms which both children and adults find attractive and readily pick them up and use them in a meaningful way.

Affect. The two primary affects of concern were fears and anger. A variety of fears were in evidence. In general, Percy experienced a free-floating anxiety which would focus on a variety of transition situations (e.g., leaving one room of the house and going to another without an adult). More specifically, he feared the dark; part of this fear revolved around bats flying into his bedroom.

The treatment procedures for these concerns were varied (see Table

Table 2. Multimodality Profile for Percy

Modality	Problem	Proposed Treatment
Behavior	Phobic reactions at night	Behavioral contract
		Tape recording
	Manipulatory behavior	Bibliotherapy
	Enuresis	Directed Muscular Activity (DMA)
	Self control	Bibliotherapy
Affect	Fears	Relaxation
		Aversion (Grandmother)
		Bibliotherapy
	Anger	DMA
		T-F-D Game
		Puppet play
Sensation-School	Speech	Speech therapy clinic
		Scriptotherapy
	Perceptual-motor	Reading help
		Retraining suggestions
Imagery	Monsters	Thought stopping
Cognition	Fears	Rational self-talk
	Values	Games (e.g. Careers)
	Sex information	Bibliotherapy
	Depression	Corrective self-talk
		Develop catalogue of rewarding activities
	Decision-making	Problem-solving practice
Interpersonal relations	Lack of friends	Friendship training
	Sibling fighting	DMA
		Bibliotherapy
	Lack of father involvement	Filial program
	Marital	Communication skills training
		Contracts
Drugs-Diet	None	No medication
	Overweight	Diet therapy

2). Considerable emphasis was placed on relaxation procedures (Lazarus, 1970). Percy practiced relaxing during the sessions; his parents were given relaxation instructions (Wolpe and Lazarus, 1966, Appendix 4), as well as copies of the tapes (Lazarus, 1970) for family use. (The father was very much in need of relaxation training.) Percy learned to apply relaxation procedures, *in vivo,* whenever he was confronted with an anxiety-provoking situation. Gradually, through the use of relaxation procedures and support and reassurance from his parents, Percy's fears subsided. Occasionally, when his grandmother was visiting, he experienced the added aversive threat of her punishing him if he left his bedroom. The grandmother also utilized the withdrawal of rewards (e.g., a trip to the bowling alley.) Additional procedures employed by the therapist included bibliotherapy, e.g., "Oliver and the Ostrich" (Gardner, 1972) in which more adaptive coping with fearful situations is described.

Percy, like many children, experienced difficulty in the appropriate expression of anger. In particular, he directed some of this aggression toward his brother. During one session he drew a picture of his brother, complete with bloody nose and black eye, on a foam rubber pillow. The therapist suggested that whenever he wanted to express anger toward his older brother, he would "beat up on the pillow." During another session his brother drew a picture of Percy with the words "help me" coming out of his mouth. When the boys were seen together and anger-producing situations arose, the therapist would request them to stop the talk or game and have them direct their feelings against their brother's picture on the pillow. They could return to their previous activity when the angry feelings were dissipated.

Games can provide a major constructive means of dealing with aggression. *Monopoly* (Percy's favorite game) was used to entice him into therapy. This game, however, is generally too time-consuming and demands too much attention to be effective for therapeutic purposes. Therefore, after two sessions with this game, it was removed from the room. A more constructive game is *The Talking, Feeling, and Doing Game* (Gardner, 1973) which confronts the child with instruction cards such as "Tell something about your father that gets you angry"; "Say something angry"; "Name three things that could make a person angry." Checkers was also used effectively (Loomis, 1964). In addition, Percy enjoyed engaging in puppetry. He would viciously attack the therapist's puppets. Sometimes this involved animals against animals while on other occasions puppets representing persons such as parents and brothers were involved.

Sensation-School. Percy had a history of speech difficulty prior to entering school. This trouble was evidenced in low volume and also in some articulation defects which necessitated that the listener ask him to repeat what he had said. Percy would become frustrated and reacted with irritation and/or by giving up. To focus directly on the speech problem, he was referred to a speech therapist. Percy initially resisted this by saying that he wanted to do other things after school. Father called the therapist and explored three strategies over the phone, finally settling on the most positive one—having his child work for short-term rewards on a weekly basis (e.g., going to chess club), as well as for a longer term goal (a bike). During Percy's psychotherapy hours (in a quiet one-to-one setting) he was usually quite understandable. Another way of surmounting this difficulty was through the use of storywriting (scriptotherapy). One depressive story was elicited with regard to Spring. "Spring is a junk yard. Spring is the worms coming out of the ground. Spring is the polluted air. Spring is the dirty water. And that's what I think of Spring." This writing was therapeutic in that Percy expressed these negative feelings and the therapist realized the similarity between the child's and father's depressive themes. The therapist then worked on these perceptions with Percy and developed more rewarding activities for him to become involved in, so as to ameliorate his negative outlook on life.

In the perceptual-motor sphere, the learning disabilities specialist noted that Percy's "ocular machinery was OK, but he hasn't learned to use it efficiently." Specific classroom suggestions were then made directly to the teacher and some special reading tutorial help was enlisted.

Imagery. One of Percy's primary difficulties (previously noted) was a wide variety of fears. Early in therapy a specific image of monsters often popped into his head. He would draw them, construct them out of paper and popsicle sticks, and so forth. A direct intervention procedure taught to him was "thought-stopping" (Lazarus, 1971). With this technique, whenever he would start forming an image of a fear-provoking monster, he would say to himself "Stop!" "Get out of here!" After much work and practice, this device enabled him to block out these feared images most of the time.

Cognition. The first three considerations under this modality in Table 2 apply to Percy, whereas the final two pertain mostly to his father. With regard to Percy's fears, the therapist diligently worked at developing new self-sentences such as (for his nighttime fears) "It was only a dream"; "Nothing can harm me here"; "Don't worry." Regarding values, a father-son similarity was again highlighted. During the playing of a game called "Careers" (sold by Parker Brothers, of Salem, Mass.), the child is called upon to develop his own success formula concerning Fame, Money, and Happiness. During the first playing of the game, Percy's favored distribution of the 60 point sum that defines success was Fame—15, Money—35, Happiness—10. After the game the formula was compared to the therapist's (15-10-35). This valuing of money was pointed out during a family session and the therapist underscored how similar this was to the father's values ("Give me $32,000 per year and I'll be happy instead of depressed''). A later game noted a shift in values to a balanced 20-20-20.

Sex education was another area covered with this child. Although most parents seem to prefer that the therapist handle this task, Percy's parents wanted to impart this knowledge to their child themselves. They were loaned two books to read with him: deSchweinitz (1953) and Winderberg (1972).

The father was basically a depressive person. Therefore, a technique of corrective self-talk was used in conjunction with the *Guide to Rational Living* (Ellis and Harper, 1961) coupled with the strategy of developing a catalogue of rewarding activities (Lazarus, 1974). During sessions with the parents, these components were worked on by having the father pick a selected irrational idea from Lazarus's (1971) adaptation of Ellis's (1962) list. He would identify and spell out his irrational self-talk. The second therapeutic component (rewarding activities) was handled as ''psychological homework'' which enabled the therapist to check up on his participation in various pleasurable activities (e.g., tennis, sex, movies, and so on).

Both parents needed help in developing effective decision-making skills. Accordingly, during the sessions problems would be confronted and an attempt would be made to solve them by generating viable alternatives. For example, some solutions to the problem of making more money for the family might be to risk a new job; to ask the boss for a raise in the old job; to have the wife go out and seek work part-time or full-time; to cut down on current family expenses; or to move to a cheaper house.

Interpersonal Relationships. Both older boys in the family seemed to lack the skills necessary to make and keep friends. Therefore, some discussion and stories dealing with such topics as meeting children, things to do with other children, and getting along with others were presented. Both boys made gains and at most recent reports were experiencing few difficulties with peer relationships.

With regard to sibling fighting, the goal was to lessen (not eliminate!) this behavior. As mentioned previously, directed muscular activity with pillows was used both during therapy as well as at home. In addition, a punching clown (''Happy Hobo'') was used during the sessions. Bibliotherapy included ''Peeper'' (Dinkmeyer, 1970)—a story in which a pecking order develops among chickens but Peeper breaks the chain. Months after Percy heard the story he remarked how similar it was to his home situation where his older brother picked on him and then he in turn would ''give it'' to his younger brother. This reaction was subsequently changed to his being a helper and babysitter for his little brother (also with financial reward).

Lack of father involvement was handled by programming time in the father's busy schedule for involvement with his children. Despite a long struggle, he gradually incorporated play time for the children. This involvement became easier for him as the children (especially the youngest) grew older and hence more verbal.

In the marital realm, communication skills between the couple were practiced during the sessions. Even though the wife reported that "I can talk about and deal with things in here which I can't at home," there was some generalization to the home scene. This training involved practice in assuming listener-respondent roles, owning feelings, and giving accurate feedback. Another useful procedure was the use of contracts (Patterson, 1971). These contracts involved such stipulations as shared activities around the home (e.g., picking up one's clothes), amount of time spent together (e.g., going to dinner one night a week).

Drugs-Diet. No particular biochemical imbalance was apparent in this case. Therefore, in this case, and in numerous other families in therapy with the author, the "D" modality centered on Diet—that is, nutritional (e.g., Feingold, 1975) or vitamin consultation (e.g., Adams and Murray, 1973; Cott, 1974; Rimland, 1968; Rosenberg and Feldzamen, 1974) with the family.

In this particular case the child was becoming a bit too heavy. Therefore, the parents read Stuart and Davis (1972), and consulted with the therapist about a balanced approach to diet, physical exercise, and the situational management of overeating. It was found that Percy prepared most of his own food and engaged in little exercise. A program was instituted in which the foods available to him were of a more balanced variety (e.g., Robinson, 1972; Fredericks, 1964). When he went food shopping with his parents he was also limited to one "junk" food per trip. In addition, he was encouraged to engage in more physical activities (e.g., playing tennis with brother or father) instead of watching so much TV. TV time was curtailed; no television was allowed on a clear day until after the evening meal. The father even devised a timed-lock system in which the TV could not be turned on until after one of the parents was home. This limit essentially forced him into other activities. By encouraging him to engage in more physical activity, and by controlling the availability of certain high calorie foods, it was expected that there would be some weight loss without highlighting this as another major problem area for the child. Both parents also noted that they could benefit from this program as well.

Discussion

This case presentation illustrates the application of a multimodal approach to the therapy of the identified client (a seven-year-old child) and his family. The BASIC ID profile was presented as a systematic approach to problem analysis and proposed treatment strategies.

In this case, therapy has been terminated for about eight months.

Toward the end, the identified client was seen rarely except on his request. His older brother would occasionally phone and say that he wanted to come in for some sessions. The parents maintained a regularly scheduled contact every three weeks for the final half year. It was expected that the therapist would maintain sporadic contacts with this family throughout the year as stress situations presented themselves (e.g., father called a week ago regarding strategies to encourage his son to attend speech therapy). The therapist could thus provide help either by phone or during the therapy hour. Contacts for the last half year, nevertheless, have been limited to periodic pleasant encounters at such places as the community swimming pool (water was one of his original clusters of fears!). It appears that this child and his family have maintained the gains made during their therapy.

References

Ahsen, A., & Lazarus, A. A. Eidetics: An internal behavior approach. In Lazarus, A. A. (Ed.), *Clinical behavior therapy,* pp. 87-99. New York: Brunner/Mazel, 1972.

Adams, R., & Murray F. *Megavitamin therapy.* New York: Larchmont, 1973.

Bedford, S. *Instant replay.* New York: Institute for Rational Living, 1974.

Beery, K. E., & Buktenica, N. *Developmental test of visual-motor integration.* Chicago: Follett, 1967.

Bender, L. *Bender Motor Gestalt Test.* New York: American Orthopsychiatric Association, 1946.

Carroll, J. F. X., Cunningham, J., Keat, D. B., Sherman, E., & Paguaga, C. A. Theoretical model to analyze adoptive parenthood. *The Catholic Charities Review,* 1969, *53,* 12-20.

Cott, A. Treatment of learning disabilities. *Journal of Orthomolecular Psychiatry,* 1974, *3,* 343-355.

DeSchweinitz, K. *Growing up.* New York: Macmillan, 1953.

Dinkmeyer, D. *Developing understanding of self and others.* Circle Pines, Minnesota: American Guidance Service, 1970.

Dinkmeyer, D., & McKay, B. *Raising a responsible child.* New York: Simon and Schuster, 1973.

Dreikurs, D., & Soltz, V. *Children: The challenge.* New York: Hawthorn Books, 1964.

Ellis, A. *Reason and emotion in psychotherapy.* New York: Lyle Stuart, 1962.

Ellis, A. *Humanistic psychotherapy: The rational emotive approach.* New York: Julian Press, 1973.

Ellis, A., & Harper, R. *A guide to rational living.* Englewood Cliffs, New Jersey: Prentice-Hall, 1961.

Ellis, A., Moseley, S., & Wolfe, J. *How to raise an emotionally healthy, happy child*. North Hollywood, California: Wilshire Book Company, 1972.

Feingold, B. F. *Why your child is hyperactive*. New York: Random House, 1975.

Freed, A. M. *T. A. for tots*. Sacramento, California: Jalmar Press, 1973.

Fredericks, C. *Nutrition: Your key to good health*. North Hollywood, California: London Press, 1964.

Frostig, M. *The developmental program in visual perception*. Chicago: Follett, 1966.

Gardner, R. A. *Therapeutic communication with children: The mutual story-telling technique*. New York: Science House, 1971.

Gardner, R. A. *Dr. Gardner's stories about the real world*. Englewood Cliffs, New Jersey: Prentice Hall, 1972.

Gardner, R. A. *The talking, feeling, and doing game*. Cresskill, New Jersey: Creative Therapeutics, 1973.

Gardner, R. A. *Dr. Gardner's fairy tales for today's children*. Englewood Cliffs, New Jersey: Prentice Hall, 1974.

Gordon, T. *Parent effectiveness training*. New York: Wyden, 1970.

Gray, W. S. *Gray oral reading tests.* Indianapolis, Indiana: Bobbs-Merrill, 1963.

Hauck, P. *The rational management of children*. Roslyn Heights, New York: Libra, 1972.

Keat, D. B. Broad-spectrum behavior therapy with children: A case presentation. *Behavior Therapy*, 1972, *3*, 454-459.

Keat, D. B. *Fundamentals of child counseling*. Boston: Houghton Mifflin, 1974. (a)

Keat, D. B. *Instructor's manual for fundamentals of child counseling*. Boston: Houghton Mifflin, 1974. (b)

Keat, D. B. Behavioral counseling with an adolescent: The green stamp case. *Pennsylvania Personnel and Guidance Association Journal*, 1974, *2*, 4-12. (c)

Keat, D. B. et al. *How can I help this child?* University Park, Pennsylvania: Cope Press, 1974.

Koppitz, E. M. *The Bender Gestalt Test for young children*. New York: Grune and Stratton, 1964.

Lazarus, A. A. In support of technical eclecticism. *Psychological Reports*, 1967, *21*, 415-416.

Lazarus, A. A. *Daily living: Coping with tensions and anxieties: Relaxation Exercises I, II, and III*. Chicago: Instructional Dynamics Incorporated, 1970.

Lazarus, A. A. *Behavior therapy and beyond*. New York: McGraw-Hill, 1971.

Lazarus, A. A. Multimodal behavioral treatment of depression. *Behavior Therapy*, 1974, *5*, 549-554.

Loomis, E. A. The use of checkers in handling certain resistance in child therapy and child analysis. In Haworth, M. R. (Ed.), *Child psychotherapy*, pp. 407-411. New York: Basic Books, 1964.

Madsen, C. K., & Madsen, C. H. *Parents/children/discipline*. Boston: Allyn and Bacon, 1972.

Mahoney, M. J. Clinical issues in self-control training. Paper presented at the 81st annual convention meeting of The American Psychological Association, Montreal, August 1973.

Mahoney, M. J., & Mahoney, F. F. A residential program in behavior modification. In Rubin, R. D., Brady, J. P., and Henderson, J. D. (Eds.), *Advances in behavior therapy* (Vol. 4), pp. 93-102. New York: Academic Press, 1973.

Patterson, G. R. *Families.* Champaign, Illinois: Research Press, 1971.

Patterson, G. R., and Gullion, E. *Living with children.* Champaign, Illinois: Research Press, 1968.

Rimland, B. High dosage levels of certain vitamins in the treatment of children with severe mental disorders. San Diego, California: Institute for Child Behavior Research, 1968.

Robinson, C. H. *Normal and therapeutic nutrition.* (14th Ed.). New York: Macmillan, 1972.

Rosenberg, H., & Feldzamen, A. *The doctor's book of vitamin therapy.* New York: G. P. Putnam's Sons, 1974.

Skinner, B. F., & Krakower, S. A. *Handwriting with write and see.* Chicago: Lyons and Carnahan, 1968.

Stuart, R. B., & Davis, B. *Slim chance in a fat world.* Champaign, Illinois: Research Press, 1972.

Wechsler, D. *Wechsler intelligence scale for children.* New York: Psychological Corporation, 1949.

Winderberg, S. *The kid's own XYZ of love and sex.* New York: Stein and Day, 1972.

Wolpe, J., & Lazarus, A. A. *Behavior therapy techniques.* New York: Pergamon Press, 1966.

Chapter 11

The Use of Hypnosis In Multimodal Therapy

Robert A. Karlin and Patricia McKeon[1]

The use of hypnosis in behavior therapy is not new (Lazarus, 1958, 1963; Wolpe and Lazarus, 1966). Several studies have reported the successful use of hypnosis within the learning theory paradigm (cf. Larsen, 1966; Feamster and Brown, 1963). More recently, Cautela (1975) and Spanos, DeMoor, and Barber (1974) have suggested the similarity of covert sensitization and counterconditioning procedures to methods used by a number of hypnotherapists. Hypnosis has even been employed in relatively strict operant conditioning research (Gaunitz, Unestahl, and Berglund, 1975). Alternately, some studies have found that hypnosis does not aid in producing more vivid imagery or more extensive change in a desensitization procedure (cf. Lang, Lazovik, and Reynolds, 1965).

The present paper explores the use of hypnosis in a multimodal framework. In order to work effectively, the multimodal behavior therapist must have at his disposal a whole range of techniques. He must be able not only to deal with problems in each of the modalities, but also to apply personalistic consideration to the particular patients who confront him. For example, he may have one phobic patient who will respond well to classical desensitization, while another may find a flooding procedure more useful. Although it is clearly unnecessary, as well as impossible, for the multimodal therapist to learn every technique that anyone has ever invented, there are a number of core procedures which he can be expected to know. It is suggested that hypnosis be considered as one of these.

A variety of factors lead some therapists to avoid the use of hypnosis. Hypnosis has a number of mystical and theatrical connotations which may be aversive to the scientifically oriented practitioner. Yet the list of psychologists who have conducted research on hypnosis includes Barber, Hull, Hilgard, London, Orne, Rosenhan, Weitzenhoffer, and Zimbardo.

Studies conducted by these and other investigators have indicated that hypnotic phenomena can be reliably produced in fully controlled laboratory environments. However, these studies have also noted some limitations of hypnotic procedures. Of interest to the clinician are the findings that not all patients are hypnotizable, and that the ability to experience specific hypnotic phenomena (e.g., glove anesthesia) is almost entirely a function of the subject's hypnotizability rather than the therapist's skill (cf. Hilgard, 1975).[2]

Despite this research, a number of common misconceptions about hypnosis remain. Many people believe that the successful induction of hypnosis requires an unusually charismatic therapist. Nothing could be further from the truth. Standard hypnotic techniques have been developed that can be used by anyone who can read. The therapist has only to read a standard induction and the hypnotizable patient will become hypnotized. However, the mystique of hypnosis is so pervasive that many people have difficulty accepting this notion. While the mechanisms by which hypnosis is induced are still not well understood in the scientific community and are currently being investigated, it is nevertheless clear that a therapist can expect to reliably produce hypnotic phenomena in most patients simply by reading some rather straightforward instructions.

Another widespread misconception is the belief that it is difficult to end a hypnotic "trance."[3] The literature clearly indicates that following appropriate instructions, patients will almost always immediately return to a normal waking state. In fact, people come out of a "trance" without being dehypnotized. A study by Orne and Evans (1966) illustrates this point. Highly hypnotizable subjects were placed in a deep hypnotic "trance." The experimenter was then called from the room to attend to an emergency. He left without providing any instructions to the subjects to end the "trance." Yet all hypnotized subjects returned to a normal waking state within 30 minutes. In clinical situations, the only occasion in which a patient may not come out of "trance" immediately occurs when he has fallen asleep. In such circumstances the therapist need only awaken the patient.

A final misconception is the belief that hypnotic treatment is of only temporary value. Hypnosis was the first victim of Freud's symptom substitution hypothesis. There is no evidence whatsoever that more "symptom substitution" occurs after hypnotically induced change than after any other type of intervention.

Hypnotic Induction

A successful hypnotic induction consists of three phases: (1) introduction to hypnosis; (2) a test of the patient's willingness to experience hypnosis; and (3) formal induction. The introduction to a hypnotic session serves to convey basic information about hypnosis and reassure the patient. The length and details of the introduction will vary from case to case. Patients who have been specifically referred for hypnotic treatment will usually require a shorter orientation than those for whom hypnosis is a novel concept.

The following brief introduction can be elaborated upon in ways which will suit the particular needs of individual patients.

> Let me tell you a little bit about hypnosis. It is something very few people know about. The first thing to know is that hypnosis is not sleep. You will be aware and in control at all times. Second, let me tell you about coming out of trance. If at any time you wish to come out of trance, for any reason whatsoever, all you have to do is say to yourself, "three, two, one, out" and you will come out of trance, relaxed and alert. When I bring you out of trance, that's all I will be doing to bring you back: saying "three, two, one, out." People sometimes get their ideas about hypnosis from the movies and are afraid they will have difficulty coming out. That's complete nonsense. In experiments on this, people in a very deep trance were left alone when the hypnotist was called out for an emergency. That left the patients alone and they all came out within half an hour. Remember, those were people who were very deeply hypnotized indeed, and they came out easily within 30 minutes. The movie version of remaining hypnotized 34 years later has no basis in fact. People come out of trance easily, relaxed and alert.
>
> Third, you will be able to hear other things besides my voice; sometimes one's hearing gets even better in a hypnotic trance. Another thing you should know is that we do not need a very deep trance for most treatment techniques. Deep trances, like the ones you've seen in the movies, are basically useful only to show the kind of spectacular things that stage magicians are interested in. For hypnotic treatment, only a light trance is necessary for almost anything. [To most patients, add: Certainly, in your case nothing deeper is needed.] Finally, you should remember everything that goes on. There is nothing about hypnosis which will cause you to forget anything that happens while you are hypnotized. Do you have any questions?

The therapist should then strive to uncover any remaining misconceptions which might prevent the patient from taking full advantage of the "trance." We find it especially useful to elicit the patient's fantasies about hypnosis as these often involve aspects of media versions which may well frighten the client, such as the image of being totally at the mercy of the hypnotist. The clinician may assuage these fears by underscoring that only a light "trance" is needed and that the patient may end the "trance" at any time merely by saying "three, two, one, out." If the patient still seems concerned with such issues, specific instructions which would relieve these fears should be given soon after the beginning of formal "trance" induction.

Upon ending the introduction, the therapist must ascertain if the patient is unwilling to be hypnotized. The concept of unwillingness can be operationalized as a refusal to engage in therapist-suggested imaginings, or as the termination of such imaginings when the patient experiences unusual events. A modification of Chevreul's Pendulum provides a simple test which allows the therapist to determine if the patient is unwilling to engage in therapist-suggested imaginings. In this procedure the patient is asked to hold a relatively lightweight pendulum with the index finger and thumb of his hand (a small object tied to a 10-inch string will suffice). His elbow is supported on the arm of the chair. He is asked to pay no attention to his arm and hand, but to concentrate on the pendulum and to imagine it moving back and forth in a direction indicated by the therapist. If the patient follows the therapist's suggestion and imagines the pendulum moving in the required direction, it will proceed to do so although arm movement will not be discernible to the patient. (Feedback mechanisms in the sensory-motor cortex cause small muscle movements which swing the pendulum in the imagined direction.)

In only two circumstances will the pendulum not swing as directed. In the first, the patient will refuse to engage in therapist-suggested imaginings. In the second, he may become so anxious about succeeding at the task that he, in effect, will try too hard and find himself unable to imagine the pendulum swinging. In either case the patient is relatively unsuited for hypnosis at that point and may benefit from further preparation. Now, assuming that the pendulum does swing in the requested direction, the therapist then asks the patient to imagine it changing direction and swinging at right angles to its former course. After a few swings in the new direction, the patient is told to imagine it completely stopped. This latter instruction serves to preclude any suspicion that the therapist is merely taking advantage of the natural movement of the pendulum. When the patient has brought the pendulum to a dead stop, the therapist takes it from the patient and proceeds with a formal induction.

Any number of formal inductions can be used. A large number of inductions can be found in Weitzenhoffer (1957). A procedure that seems particularly suitable for clinical use is the Hypnotic Induction Profile (Spiegel, 1974).[4] The straightforward nature of this induction is illustrated in the following excerpt.

Take a deep breath, hold. Now exhale, let your eyes relax and let your body float. Concentrate on a feeling of floating, floating right down through the chair. There will be something pleasant and welcome about this feeling of floating. Now while you concentrate on this floating, I'm going to concentrate on your left arm and hand. In a while I am going to stroke the middle finger of your left hand. After I do, you will develop movement sensations in that finger. Then the movement will spread causing your left hand to feel light and buoyant and you will let it float upward. Ready? (p.9)

Among the many advantages of Spiegel's induction is that it includes instructions for self-hypnosis as part of the formal induction. In all future inductions the patient may be asked to put himself into a light "trance" state using the self-hypnosis procedure. Thus, in all but the first induction the therapist's role becomes limited to the use of standard deepening techniques.

One final point: hypnotic induction has been presented here in a standardized and somewhat mechanistic fashion. As with any other procedure, the practitioner may wish to make minor modifications in the technique so that it becomes more consonant with his personal style. Such changes are just as feasible with hypnosis as they are with any behavioral technique.

Having presented a brief overview of some procedures used in the induction of hypnosis, we would like to turn now to two cases illustrating the use of hypnosis in a multimodal framework.

The Case of Carol

Carol was a 29-year-old white female finishing her second year in a local college. She had returned to school two years before, after working for several years as a dental technician. Carol came from a working-class background and had a strong upwardly mobile orientation. She wished to continue her studies until she received a masters degree, and was being encouraged to do this by a number of her professors. At the time of initial referral, Carol's presenting problem was the occurrence of severe anxiety attacks. As Woolfolk (1976) noted in this volume, a multimodal analysis of anxiety requires an appreciation of a number of interactions between modalities. Carol's anxiety attacks will be considered from this point of view.

When Carol found herself in an uncomfortable situation, her heartbeat accelerated and she experienced difficulty in swallowing (Sensory Modality). These sensations occurred in such situations as parties and college examinations, and immediately triggered the fear that she would experience an anxiety attack (Affective Modality). Cognitions that she was inadequate and unable to cope with her environment would also occur (Cognitive Modality). Her preoccupation with these thoughts and fears often resulted in interpersonal clumsiness (Interpersonal Modality). To compound matters, these cognitions were often accompanied by the physical sensation of nausea (Sensory Modality). The nausea was especially noteworthy as Carol often imagined herself vomiting in public (Imagery Modality). Since she was phobic about vomiting in general, and vomiting in public turned out to be the highest item in the hierarchy, the image of herself vomiting clearly added to her anxiety (Affective Modality). By this point, Carol perceived herself as being in the midst of an anxiety attack, which would often become incapacitating. Fear of anxiety attacks led her to avoid numerous activities she might otherwise have enjoyed (Behavioral Modality).

Although anxiety attacks were only one of several difficulties which Carol confronted (see Table 1), she considered them her primary problem. In beginning to solve such a problem the multimodal therapist must ask, "In which modality is it most profitable to intervene first?" One strategy viewed as clearly helpful was to teach Carol to relax whenever she began to feel the sensations associated with anxiety. Relaxation training was judged to be especially important since it would enhance the treatment of the vomiting phobia by desensitization. Other aspects of the treatment plan would also be facilitated if Carol could master deep muscle relaxation.[5]

Carol's strong achievement motivation and performance anxiety suggested that a straightforward relaxation regimen would provide her with just one more task at which to "try to succeed," resulting in anguish rather than serenity. The hypnotic paradigm makes it possible to avoid this type of problem.[6]

Towards the end of the first session, the therapist indicated that some of Carol's problems might be amenable to treatment with hypnosis. Carol was told, "It would be very nice if we can use hypnosis, although there are several other things we can do if we can't." During the second session she was tested for hypnotizability using the Hypnotic Induction Profile (Spiegel, 1974). Carol proved to be moderately hypnotizable and responded to the "trance" induction with a major decrease in physical tension, as measured in differences in arm muscle flaccidity and neck muscle rigidity before and during hypnosis. After "trance" had been induced, Carol was asked to numb her right hand. She was told: "Just imagine a glove full of novocaine covering your hand. Feel the novocaine penetrating into every cell. All the nerves, the muscles, flowing through the bloodstream and your hand gets more and more numb, more and more numb. When you have made your hand numb, you may reach over and pinch it with your other hand." The therapist then suggested to Carol: "In the week to come, you will be less than half as tense as you have been."

The choice of a comparative phrase ("half as tense as you have been") was made in order to provide Carol with a framework that would help her observe the diminution in her ongoing level of anxiety. She was also given a Positive Self-Statement (PSS) at this point—"I am a competent and worthwhile person." Then Carol was brought out of "trance." She was instructed to practice a self-induced "trance" at least half a dozen times a day. These "trances" were to include the positive self-statement. (One problem with assigning PSSs is that patients will often not use them; the hypnotic "trance" functions as a clear discriminative stimulus for PSS and makes their use more frequent. It should also be noted that the practice of these self-induced "trances" requires no more than one minute per session; time demands on the client are not inordinate.) Most important, Carol was also instructed to use this "one minute trance" whenever she began to feel anxious; this gave her a tool with which she could decrease the sensations related to anxiety. By the use of hypnosis, her physical sensations of tension now led to a short period spent in "trance" and consequent relaxation, not to a vicious circle of increasing fear, self-denigration, interpersonal clumsiness, and images of vomiting.

Once Carol was able to use self-hypnosis to deal with her anxiety attacks, work on the other modalities was greatly facilitated. For example, desensitization for her vomiting phobia was easily accomplished. Cognitive restructuring was also helped by her use of the positive self-statements she repeated in "trance."

Within two weeks after the original hypnotic induction, Carol's anxiety had markedly decreased. She reported feeling calm when taking college examinations—she had previously taken 2 mg. of Stelazine (trifluoperazine hydrochloride) on such occasions. As a result of her control over the anxiety she had ceased to think that something was wrong with her and she now conceived of herself as an adequate person. She no longer reported feeling anxious about being alone, nor did she find it difficult to fall asleep. She no longer experienced any of the aversive sensations reported during the first session.

Another important outcome of the first session was her referral to an internist because she was underweight (Drug Modality); the diet he prescribed caused her to gain about one pound each week. This weight gain was aided by the ongoing desensitization of the vomiting phobia; as treatment progressed, she was able to eat a wider variety and larger amounts of food, as she was no longer so afraid of feeling nauseous.

The remaining problems were largely centered in the Interpersonal Modality; they included her fear of involvement with others, especially men, as well as a hostile relationship with her mother. However, at this point a BASIC ID assessment revealed an additional troublesome aspect in the Cognitive and Interpersonal Modalities. Carol had experienced a good deal

Table 1. Carol: Problem Assessment by Modality

Behavior

Avoids stressful interpersonal situations
Avoids being alone
Undereats
Frequent difficulty falling asleep

Affect

Frequently anxious
Fear of anxiety attacks and vomiting
Hostile feelings toward mother

Sensation

Food doesn't taste good
Severe headaches
Tenseness in neck
   (During anxiety attacks)
   Feels nauseous
   Eyes jittery
   Heartbeat fast
   Feels tightness across chest
   Difficulty breathing
   Throat closes, cannot swallow

Imagery

Self and others vomiting
Anxiety attack during school or at party

Cognition

Excessively perfectionistic standards
Inappropriately low assessment of achievement
Negative self-statements

Interpersonal relationships

Excessive distancing of self from others
Mutually hostile relationship with mother

Drugs

Underweight, possibly anemia or metabolic problem
Takes Librax (one or two each day for anxiety and nausea)
Takes Stelazine (2 mg.) before college examinations

of change over the course of the month, but to some degree, she viewed it as brought about by the therapist, not by herself. Although she had actively participated in the process, the degree of change that had taken place during this short period seemed disproportionate to the relatively small amount of energy she had expended. (Let us note that the literature on change strongly suggests that it is best for patients to ascribe changes to their own efforts. In this instance, the very simplicity and ease of hypnosis had, to some extent, deprived Carol of this opportunity. It seemed necessary to take this factor into consideration when deciding on a strategy for working through Carol's difficulties in the Interpersonal Modality.)

Since the problems with Carol's mother seemed more amenable to immediate change, the major emphasis of the fifth week was centered there, rather than on her problem with men. As family therapy would have been difficult, given the mother's antipathy toward psychologists, treatment centered on changing Carol's beliefs and feelings, especially her maladaptive belief that she in no way resembled her mother. It seemed likely that if Carol could be made aware of the ways in which they did in fact resemble one another, both the intensity of her hostile feelings toward her mother and the severe conflict between them would be reduced. Even if her feelings were not directly affected, the shift in her belief system might provide a rationale for an adaptive change in behavior towards her mother, which we hoped would result in a mutually reinforcing behavior cycle.

A number of hypnotic techniques are available which could have helped Carol to change her beliefs. At this stage of therapy, however, it was clear that hypnosis would prevent her from attributing change to her own efforts. It seemed necessary to use a technique that would cause Carol to exert more effort than hypnosis would require; this effort would promote cognitions that she herself had brought about the changes she was experiencing. Consequently, the "empty chair technique" (cf. Perls, 1969) was employed to help her recognize areas in which she in fact did resemble her mother. As a result of her experiences with this technique, and her subsequent need to organize and integrate her reactions, Carol was forced to spend a great deal of time and energy in beginning to reassess her feelings and change her behavior toward her mother. Within two weeks she and her mother were on much better terms; this was evidenced by Carol's cooking for the family and her mother's offering to give Carol five hundred dollars toward a summer vacation. Most important, she now believed that she had brought about the change in herself, not just in this matter but throughout therapy.

Hypnosis was an extremely helpful adjunct to the initiation of the therapeutic process. In the treatment of this case it facilitated quick problem abatement over a series of modalities. However, it was necessary to continue to engage in ongoing multimodal assessment; this enabled the therapist to determine when hypnosis was contraindicated. Only a thorough analysis of all seven modalities revealed the occasions when hypnosis was appropriate and when the use of another technique was indicated. This is not to say, however, that other techniques could not have been used to treat Carol even at the beginning of therapy. In this way, Carol's case is unlike the case of Betty, which will be described next. In Betty's case no treatment other than hypnosis had a high likelihood of success.

While hypnosis will often work to facilitate treatment in a variety of modalities, it is sometimes necessary to work with other modalities before hypnotic treatment can be effective. The case of Betty illustrates this point.

The Case of Betty

Twelve years ago, when Betty was 17, she became pregnant and married a man she did not particularly like. When her child was two months old, she asked her husband to carry a diaper pail from one room to another. When he refused, she attempted to do so herself but could not "straighten up" as she found herself in severe pain. Within two months she underwent disc surgery twice, which appeared to correct the problem; in six months she was again functioning well. During the following year she separated from her husband; the marriage finally ended in divorce. Slightly less than three years ago, after a period of severe stress following the termination of a love affair, Betty again began to experience intense back pain. The locus and severity of the pain were the same as they had been nine years earlier. This time, however, medical examinations by a number of orthopedists and neurosurgeons failed to reveal any physical basis whatsoever.

When Betty came for hypnotic therapy, she had been experiencing constant pain for over two and a half years and had been taking between 5 and 15 grains of codeine phosphate per day without appreciable relief. She had recently ceased almost all of her former activities because of the pain.

From the beginning it was apparent to the therapist that Betty needed to address problems in other modalities, although she herself did not believe that therapy was needed in any area other than the alleviation of pain. Furthermore, because of this pain, assessment of other modalities was limited. For example, it was initially unclear whether the cognition "I am helpless," which seemed to pervade her thoughts, was directly a product of her pain or whether it had other implications. For Betty, relative freedom from pain was a necessary prerequisite to any further therapuetic attempts to examine other problems. At the outset of treatment, she would have been unwilling to participate in any therapy not directly related to relieving her pain. Since all conservative medical strategies had been or were being employed with no results, and there was no indication of structural or neurological trauma, hypnosis appeared to be indicated.

Betty proved to be highly hypnotizable, entering a deep trance during the Chevreul Pendulum Test. She was instructed to create a glove anesthesia in her left hand (as described in the case of Carol). Once numbness was experienced she was instructed as follows: "Place your numb hand on the part of your body which hurts most and transfer the numbness from the hand to that part of your body. Remove your hand again when your are free from pain." Betty followed these instructions and two to three minutes later, after having touched her back and leg, signaled that she was no longer feeling pain by replacing her hand in her lap. She was then instructed to maintain that pain-free state as much as possible during the following week. It was finally suggested that, through self-hypnosis, and by using the hand-numbing procedure, she could control any remaining pain. Betty left the office without pain; on her return the following week, however, she noted that she had not been able to maintain her pain-free state, nor could she control the pain by self-hypnosis. The next two sessions yielded similar results; Betty experienced a short period of relief during and immediately following hypnosis, but found that the pain would return within an hour. It became clear that direct confrontation of the sensation of pain with hypnotic analgesia would prove inadequate for lasting relief. Further, the initial demonstration that she had control of the pain was insufficient to change her cognitions and affect. Betty still thought of herself as helpless, and not in control of the pain; moreover she still believed the pain had a physical basis.

Being a psychologist, and not a physician, it was impossible for the therapist to state with any degree of expertise that there was no physical basis for the pain. Betty was therefore referred for brief treatment to a general practitioner who had worked extensively with hypnotic phenomena. During the course of his treatment of Betty, the physician played a "bad guy" as opposed to the therapist's "good guy" supportive role. The physician attacked Betty's maladaptive beliefs about the physical origin of her pain and confronted her with the benefits she was accruing from adopting a sick role. (For example, her income was largely derived from a medical disability insurance program which would cease if she were no longer disabled.) During this period Betty's therapist intervened only to ensure that Betty would continue seeing the physician despite her conviction that he was "crazy and the rudest man I've ever met." After three sessions the patient returned to treatment with the therapist. Using his status as a "good guy," he was able to help Betty integrate the physician's challenges. She began to accept the notion that she might have reasons for creating pain, and that she was deriving a number of benefits from it. When it became clear that Betty accepted these ideas, hypnosis was again employed, and this time Betty was able to maintain freedom from pain for two and a half weeks. After this period she again experienced pain for five days.

During the two and a half weeks during which Betty reported being free of pain, to her surprise, although not to the therapist's, she remained emotionally distressed. A depression centering around loneliness, feelings of rejection, and dissatisfaction about her interpersonal relationships emerged as a major problem. After consultation, the family physician placed Betty on 75 mg./day of Tofranil (imipramine hydrochloride). However, when pain was reported during this period, hypnosis was again employed to rid her of pain. This time the self-induction procedure centered around the Chevreul Pendulum. Betty was asked to carry out the usual pendulum procedure, except that she was instructed: "When you've brought the pendulum to a stop you will be in a trance. Let your hand relax and give yourself the signal 'Blue Mountain Lake' (a phrase which had been used as a signal to deepen the 'trance'). Then count to ten, numb your hand and get rid of the pain." Since the implementation of this procedure, Betty has experienced only moderate and intermittent pain. Her reaction to the Tofranil has also been encouraging and she is at present discussing the possibility of returning to work after spending the summer with her son.

Although Betty continues in therapy, and the eventual outcome is still unclear, treatment is now focused on all the modalities, a possibility which seemed remote when Betty's only concern was with freedom from pain. Without hypnosis, her treatment could almost certainly not have progressed to this point.[7]

Conclusion

A clinician can occupy three distinct roles: comforter, repairman, and change agent. When we are confronted with problems that we can do little about, we must at times assume the role of comforter. In this role we can only hope that time, or some other factor, will ameliorate our patient's distress. For most therapists, especially those interested in multimodal therapy, acting as a comforter is an unsatisfying role. As repairman we use well-established techniques to attack problems which, once eliminated, have no further consequences for the patients. Unfortunately, recent reports (cf. Lazarus, 1974) cause us to doubt the long-term effectiveness of the repairman role for some patients. This does not represent a return to the symptom substitution hypothesis. We are merely recognizing that patients often possess a large variety of maladaptive overt and covert behaviors.

When dealing only with the presenting problem many of these less obvious behaviors remain intact and cause problems which soon emerge into the forefront of the patient's life.

In the role of change agent, the clinician will wish to look beyond the immediate problem and yet "think small' enough to produce incremental change. The multimodal framework helps to bring this goal into closer view. It forces us to assess the patient both in terms of what we identify as maladaptive and precisely what we can do to foster change. In a sense, it provides a salutary exercise in self-discipline for us, in that it does not allow therapists to be satisfied with the role of comforter when change is possible, nor does it allow us to work only on those aspects of the patient's problems which are most easily accessible. Finally, it forces us to take cognizance of our patient's many strengths.

In many ways, hypnosis seems tailor-made for the multimodal therapist. When we are confronted with a problem in which the repairman role will suffice, hypnosis is one of the many techniques which the multimodal therapist may use. In more complex problems, as illustrated above, hypnosis may be employed along with other techniques to gain access to various modalities. One major advantage of hypnosis is that it can be used in several modalities, whereas most techniques are limited to one. Further, the constant ongoing assessment that is so essential in multimodal therapy forces the therapist to question when hypnosis is appropriate and when it is not. Finally, work with other modalities may facilitate hypnotic treatment. Hypnosis then is neither a gimmick nor a panacea, but may be viewed as one of the many tools which ought to be included in the armamentarium of the multimodal therapist.

Notes

1. The authors wish to acknowledge the assistance of Dr. L. S. Wolfe of Hellerton, Pa., in the treatment of the second case discussed in this paper.

2. The test-retest reliability of hypnotizability measurement in the different forms of the Stanford Hypnotic Susceptability Scale (SHSS) is commonly reported as being about .90 (Hilgard, 1975). Further, a recent study by Morgan, Johnson, & Hilgard (1974) has shown that when students at Stanford University were retested ten years later, the test retest reliability on the SHSS Form A was about .60. These data compare favorably with the product moment coefficients found in the reliability measurement of IQ: they make it clear that hypnotizability is most accurately conceptualized as a relatively stable individual difference. Thus, the problem encountered by the new hypnotist lies not in his inability to hypnotize patients, but rather in a series of common and mistaken impressions he may have assimilitated about hypnotic

phenomena. Like most individual difference dimensions, hypnotizability appears to be normally distributed throughout the population. Few clients will manifest the more bizarre and dramatic hypnotic phenomena, such as global post-hypnotic amnesia; these phenomena are regularly experienced only by the most highly hypnotizable, 2 percent or so of the population. The hypnotist who considers this kind of dramatic event as the only evidence that a patient has been hypnotized will find that he is, indeed, able to hypnotize few people. However, there are a number of distinctive phenomena requiring only a light trance state for their production. These include glove anesthesia and hand levitation. Such responses can be produced by large percentages of the population and can be used to reassure both patient and therapist that hypnosis has been induced.

3. A current controversy in the literature on hypnosis revolves around the meaning of the concept hypnotic "trance." The interested reader is referred to the work of Orne (1971) and Barber (1974) for a discussion of this issue. However, we find the term "trance" to be convenient in discussing hypnotic phenomena, although throughout this paper we have enclosed it in quotation marks to acknowledge its controversial status.

4. The authors believe that Spiegel places undue emphasis on a test of hypnotizability centering on eye movement. The induction is in no way harmed if these instructions are read and eye movement is used merely as a specific cue for "trance" induction.

5. It can be noted here that the work of Lang and his colleagues (Lang, Lazovik, and Reynolds, 1965; Lang, 1969), concentrated on relationships between desensitization and hypnosis which are only tangentially related to the present discussion.

6. Although relaxation is not a necessary characteristic of the hypnotic state, patients will almost always physically relax while hypnotized since they believe that hypnosis connotes a state closer to sleep. (Popular views about hypnosis can be traced back to the models of hypnotic trance presented in Thomas Mann (1931) and George du Maurier (1895). Du Maurier's *Trilby* has influenced most of the later popular views of hypnosis.) Since behavior under hypnosis will invariably conform to expectations, in our modern society it tends to took like relaxation. Yet the hypnotic state has appeared quite different in the past. For example, Mesmer's patients experienced hysterical seizures followed by sleep; upon awakening they were free from symptoms. In an experiment by Orne (1971), one class of college students witnessed a demonstration of hypnosis in which the subject developed "catalepsy of the dominant hand." This phenomenon was presented as being integral to the hypnotic state. The demonstration given to a second class of college students involved no such catalepsy. When the students in the two classes were subsequently hypnotized, a new characteristic of hypnotic behavior emerged, catalepsy of the dominant hand. Not surprisingly, this new phenomenon was observed only in the members of the first class. Thus it is evident that people's expectations about how one should look when hypnotized play an enormous role in how they themselves look under hypnosis. And, since modern patients

associate hypnosis with relaxation, they will almost always exhibit major decreases in muscle tension when exposed to hypnotic procedures.

7. As this book goes to press, Betty has been pain-free for five months. She is functioning well in all areas and is no longer in treatment.

References

Cautela, J. The use of covert conditioning in hypnotherapy. *International Journal of Clinical and Experimental Hypnosis,* 1975, *23,* 15-27.

DuMaurier, G. *Trilby,* New York: Harper, 1895.

Feamster, J., & Brown, J. Hypnotic aversion to alcohol: Three-year follow-up on one patient. *American Journal of Clinical Hypnosis,* 1963, *6,* 164-166.

Gaunitz, S., Unestahl, L., & Berglund, B. A posthypnotically released emotion as a modifier of behavior. *International Journal of Clinical and Experimental Hypnosis,* 1975, *23,* 120-129.

Haley, J. (Ed.) *Advanced techniques of hypnosis and therapy: Selected papers of Milton Erickson,* New York: Grune and Stratton, 1967.

Hilgard, E. Hypnosis. In Rosenzweig, M. R. & Porter, L. W. (Eds.), *Annual Review of Psychology, 26,* pp. 19-44. Palo Alto: Annual Reviews, Inc., 1975.

Lang, P., Lazovik, A., & Reynolds, D. Desensitization suggestibility and pseudotherapy. *Journal of Abnormal Psychology,* 1965, *70,* 395-402.

Lang, P. The mechanics of desensitization and the laboratory study of human fear. In Franks, C. M. (Ed.), *Behavior therapy: Appraisal and status,* pp. 160-191. New York: McGraw-Hill, 1969.

Larsen, S. Strategies for reducing phobic behavior, *Dissertation Abstracts,* 1966, *26,* 6850.

Lazarus, A. Some clinical applications of autohypnosis. *Medical Proceedings,* 1958, *14,* 848-850.

Lazarus, A. Sensory deprivation under hypnosis in the treatment of pervasive ('free-floating') anxiety: A preliminary impression. *South African Medical Journal,* 1963, *37,* 136-139.

Lazarus, A. Multimodal behavior therapy: Treating the "BASIC-ID." *Journal of Nervous and Mental Disease,* 1973, *156,* 404-411.

Lazarus, A. Multimodal therapy. *Psychology Today,* 1974, *7,* 59-63.

Mann, T. *Mario and the magician,* Lowe-Porter (Trans.). New York: Knopf, 1931.

Morgan, A., Johnson, D., & Hilgard, E. The stability of hypnotic susceptibility: A longitudinal study. *International Journal of Clinical and Experimental Hypnosis,* 1974, *22,* 249-257.

Orne, M. Hypnosis, motivation and the ecological validity of the psychological experiment. In Arnold, W., & Page, M. (Eds.), *Nebraska symposium on motivation: 1970.* Lincoln: University of Nebraska Press, 1971.

Orne, M., & Evans, F. Inadvertent termination of hypnosis with hypnotized and simulating subjects. *International Journal of Clinical and Experimental Hypnosis,* 1966, *14,* 61-78.

Perls, F. *Gestalt therapy verbatim,* Lafayette, Ca.: Real People Press, 1969.

Spanos, N., De Moor, W., & Barber, T. Hypnosis and behavior therapy, common denominators. In Strupp, H. et al. (Eds.), *Psychotherapy and behavior change 1973,* Chicago: Aldine, 1974.

Spiegel, J. *Manual for the hypnotic induction profile.* New York: Soni Medica, 1974.

Weitzenhoffer, A. *General techniques of hypnotism.* New York: Grune and Stratton, 1957.

Wolpe, J., & Lazarus, A. *Behavior therapy techniques.* Oxford: Pergamon Press, 1966.

Woolfolk, R. A multimodal perspective on emotion. In A. A. Lazarus, *Multimodal behavior therapy.* New York: Springer, 1976.

Chapter 12

Group Therapy and the BASIC ID

Arnold A. Lazarus

It seems axiomatic that thorough and complete methods of therapy depend upon asking the right questions (adequate diagnostic evaluations) and eliminating all relevant problem areas (comprehensive intervention). Faulty problem identification (inadequate assessment) is probably the greatest impediment to successful therapy. The distinctive feature of behavioral approaches to assessment and therapy is the emphasis upon response-specificity and problem specification within the context of precipitating events (antecedents) and maintaining factors (consequences). *But the foregoing precepts do not guarantee clinical thoroughness.*

Are Franks and Wilson (1974) correct in assuming that, as far as problem identification is concerned, there is no significant difference between the BASIC ID schema and the assessment framework outlined by Kanfer and Saslow (1969)? And is it true that advocates of the BASIC ID (multimodal) approach "have no explicit criterion for the choice of different techniques. . . [and rely on] intuition and subjective judgment" (Franks and Wilson, 1974, p. 674)? The present paper endeavors to show that the BASIC ID orientation transcends the innovative multifaceted assessment strategies outlined by Kanfer and Saslow (1969). Furthermore, we hope to demonstrate that the choice of particular techniques within each modality is anything but capricious. At the same time, since group settings provide an excellent medium for the implementation of multimodal therapy, the emphasis will be centered on "group therapy and the BASIC ID."

From the *Annual Review of Behavior Therapy: Theory and Practice*, Vol. 3, ed. C. M. Franks and G. T. Wilson. Copyright 1975 by Brunner/Mazel, Inc. Reprinted by permission.

Selection of Group Members

Extremely depressed, hostile, paranoid, or deluded individuals often have a disruptive effect on treatment groups. Similarly, people with severe obsessive-compulsive problems who are locked into their own rituals have tended to respond poorly in multimodal groups. The foregoing are treated individually, or in the context of conjoint or family sessions.

Generally, clients are assessed individually before being invited to join a group. Some people are opposed to the idea of joining a therapy group and need to be disabused of the idea that a premium on privacy and seclusiveness is personally advantageous. However, those who remain disinclined to join a group are never coerced into doing so.

Many people require some schooling in learning how to extract maximum benefits from group exposure. One of the major skills group members need to acquire is the capacity to abstract personally relevant information and helpful hints even when the spotlight of attention is not directly focused on them. Thus, an unmarried person listening to the tribulations of a married couple may erroneously conclude that since he or she is single, there is little to be gained by attending to other people's marital conflicts. However, whether the particular emphasis is on husband-wife, parent-child, employer-employee, or any other specific relationship, there is always a chance to extract valuable clues for achieving more satisfying *interpersonal relationships* in general. Throughout the group proceedings, the members are shown how to derive individual benefits from general procedures. Vicarious learning is an important component of any productive group.

The most efficient multimodal groups to date have consisted of ten to twelve members. Groups are held weekly for two to two-and-a-half hours, and an attempt is made to have more or less equal numbers of men and women.

The emphasis in multimodal groups is different from group desensitization (Lazarus, 1961) or assertion training groups (Lazarus, 1968). When a group of people are the simultaneous recipients of individual behavior therapy, we are dealing with *behavior therapy in a group*. This is contrasted with *group behavior therapy* where all the members serve as active change agents for themselves and for one another. In group desensitization, the lines of therapeutic demarcation are primarily from each individual to the therapist. Each person in the group pictures his or her own hierarchical image, and there is limited interaction among and between group members. Multimodal groups afford a constructive setting in which members are deliberately encouraged to monitor their own and every other group member's specific problems across each basic modality.

Multimodal Group Processes and Procedures

The raison d'être for conducting multimodal group sessions is that they are often more expedient, more practical, and less expensive than individual therapy. Initial anxieties are usually quelled by the group leaders' orienting remarks emphasizing cooperation, the pooling of resources, constructive rather than destructive criticism, a sense of helpful togetherness, confidentially, and the absence of unbridled anger (cf. Lazarus, 1968, 1971, 1974a). Thereafter the multimodal orientation *per se* is outlined. The level of group sophistication will determine the manner in which the BASIC ID is presented. In a recent group of professionals, the following introduction was provided:

> Descriptively, we are moving, feeling, sensing, imagining, thinking, relating, and biochemical beings. All significant events will influence the way we behave, feel, think, relate, and so forth. Our problems will affect us in each of these areas. Some difficulties will show up more clearly in one area than another, but it is important to track down the effects in all relevant areas. For example, a man complained that he was afraid of driving his car. He had been in a collision and immediately thereafter found himself especially fearful at the wheel of a car. Tracking the impact across each major dimension we came up with the following profile:

> | | |
> |---|---|
> | Behavior: | Avoided driving his own car. |
> | Affect: | Felt highly anxious. |
> | Sensation: | Complained of tense feelings at the back of his neck and butterflies in his stomach. |
> | Imagery: | Vividly relived the accident in which he had been involved. |
> | Cognition: | Believed that he was in great danger when at the wheel of his car. |
> | Interpersonal: | His wife was now chauffeuring him to and from work. |
> | Drugs: | He was taking tranquilizers that his doctor had prescribed. |

This list provides the therapist with specific clues for taking constructive action. First, the man could be taught "differential muscle relaxation," especially in his neck and stomach. He could also be taught "thought blocking" to enable him to switch off the negative imagery concerning the accident and to dwell on pleasant scenes. He could be shown how to dispute his irrational thoughts by saying over and over, "I am in no great danger if I keep alert and do not speed." The therapy could then be divided into two main activities: (1) having him drive progressively longer distances while carrying out his differential relaxation, plus thought blocking, plus positive imagery and rational self-talk exercises, and (2) examining the relationship between his wife and him to determine whether there were any payoffs for him to become dependent on her.

Group members then discuss the foregoing, and the various points are clarified. The BASIC ID acronym is provided, and each group member gains the opportunity to evaluate some of his or her own current problems across each modality.

Thus far, there is probably no fundamental difference between the foregoing procedures and most behavior therapy programs or indeed many other forward-looking therapy programs. In the case of the "car phobia," some behavior therapists may have employed imaginal desensitization rather than *in vivo* procedures, and there may be some differences in the various antianxiety measures applied. Perhaps a few therapists would overlook the marriage dyad, but on the whole, "broad-spectrum behavior therapy" (Lazarus, 1971) would use several techniques that are likely to potentiate the client's nonanxious responses, while searching for maintaining factors in significant person-to-person interactions. However, as we hope to show, the multimodal approach ensures a greater diagnostic thoroughness, and provides a series of methods for eliciting data that elude other avenues of inquiry. The thoroughness of this approach emerges when examining the typical ABC's (Antecedents-Behaviors-Consequences) through the viewpiece of each separate but related modality.

It should now become apparent that the multimodal approach enables one to conduct a thorough functional analysis of significant antecedent and maintaining factors across the fundamental parameters of each client's problem areas. The BASIC ID profile serves two main purposes: (1) it thoroughly dissects presenting complaints into several discrete yet interrelated components; and (2) it permits the therapist to direct ongoing procedures into productive channels. Emphasis is placed upon the fact that patients are usually troubled by a multitude of specific problems and that effective therapy requires a similar multitude of specific treatments. A slightly condensed group protocol might lend substance to the various assertions outlined above.

Illustrative Group Protocol

Martin:	This week has been hell for me again. I can't seem to get rid of the anxiety. It's with me all the time. I don't know where it comes from and what it's all about.
Norman:	Well, we know it is tied up to some extent with your work.
Martin:	But work has been just fine this past week.
Therapist:	Well let's track it. Are you feeling the anxiety right now?

Martin:	Sure am!
Therapist:	Can you close your eyes, get into it, and share all your feelings with us?
Martin:	(After about 30 seconds) My breathing seems tight. I can feel tension in my jaws and stomach. It's as if I'm in danger. (Opens eyes) Look how my hands are sweating.
Alice:	Is the group making you so uptight?
Martin:	No, it's really got nothing to do with being in the group. This is how I've been feeling all week long.
Betty:	Perhaps some breathing exercises and relaxation will help you.
Therapist:	Before we work on getting rid of the anxiety let's see if we can spot some precipitating causes. Would you close your eyes again, Martin, and concentrate on the tight breathing sensations as well as the tension in your stomach and jaws? Now really get into those sensations. (Pause of about 20 seconds) Now as you feel those negative sensations, see what images or mental pictures run through your mind.
Martin:	(After about 30 seconds) A whole lot of things went flashing through my mind.
Sheila:	Like what?
Martin:	I don't know. It's hard to find the right words.
Bert:	Stop being Mr. Perfect. Find any words even if they are not right on target.
Martin:	(Closes his eyes) There seem to be two main pictures involved. It's funny. I don't see what relevance they have to each other or to anything else.
Betty:	So tell us already.
Martin:	Well, you remember I told you about the time when I knocked up that girl when I was 16? Well, what I didn't tell you was that her father, a big brute of a guy, beat the hell out of me. (Turning to therapist) When you mentioned images, that beating came back to me all too clear.
Neil:	(Facetiously) So who've you knocked up this week?
Martin:	Actually my girlfriend thinks she may be pregnant. Could this be getting me so upset?
Therapist:	Well, how does it feel to you?
Martin:	It doesn't make sense.
Therapist:	Well, if Milly is pregnant, what do you intend to do?
Martin:	I don't know.
Alice:	What do you mean you don't know?
Martin:	She's got religious scruples. I don't know if I'm ready to get married or if it would be a good thing or not.
Bert:	And he wonders why he has been feeling anxious!

(The group then focused upon various options that were open to Martin coupled with a clearer exploration of his feelings regarding marriage, being a father, and so forth. It soon became evident that, despite his denials, this was a potent source of his anxiety. Behavior rehearsal was employed to increase the probability that he would discuss his genuine feelings and conflicts with his girlfriend. At the next meeting the following dialogue ensued.)

Therapist: Martin, how have you been feeling this past week?
Martin: Slightly better, but I'm still feeling some anxiety.
Betty: What happened with your girlfriend?
Martin: Oh, by the way, she isn't pregnant.

(Group discussion focused on this revelation for a short time.)

Therapist: Martin, last week when you were focusing on your sensations you said you had *two* images. You shared one with us but can you still remember the second one?
Martin: Yes, but I don't think it has anything of any value. It was just a random sort of thing.
Bert: What was it?
Martin: A train.
Mary: A train?
Therapist: Clue us in some more.
Martin: This is ridiculous. I got this image of a train in the station. As I said, I'm sure we're barking up the wrong tree.
Therapist: Let's stay with it a little longer. Will you close your eyes and focus on the train again and tell us what is the clearest part of the image?
Martin: (After about 20 seconds) It's the steam. You know how the trains have that white steam while they stop at stations.
Therapist: Concentrate on the steam. What other images do you get?
Martin: (Pause) The kettle boiling on the stove. When I was recovering from polio I would sit in the kitchen. My mother would make tea or she had a pot of coffee boiling on the stove.
Therapist: Can you tie that into your anxiety in any way?
Martin: Could it be that when I feel anxious I tie it in with physical illness and I become afraid of getting sick again?
Therapist: Does that ring any bells for you?
Martin: I think so. I need to divorce my feelings of anxiety from the idea that I will get ill. I think this fear only makes the anxiety worse and keeps it alive.
Therapist: Well why not try some cognitive disputation to begin with. Say over and over to yourself: "I will not die from anxiety. Anxiety will not make me ill."

Discussion of Protocol

The dialogue before the discussion of the train image is fairly typical of "behavior therapy groups." No time is spent "promoting insight into unconscious processes," or "lifting repression." Although Martin seemed to be unaware of the source of his current anxiety, and although the focus of group attention was on unearthing basic events, this is not synonymous with delving into the unconscious. A more articulate person may have stated outright that he felt anxious over the fact that his girlfriend might be pregnant. A direct inquiry such as, "Is anything on your mind?" may have elicited the same information, although Martin usually responded with "I don't know" to most direct questions. Using simple sensory and imagery procedures proved productive in eliciting (what appeared to be) a central source of anxiety. Note that the techniques selected to deal with the problem areas were based not upon subjective whims but upon the fact that well-established data exist regarding the efficacy of modeling, behavior rehearsal, and cognitive restructuring (or modified self-talk).

Clients who are introspective and highly verbal usually have little difficulty in stating their complaints without the aid of therapeutic probing: "I've been feeling extremely anxious all week. I think it's tied up with my girlfriend's suspected pregnancy, and the fact that I seem to connect my feelings of anxiety with dreaded illnesses—probably stemming from my bout with polio." However, few people are that articulate, and a certain amount of exploration is usually necessary. By asking specific questions about behavior, affective responses, sensory reactions, imagery, cognitive input, and interpersonal consequences, the clinician leaves no stone unturned. People who have poor verbal facility, as well as those who tend to over-intellectualize, usually provide important therapeutic clues when asked to focus upon sensory and imagery modalities.

The discussion of the train image illustrates the use of *associated imagery* in tracking down potential sources of anxiety. It is conceivable that the demand characteristics of this procedure together with probable response acquiescence may yield false positives. However, in practice, this method so often seems to prove clinically productive that it would be an error to dismiss it out of hand. Certainly, the value of associated imagery can be experimentally verified. Of course, clinicians from non-behavioral disciplines often use procedures similar to "imagery association" but a technically eclectic orientation would preclude any espousal with the mystical and esoteric theories that often underlie these methods in other clinicians' hands.

It should be evident from the foregoing that while many behavior therapists deal with each modality contained in the BASIC ID, they do not duplicate the clarity and intensity with which each modality is assessed in multimodal therapy. The usual behavior therapist does not devote as much attention to imagery techniques as we are advocating (even when using imaginal desensitization and covert reinforcement procedures), nor does he delve meticulously enough into sensory reactions or cognitive material. Perhaps above all, the tendency is to neglect pertinent philosophical values and their bearing on an individual's self-worth.

In case it is still not clear how, from an assessment standpoint, the BASIC ID or multimodal framework goes beyond the comprehensive behavioral diagnostic procedures of Kanfer and Saslow (1969), the following points need to be underscored. Within the seven guidelines of assessment and problem identification which Kanfer and Saslow rightly consider essential for a thorough functional analysis, a multimodal therapist, whenever feasible, would scrutinize each response through the viewpiece of the seven modalities. Thus, when looking into behavioral excesses, or deficits, or when examining behavioral assets, one would take careful stock of overt behaviors, affective responses, sensory reactions, imagery (positive and negative), cognitive components, interpersonal assets and liabilities, as well as organic or biochemical factors, whenever relevant. It also needs to be emphasized that these seven modalities are not a random choice, or a *sui generis* creation. They constitute distinct yet related areas that have been the main subject matter of general psychology for over a hundred years.

Different Ways of Conducting Multimodal Groups

My initial multimodal groups tended to be somewhat rigid and stylized (Lazarus, 1975). Considerable time was spent drawing up detailed "modality profiles" for each group member, and several sessions tended to adhere to a fixed format. More recently, two multimodal groups were conducted quite differently from past ones and from each other. The one group avoided any discussion of the BASIC ID rationale with its members, but the co-therapists systematically applied the relevant modalities to each problem area that emerged. In the second group, the BASIC ID was discussed with the members and they were asked to make lists of behaviors, feelings, sensations, images, and thoughts (a) that they wished to increase, and (b) that they wished to decrease. One client provided the following fairly typical list:

Behaviors that you wish to increase:
1. Actively seek out opportunities to speak in public.

2. To spend more time with my children and to be more patient with their difficult and stubborn behaviors.
3. To get more exercise.
4. To get closer to my brother by sharing intimate thoughts and feelings.
5. To play the guitar more often.

Behaviors you wish to decrease:

1. To become less aggressive, especially when I disagree with my wife.
2. To be less critical and quick to put down other people's ideas.
3. Stop avoiding certain people just because they displease me.
4. Overeating, especially when going out

Feelings you wish to increase:

1. Feelings of self-acceptance and self-confidence.
2. Calm feelings and restful feelings.
3. Feelings that provoke a feeling of fun and laughter.

Feelings that you wish to decrease:

1. Feelings of guilt, especially about being selfish at times.
2. Feelings of anxiety when having to speak in public.
3. Feelings of tension at meeting new people.
4. Feelings of anxiety around doctors and hospitals.

Sensations that you wish to increase:

I want to be able to get more pleasure from all my senses—to enjoy art and what I see, music and what I hear, my sense of taste, smell, and touch.

Sensations that you wish to decrease:

1. Occasional sensations of dizziness and light-headedness.
2. Butterflies in my stomach.
3. Unpleasant tingling sensations in my feet when I feel tense.

Images that you wish to increase:

1. My wife and I being more physical with each other.
2. Scenes of me running my own business.

Images that you wish to decrease:

1. Scenes of my father when drunk.
2. My friend's body after drowning.

Thoughts you wish to increase:

1. I am a capable person.
2. I am warm and loving.

Thoughts you wish to decrease:

1. I am incompetent.
2. I am inferior.

The present approach is similar to the "problem-oriented record approach" in psychiatry as exemplified by Hayes-Roth, Longabaugh, and Ryback (1972). As one studies each excess or deficit under "thoughts," "feelings," "sensations," and so forth, it is clear that several specific, task-oriented, and goal-directed procedures may be devised for overcoming each particular problem. Again, the selection of techniques is neither random nor subjective but is made in concert with idiosyncratic needs of the client and with objective data in the literature.

Clients continually update their modality profiles by adding new items that come to mind; often group members or the group leader may suggest new items in the light of group processes.

It is worth mentioning in passing that, of 40 clients who have attended 25 or more sessions of multimodal group therapy, 37 seem to have derived marked benefits. Not only has there been "symptomatic relief" (e.g., agoraphobics now travelling on their own, impotent men now fully potent, depressed people now emitting optimistic statements and apparently enjoying life, compulsive individuals now in control of ritualistic behaviors), but, in addition, these ex-group members seem to have acquired a facilitative interpersonal style, a nonperfectionistic outlook on life, and a modus vivendi which, in the words of certain existential writers, tends toward "self-actualization."

References

Franks, C. M., & Wilson, G. T. *Annual review of behavior therapy: Theory and practice*. Vol. 2. New York: Brunner/Mazel, 1974.

Hayes-Roth, F., Longabaugh, R., & Ryback, R. The problem-oriented medical record and psychiatry. *British Journal of Psychiatry,* 1972, 27-34.

Kanfer, F. H., & Saslow, G. Behavioral diagnosis. In C. M. Franks (Ed.) *Behavior therapy: Appraisal and status,* pp. 417-444. New York: McGraw-Hill, 1969.

Lazarus, A. A. Group therapy of phobic disorders by systematic desensitization. *Journal of Abnormal and Social Psychology,* 1968, *63,* 505-510.

Lazarus, A. A. Behavior therapy in groups. In G. M. Gazda (Ed.), *Basic approaches to group psychotherapy and group counseling,* pp. 149-175. Springfield, Ill.: Charles C. Thomas, 1968.

Lazarus, A. A. *Behavior therapy and beyond.* New York: McGraw-Hill, 1971.

Lazarus, A. A. Multimodal behavior therapy: Treating the "BASIC ID."*Journal of Nervous and Mental Disease,* 1973, *156,* 404-411.

Lazarus, A. A. Multimodal therapy: BASIC ID.*Psychology Today,* 1974,*7,* 59-63.

Lazarus, A. A. Understanding and modifying aggression in behavioral groups. In

A. Jacobs and W. Spradlin (Eds.), *The group as agent of change*, pp. 87-99. New York: Behavioral Publications, 1974 (a).

Lazarus, A. A. Wanted: A multimodal theory of personality. *Fields within Fields*, 1974, *13*, 67-72. (b)

Lazarus, A. A. Multimodal behavior therapy in groups. In G. M. Gazda (Ed.) *Basic approaches to group psychotherapy and group counseling* (2nd edition), pp. 150-174. Springfield, Ill.: Charles C Thomas, 1975.

Chapter 13

Multimodal Treatment of Spastic Colitis and Incapacitating Anxiety: A Case Study

Dan W. Briddell and Sandra R. Leiblum

For reasons of practical as well as conceptual economy, clinicians often seek unitary solutions to very complex problems. It is therefore understandable why so many therapists choose to emphasize one particular aspect (modality) of psychological functioning as being fundamental to the problems their clients present. For example, insight (the cognitive modality) may receive exclusive attention by the more traditional therapist whereas the importance of warm, open, and supportive familial/social relationships (interpersonal modality) is emphasized by other clinicians. By contrast, the behavior therapist relies primarily on observable process—the behavior modality. However, what most systems of therapy regard as necessary and sufficient conditions for durable therapeutic change are frequently shown to be unnecessary or insufficient (Jurjevich, 1973; Lazarus, 1969).

The present report illustrates the successful application of the multimodal schema to a complex clinical case considered intractable by previous therapists.

Case History

Mr. M., a 27-year-old junior buyer for a large electronics part manufacturing firm, had been recently divorced from his wife. He was referred to us by his general physician because of various somatic complaints for which no

D. W. Briddell was the primary therapist in the treatment of this case. S. R. Leiblum provided continual consultation during the course of therapy.

disease process had been isolated. No treatment gains had been effected by several independent physicians and specialists. The client was first troubled in 1969 by recurrent bladder infections and prostatitis which did not respond well to medical treatment. These complications were superseded by intermittent (every two to three months) internal bleeding (gastrointestinal). The internal bleeding was in turn supplanted by chronic spastic colitis—the presenting problem in this case. Mr. M. was often in severe discomfort: he would experience abdominal and rectal cramping prior to, and painful burning sensations following, elimination. The pain associated with defecation as well as the passage of stools consisting almost entirely of mucus was of greater concern to the client than the inconvenience of making eight to ten bathroom trips per day. Mr. M. also reported feeling chronically anxious for the last four years, and experiencing several severe anxiety attacks (muscular shaking, internal tremors, excessive smoking, and feelings of panic) within the last year while at work. The client believed that his high levels of anxiety and tension and the resultant impairment of his functioning contributed to the break-up of his marriage and were currently threatening his job, as he had been recently forced to take several "vacations" in order to "work out his problems."

Additionally, Mr. M. reported a history of cross-dressing. Shortly after marrying, he began dressing in women's clothes (his wife's undergarments and nightgown) during the foreplay period prior to intercourse. He indicated that his wife responded with amusement, and actually encouraged his trying on her clothes, curious to see how he would look. A satisfying sexual encounter almost always followed the cross-dressing and foreplay, suggesting to us that his erotic feelings and subsequent orgasm—in addition to his wife's verbal encouragement—served to strengthen the behavior. He reported feeling satisfied and relaxed after intercourse (still wearing his wife's clothing)—the cross-dressing thus also being reinforced by the pleasant sensations of postorgasmic relaxation. He subsequently began to cross dress independently of sexual encounters with his wife, stating that it helped him to relax. She gradually began to question the appropriateness of this behavior, particularly as the frequency of cross-dressing increased and often interfered with "their" plans to go out. Mr. M. felt that his cross-dressing was not instrumental in breaking up his marriage but admitted that it may have contributed to already existing problems. He enjoyed cross-dressing (the behavior having both sexually gratifying and anxiety-reducing components) but saw it as a problem in that he felt guilty afterwards, feared detection, and was uncertain as to the role this behavior would play in future relationships with women.

Assessment

A detailed multimodal assessment (summarized in Table 1) revealed the complex and interrelated nature of the client's problems. For example, the relaxing fantasies of cross-dressing (imagery modality) were often evoked by Mr. M. to combat inner tremors and intestinal spasms (sensory modality) which resulted from an inability to be appropriately assertive (behavior modality) with an overly demanding employer. Table 1 also summarizes the therapeutic interventions eventually employed for each identified subproblem within the various modalities of Mr. M's functioning.

The three general problem areas (as initially presented by the client) were defined operationally and monitored during the course of therapy to evaluate the impact of specific interventions within each modality on the overall "clinical picture." These definitions were: (1) *Job-related anxiety*—defined as (a) smoking more than two packs of cigarettes per day, (b) being forced to leave his desk or office in order to "cope with anxiety," and (c) subjective feelings of panic. The occurrence of any two of these three components during the working day resulted in the day being recorded as an "anxiety day." (2) *Colitis*—four or more bowel movements during a 24-hour period and/or any bowel movement associated with pain or intense discomfort. (3) *Fetishistic cross-dressing*—putting on any article of feminine apparel.

The simultaneous monitoring of several problem areas (multiple baseline) was not experimentally employed here to parcel out "active ingredients" of discrete and separate interventions, but rather to reflect discrete and measurable changes in clinically relevant target behaviors resulting from the multiple and simultaneous interventions characteristic of "multimodal behavior therapy."

Treatment

Although Table 1 presents an encapsulated overview of the assessment and treatment, selected phases of the therapy with examples of specific interventions will be described more fully below to illustrate the application of the multimodal schema in the treatment of Mr. M.

It was decided to direct initial treatment efforts toward the management of the job-related anxiety attacks, as Mr. M. was in immediate danger of losing his job. The management of anxiety was also a presumed necessary condition for the successful treatment of the colitis.

An assessment of the cognitive modality revealed that Mr. M.'s maladaptive cognitions (re: his boss and job situation) were fundamentally related to the anxiety attacks at work and perhaps less directly to the spastic colitis. Mr. M.'s office supervisor was notorious for making unreasonable

Table 1. Modality Profile

Modality	Problem	Treatment
Behavior	Lack of assertiveness	Desensitization, behavior rehearsal, in-vivo assertion assignments
	Cross-dressing	Self-monitoring, discard female clothes, relaxation training
	Excessive smoking	Self-monitoring, incompatible exercises (straighten materials on office desk), peaceful images
Affect	Anxiety and panic attacks	Relaxation training, focusing tasks (performing easy on-the-job tasks incompatible with anxiety attacks), coping imagery
	Mild depression	Scheduling of reinforcing activities and reassurance
	Chronic fear of disapproval	Rational Emotive Thinking, implosion
Sensation	Headaches	Relaxation of frontalis muscle
	Inner tremors, painful intestinal spasms and rectal burning, cardiac palpitations	Autogenic training, hypnotic relaxation with suggestions of colon and abdominal anesthesia
Imagery	Boss berating him verbally	Counterimage of boss in ridiculous and vulnerable situations
	Insides rotting	Hypnotic counter suggestions
	Mother discovering female garments	Discarding female clothes
	Cross-dressing fantasies	Fading of clothes back on to female-orgasmic reconditioning
Cognitions	Irrational self-talk: "I am physically sick." "I am sexually maladjusted." "I am an incompetent employee." "My situation is hopeless." "My boss is always right."	Corrective self-instruction, rational disputation (RET)
Interpersonal relationships	Overly compliant with boss	Assertion training
	Withdrawn from fellow employees	Role playing interpersonal encounters
	Overly dominated by mother	Explain secondary gain to patient, training in confrontative behaviors
	Little social contact and dating	Desensitization, systematic encouragement and exploration of potential social /sexual encounters
Physiology (drugs)	Colitis, complaints of associated internal "disorders"	Previous medical workup—no organic pathology or medication indicated, explain relationship between somatic complications and "emotional state," reading assignments

demands on employees—Mr. M., because of his junior status, was a prime target. Unfortunately, the client was disposed to think of himself as worthless and incompetent when unable to meet the demands no matter how outrageous or unreasonable: ''I must be a real loser if I can't complete the factory inventory by lunchtime.'' The relationship between the cognitive modality and the experience of anxiety (affective modality) was explored with the client. He was thoroughly familiarized with the Ellis model of Rational Emotive Therapy (1962) and was encouraged to monitor the situations in which he felt anxious—analyzing cognitions and self-statements, and substituting more adaptive thoughts for irrational ones.

This initial approach was ineffective. Mr. M. indicated that he felt completely overwhelmed with feelings of anxiety and panic *before* he could initiate the corrective rational self-instruction. An inquiry into the *behavior* responses associated with the attack revealed that Mr. M. would typically leave his desk, walk around his office, and try to distract himself from agonizing by the ritualistic handling of various electronic parts, and by re-reading employee memorandums. It was decided to fortify the attempts at cognitive restructuring with a more ''therapeutic'' ritual. Mr. M. was instructed to prepare the ''equipment'' for relearning the ''A-B-C's'' of rational emotive thinking. Mr. M. was requested to construct a poster bearing the letter ''A'' and attach it to one wall of his office; a second poster (''B'') and a third (''C'') were mounted on the other walls of the office. The ''A'' poster was to represent all *antecedent events* which typically led to anxiety responses (e.g., phone calls, directives from superiors, etc.). The ''C'' poster symbolized the *consequent feelings* resulting from the anxiety events (e.g., feelings of worthlessness, depression, etc.). The mediating *belief* system with its attendant irrational cognitions (e.g., ''I should be able to finish that job,'' ''my boss has the right to expect that of me,'' etc.) was represented by poster ''B.''

At week four of therapy, Mr. M. was instructed to start each working day by manufacturing 100 paper spitballs and placing them strategically in his center desk drawer. When any event occurred which had been previously associated with feelings of anxiety or panic, Mr. M. was to close his office door, reposition himself behind the desk, and bombard poster ''A'' with at least two or three spitballs, followed by a subvocal description of the event that had just occurred—''my boss just ridiculed me with the following statement. . . .'' After hurling spitballs at poster ''C,'' the client was to subvocally identify and describe his affective response to the event. Then, when poster ''B'' had been similarly shelled, the irrational cognition was to be identified and a more rational self-statement or thought was to be substituted and rehearsed subvocally at least three times. If feelings of panic intruded at any stage of the sequence, Mr. M. was instructed to improve the accuracy of his spitball bombardment with ten practice shots (a distracting and anxiety incompatible behavior) and to resume the sequence of cognitive restructuring after becoming more relaxed.

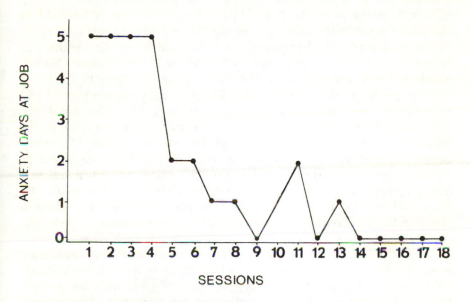

Figure 1. Number of days per week which were rated by the client as "anxiety days" at work.

A substantial reduction in the number of "anxiety days" per week was observed (Fig. 1). The A-B-C ritual was presumably effective through the active focusing of the client's attention on the various components of his cognitive-affective functioning. The procedure assisted the client in defusing the high levels of anxiety which had previously disrupted other forms of self-monitoring and cognitive restructuring. After two weeks the client was able to effectively self-monitor irrational cognitions and make the necessary corrective self-instructions without the use of posters and spitballs.

Assessment within the *behavioral* and *interpersonal* modalities revealed Mr. M. to be deficient in assertion skills. He was unable, as might be expected, to refuse unreasonable requests. Even after three sessions of behavior rehearsal and two sessions of relaxation-desensitization, he was still unable to carry out in vivo assertion assignments (an encounter with his boss). Re-exploration of the factors responsible for Mr. M.'s lack of success in carrying out the assertion assignment revealed that the intrusive *image* of his boss berating and ordering him to report to the paymaster for severance pay always preceded and accompanied the failure to carry out the assignment. A prescribed counterimage of the boss delivering the "orders" while firmly planted on the office toilet seat enabled Mr. M. to proceed. Mr. M. reported that "priming" the assertive response with the ridiculous image made the boss appear less formidable and helped to eliminate the intrusive image. By the eighth week the client was carrying out the graded assertion assignments with little difficulty. By Session 12, he indicated that his boss seemed to be making fewer unreasonable demands and was now requesting Mr. M.'s "informed opinion."

At Session 8, the client reported feeling less anxious in general and remarked that the colitis had diminished in intensity (pain) but that it was still a daily inconvenience (eight to ten bowel movements per day). It was decided now to direct treatment toward the somatic aspects of anxiety control, as well as to continue to facilitate the client's management of life-stressing events. At the beginning of the session, Mr. M. mentioned having recently seen a TV program during which hypnosis was used in the successful treatment of a "nervous problem." Mr. M. was given a rationale for the "power of deep relaxation and hypnosis" to meet the client's covert request and expectancy set regarding the efficacy of hypnosis. The relevance of developing control over the bodily *sensations* associated with colitis was stressed. After preparing the client (Hartland, 1971), a formal hypnotic procedure was administered utilizing an eye-fixation technique and several induction suggestions that the client himself had indicated (during the prehypnotic briefing) would be "especially effective." Mr. M. was given specific suggestions, augmented with goal directed imagery (Spanos, 1971) of colon and abdominal anesthesia. He was then told to imagine and experience the sensations associated with the colitis and following that to re-experience analgesia and the disappearance of the troublesome sensations. He was instructed to focus on the difference between the two sensations and to be aware that he could learn to turn *"on* and *off "* the sensations of colitis even during the "waking state." It was suggested that with continued practice he would gain increasing control over his bodily responses. The importance of the continued use of previously learned anxiety management procedures was also reemphasized. At the close of the session, the therapist said, "I would be surprised if the spastic colitis didn't improve somewhat by the next session."

At the following session, Mr. M. reported that he had been symptom free for the entire week—he experienced no more than three bowel movements in any given day nor any associated pain. Therapy continued with training in self-hypnosis, autogenic relaxation, and in devising other methods of highly portable, self-initiated forms of relaxation, and "aversive *sensation* elimination."

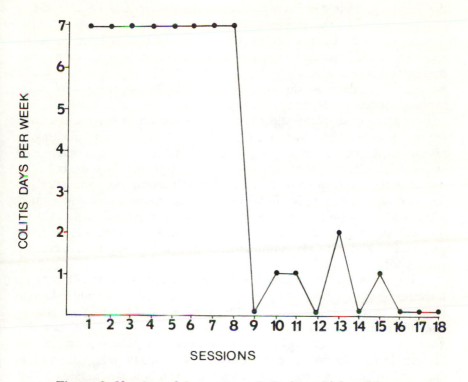

Figure 2. Number of days per week during which colitis was problematic.

Although Mr. M.'s accounts of the cross-dressing episodes were the most "sensational" and "provocative" of the problems presented, the behavior itself was not targeted for modification at the outset of therapy. It was clear that Mr. M. enjoyed the erotic gratification and relaxation associated with cross-dressing and he was not sure he was "worried enough about it to stop." The therapist's insistence that treatment be directed towards the elimination of the cross-dressing would have been inappropriate and undoubtedly would have resulted in Mr. M.'s premature termination of therapy. However, after substantial progress had been achieved in other areas, and following a discussion of Mr. M.'s *interpersonal* functioning and goals regarding future relationships and anticipated sexual encounters, the client spontaneously initiated a re-evaluation of the "problem" area. He openly discussed his feelings about cross-dressing and acknowledged that it was no longer necessary or functional as a means of coping with his generalized anxiety (which by this time had significantly diminished). In addition, Mr. M. realistically concluded that cross-dressing may complicate his present and future heterosexual relationships. Initially, Mr. M. was simply asked to record the incidence of cross-dressing episodes. During a subsequent session he revealed that the actual recording of the cross-dressing made him "feel funny," and, furthermore, that the assignment was interfering with the fantasies which were typically associated with the cross-dressing. It was during this session that the client explicitly stated his desire to terminate the cross-dressing altogether. Mr. M. was asked to supplement the recording procedure (when experiencing the urge to cross dress) by writing down the actual articles of clothing he planned to put on. He was also required to list the color, fabric content, and to detail the sequence of adornment and the setting in which the behavior would occur. As expected, this form of self-monitoring and attention focusing proved incompatible with the erotogenic *imagery* and fantasy which had always preceded and accompanied the cross-dressing. Cross-dressing, previously occurring three to four times per week, ceased to be problematic and Mr. M. continued heterosexual dating with increased confidence.

The client was much improved at termination (Session 18) as he no longer experienced debilitating anxiety, had achieved a dramatic reduction in his psychosomatic condition, and no longer cross dressed. More important, the client seemed to have demonstrated the skill to maintain this improvement by employing the various anxiety management techniques on his own. During the last three sessions he was trained to anticipate problem areas and to devise his own coping and self-treatment strategies. Mr. M. was specifically taught to utilize the multimodal schema in his own "self analysis" and was encouraged to continually monitor his level of functioning within the seven modalities.

Follow-up

Mr. M. was contacted by phone at six and twelve months following termination. He reported that the colitis stabilized following treatment—being problematic no more than once or twice every three to four weeks. The client indicated that he was feeling much more relaxed around others, and in fact, reported (at 12 months) that he had taken a new job and had recently been promoted to the position of director of the *personnel* department. He reported no instances of cross-dressing.

Discussion

Multimodal assessment, intervention and continued evaluation was particularly helpful in working with Mr. M. who, like most clients, displayed a wide variety of dysfunctional adaptational patterns. A survey of the modalities revealed the problem areas to be interrelated and interdependent. As an example, the distressing *sensations* (headaches, intestinal spasms, and cardiac palpitations) were seen to be functionally related to behavior within the *imagery* and *cognitive* modalities, namely his intimidating visual images and irrational self-messages. A continual re-examination of Mr. M.'s functioning within the seven modalities allowed treatment to progress on several "fronts." Such an approach may reduce the likelihood of relapse in that therapeutic attention is directed to the numerous areas of individual functioning, which, if left untreated, could ultimately contribute to new presenting problems. The multimodal schema alerts the clinician to the client's potential areas of difficulty and encourages creative and flexible approaches to treatment. In the present case, numerous and diverse strategies were employed. When stymied by a particular intervention's lack of effectiveness, or when general progress slows, it is often possible to re-explore the other modalities and find neglected areas of concern. The subsequent re-orienting of treatment efforts will typically remove the block to progress. Finally, the analysis of, and work within the various modalities not only permits the pinpointing of numerous deficiencies, but also enables the identification of the individual's strengths which can be effectively utilized in treatment.

References

Ellis, A. *Reason and emotion in psychotherapy*. New York: Lyle Stuart, 1962.

Hartland, J. *Medical and dental hypnosis: And its clinical applications*. Baltimore: Williams and Wilkins, 2nd Edition, 1971.

Jurjevich, R. R. *Direct psychotherapy*. Coral Gables, Fla.: University of Miami Press, 1973.

Lazarus, A. A. Relationship therapy: Often necessary but usually insufficient. *The Counseling Psychologist*, 1969, *1*, 25-27.

Lazarus, A. A. Multimodal behavior therapy: Treating the "BASIC ID." *The Journal of Nervous and Mental Disease*, 1973, *156*, 404-411.

Spanos, N. P. Goal-directed phantasy and the performance of hypnotic test suggestions. *Psychiatry*, 1971, *34*, 86-96.

Chapter 14

A Multimodal Approach
to the Treatment of Obesity

William L. Mulligan

Background Information

The client (hereafter referred to as Ms. G.) was a 43-year-old, single Caucasian female, who requested therapy to help her lose weight. A Life History Questionnaire (See Appendix 1) was sent to her before our first session. The completed questionnaire revealed that she had never been married and was living with her parents. She had obtained a masters degree and was employed as an elementary school teacher. Ms. G. had been overweight for many years, but her weight significantly increased during the two years prior to therapy. At the time she requested therapy she weighed 210 pounds at 5'5'' in height. Although distressed about her weight, she had not previously contacted a mental health professional for assistance. She had been able to lose 22 pounds on one occasion by attending Weight Watchers.

Ms. G.'s parents were both living. Her father was 65 years of age and her mother was 63. While they were also considerably overweight, they were both in good health and led exceedingly active lives. The client described her mother as a very strong-willed woman who often attempted to induce guilt and who played the martyr role. In a sentence completion exercise, she provided the following answers: (a) one of the things I feel guilty about is . . . "my earlier feelings about my mother"; (b) Mother was always . . . "angry and insensitive"; (c) What I needed from mother and did not get was . . .' "understanding and a listening ear." Ms. G.'s relationship with her mother was frequently strained. Tensions were most

170

evident when Ms. G. was younger because she was not always a passive and compliant daughter. Although Ms. G. felt that her father was more approachable and understanding than her mother, she did not feel that they really understood her.

In response to the question, "What are your five main fears?", she replied: "(1) dependency in old age upon others; (2) lack of sufficient funds in old age; (3) incapacitating illness in old age; (4) parents will become chronically ill in the last years of their lives; (5) my reaction to my parents' deaths."

When asked which of a large number of problems applied to her, she checked "feel tense," "conflict," "fatigue," and "unconfident (in certain situations)." When asked if she had ever lost control, she replied with the following: "I would say that I'm a very controlled person. However, recently (last two years) I have become tearful in emotional situations, even ones which are not really that distressing." In addition, she selected the following adjectives to describe herself: "worthwhile," "sympathetic," "intelligent," and "considerate." In general, it appeared that the client was anxious and also suffered some underlying depression, but she was able to maintain a fair degree of self-esteem.

Ms. G. also seemed to be a nurturant person who in her own words "feels deeply for people." She reported having several female friends, but she lacked male friends and there was evidence that she was afraid of being dependent upon others. Another sentence completion item revealed the following: What I need and have never received from a man is . . . "love."

In essence, the questionnaire data described a woman who seemed to be functioning well in many areas of her life, but who had significant areas of anxiety and frustration. However, she regarded overeating as her only problem, and wanted to be treated by a behavior therapist. She hoped that therapy would last no more than three to four sessions. She denied being dissatisfied with any other aspect of her life. She had many hobbies and was active in community affairs. She said she made friends easily and kept them. None of her responses was blatantly suggestive of neurotic or psychotic processes. On the other hand, several factors contributed to a less optimistic prognosis: she was single and living with her parents; her parents were both considerably overweight; her obesity problem was severe and of long duration. There was reason to suspect that, in addition to a strict behavorial treatment of her overeating, she would benefit from an exploration of (a) her emotional lability; (b) dependency issues vis-à-vis her parents, (c) her thoughts and feelings regarding her parents' inevitable deaths; and (d) her social life, particularly her lack of durable relationships with men.

Treatment

Ms. G. was seen once per week for 40 individual sessions followed by 10 group therapy sessions.

The first few sessions were devoted to examining and clarifying her responses to the Life History Questionnaire and conducting a functional behavior analysis. These sessions produced the data necessary to formulate the multimodal profile presented in Table 1. This profile was useful in delineating specific problem areas that could be ameliorated by therapeutic attention. I did not feel that psychological testing was necessary in this case either for diagnostic or for treatment purposes. Periodically during the course of therapy Ms. G. was seen by a physician who monitored her physical condition.

Table 1. Ms. G.'s Multimodal Profile

Modality	Identified Problems
Behavior	Overeating
	Situational passivity
Affect	Emotional (tearful) episodes (underlying depression)
	Emotional constriction
	Occasional anxiety
Sensations	Bodily tension associated with anxiety
Imagery	Negative body image
Cognitions	Irrational self-talk
	a) "I am crazy"
	b) "I am unattractive"
	c) "It is a disgrace to be single"
	d) "I am too old to make changes"
	Sexual misinformation
	Puritanical attitudes regarding work and play
Interpersonal relationships	Lack of close peer friendships, particularly with males
	Dependency on parents and others
	Role as family nurse maid
	Passivity in interactions with others
Drugs	Not required

My approach to treatment was conceptualized within the multimodal framework. Treatment here initially focused upon the behavior modality, because this was least threatening to the client and because it included the eating behaviors, which she regarded as her primary problem.

Behavior

Ms. G. was weighed at the first and at each succeeding session. Her weight before the first session was 210 pounds. As noted above, a functional behavior analysis was undertaken to determine which environmental factors influenced her eating habits. This analysis and the corresponding treatment recommendations included the following:

1. She was in the habit of having a few cocktails in the evenings at home. She said the drinks relaxed her, but they also seemed to trigger eating binges by reducing her inhibitions and controls. Thus, she was trained in systematic deep muscle relaxation (predominantly a sensory modality). She also agreed to stop drinking, since alcohol was incompatible with the Weight Watchers Program (see below).

2. She seemed to have more difficulty controlling her eating on weekends (i.e., when she was alone and without the structure and stimulation of her work). We discussed ways in which she could more constructively and enjoyably occupy herself when away from her job.

3. Ms. G. was told that she would have to alter her eating habits on a permanent rather than on a temporary basis. It was recommended that she (a) only eat when she was sitting at her kitchen table; (b) write down everything she planned to eat just before doing so; (c) place her silverware on the table after each mouthful, and (d) chew her food 25-30 times before swallowing. These procedures were designed to slow down the rate at which food was ingested, and to change eating from an automatic, habitual response to a set of specific behaviors over which Ms. G. could gradually gain conscious control.

4. She agreed to attend Weight Watchers meetings and to adhere to their recommended diet. In connection with her dieting, we made the following contract: she would call me—any time day or night—if she felt she was about to go off of her diet. This contract was presented to her as an agreement based on trust, and I said that I expected her to honor it. I reminded her of the contract at several times during the course of therapy.

After 25 individual sessions, Ms. G. weighed 130 pounds which represented a loss of 80 pounds from her initial weight of 210 pounds. Her weight loss was surprisingly steady and consistent during this initial phase. Once she reached the 130 mark, our efforts were devoted to maintenance within the 130-135 range. In the ensuing months prior to termination of therapy her weight fluctuated. She occasionally went as high as 140, but for the most part was able to keep her weight below 135. On many occasions she exercised remarkable restraint when faced with culinary temptations. Whenever she reported such instances, I freely praised her. Throughout the course of therapy I was liberal with praise and compliments whenever positive changes were evident in Ms. G.'s behavior. In addition the weight loss itself was reinforcing, since others began complimenting and praising her on her new figure. At each session for about two months she reported new instances of positive reinforcement she was receiving from others for her weight loss. Fortunately, Ms. G. was very pleased to receive social reinforcement from friends and colleagues, unlike some clients who find attention and compliments unpleasant.

Affect

Ms. G. was initially tense in the sessions and appeared quite ambivalent about discussing issues not directly related to her eating problem. She mentioned that she was shocked by the amount of information and the intimacy of the material requested in the Life History Questionnaire, since she had expected a very narrowly focused behavorial treatment. Yet she had identified her overemotionality (i.e., breaking into tears unexpectedly) as "an annoying problem." Several other affective problems (as noted in the Background Information Section) seemed in need of some attention as well.

My questions were initially limited to exploring nonthreatening, impersonal areas. However, using standard Rogerian techniques, I gradually and cautiously encouraged her to talk about additional issues which seemed to be emotionally laden. As she loosened up and began talking more, she dwelled on a number of these highly charged areas. It was easy to identify those issues which posed affective problems for Ms. G. Her eyes inevitably became red and teary as we approached emotionally laden areas. The process was not characterized by relentless probing but was based upon encouraging her to talk, making empathetic statements, pointing out the emotion apparent in her face, and supporting her as she expressed her feelings, cried, and so on. As noted above, Ms. G. initially regarded her "emotional outbursts" as "an annoying and bewildering problem." Expression of strong emotion was clearly incompatible with this woman's concept of herself as a competent, strong, independent person. In the initial phase of therapy, Ms. G. chastized herself for being so emotional and for losing control. I countered these irrational, self-deprecating cognitions by asking her why she was being so hard on herself and what was so terrible about crying and expressing her feelings. These sessions allowed Ms. G. to release much pent-up emotion and to change her cognitions so as to enable her to accept her feelings as a legitimate and valuable part of herself.

The manner in which I gently encouraged her to discuss issues and to express her feelings, along with my acceptance of what she was experiencing, undoubtedly played a significant role in the course of therapy. Whether or not these factors were essential for weight loss (and subsequent maintenance of that loss) cannot be stated. I believe it was probably a critical factor in the development of a strong positive relationship between Ms. G. and myself. She became comfortable discussing personal issues of any kind with me and this social ease transferred somewhat to her interactions with others. Ms. G.'s mood and self-confidence improved. The overemotionality of which she complained prior to therapy (i.e., suddenly and unexpectedly breaking into tears) ceased.

Sensations

As noted above, Ms. G. reported occasionally feeling tense and anxious when returning home from work. It was particularly at these times that she would have a few cocktails. The other method she used to deal with tension was to go to sleep. I suggested that it might be better if she could learn to eliminate some of her tension by means of deep muscle relaxation (Jacobson, 1964). A portion of several sessions was devoted to teaching her relaxation exercises which she practiced at home.

Imagery

Ms. G. failed to report any troubling images, other than the realistic image of herself as an obese woman. She spontaneously reported using this negative image to help her avoid eating unacceptable foods. I encouraged her to use this technique since she found it helpful. Whenever faced with food not on her diet, she would evoke an image of herself as she looked prior to therapy. As she turned away from the unacceptable food, she would replace the aversive image with a postive picture of herself as a trim woman in a bathing suit being admired by others.

Cognitions

When dealing with the client's cognitions I made use of techniques and ideas suggested by Albert Ellis in his publications on Rational-Emotive Psychotherapy (Ellis, 1962, 1973; Ellis and Harper, 1961). Happily, Ms. G. was free from the most debilitating, irrational cognitions which revolve around feelings of worthlessness, self-abnegation, and malignant self-criticism. However, she held a number of interrelated attitudes which I questioned and challenged. For example, in a variety of ways I communicated my general belief that it is desirable to express feelings and that the expression of emotion does not reflect weakness or incompetence. I also suggested that there is more to living than hard work, self-denial, and selfless devotion to others. I attempted to replace some of her cherished Puritan (religiously based) notions with a view of life that places as much of a value on happiness and enjoyment as it does on work and making a contribution to society.

Some sexual counseling was also provided during the course of therapy. I gave Ms. G. several books to read and we discussed a variety of issues dealing with sex and masturbation.

Ms. G. believed that she was exceedingly ugly. I shared with her my opinion that she was a good, worthwhile person and that this was more important than physical appearance. I also told her that while everyone looks more attractive when not obese, I thought she had a very pretty face; I have continued to convey my genuine feelings that she is an attractive woman.

In one session, I asked Ms. G. why she wanted to lose weight. She gave the following reasons: (a) it is healthier for me not to be overweight, (b) I feel better physically, (c) I look better, and (d) I feel better about myself. The first three reasons sounded quite rational, but when I asked her in what ways she felt better about herself when slimmer, she replied that when she is overweight or goes off her diet, she thinks of herself as a worthless slob, as a total failure, and as completely unattractive. I told her that it was to be expected that sooner or later she would eat something that was off her diet and that this would not make her a worthless slob. Continuing, I emphasized that the important thing was to catch herself and get back on the diet rather than to chastize and ridicule herself, which was irrational as well as destructive.

Another irrational cognition held by Ms. G. was that she had missed her opportunity for a more exciting, active life. She felt that because she had not made certain critical decisions earlier in life it was too late to change things. I stressed that it was hardly ever too late to make desired changes and that there was no such thing as a critical period for decision-making.

A final area handled cognitively concerned Ms. G.'s difficulty in tolerating frustration. Over the years she had repeatedly told herself that she could not stand being anxious and that she had to have a drink and/or gorge herself to reduce the tension. Acting on the basis of these cognitions produced two problems where there once was only one; she became overweight as well as anxious. She repeated the same things to herself about her inability to control her overeating as she had said about her inability to tolerate anxiety: ''I want to eat that food now and I cannot refrain from doing so; it would be too intolerably painful to keep myself on a diet.'' After therapeutic intervention and considerable effort on her part she was eventually able to challenge such self-defeating statements.

Interpersonal relationships

A considerable amount of therapeutic attention was devoted to discussions of Ms. G.'s relationships with other people. It was clear from her responses to the Life History Questionnaire that she was greatly concerned with her parents' eventual deaths and with her own adjustment to their demise. During the first few sessions, Ms. G. stated that several stressful events had occurred during the year preceeding therapy: (a) she attended the 25th reunion of her high school class and saw many former classmates who were married with families of their own; (b) a social club, to which she belonged for ten years, was to be disbanded; and (c) her sister and her sister's family moved out of state, thus virtually terminating what had been a very close sibling relationship. Each of these issues shared the common theme of losing close friends and loved ones and/or heightening her awareness of being alone. We spent a good deal of time discussing her decision to live with her parents, what it was like living with them, and how her life would be affected by their absence.

It soon became obvious that she needed training in assertive behavior. The question I repeatedly presented to her was the following: "Once you have determined what your feelings and needs are, as compared to the needs of others, how can you calmly but firmly assert yourself?" We used behavior rehearsal to practice new ways of interacting with specific individuals. For example, whenever Ms. G.'s mother did not get her own way, she assumed a stony silence, instead of sharing her feelings and thoughts in an assertive manner. We worked on ways in which Ms. G. could confront her mother and help her express her feelings. Ms. G. was urged not to reinforce her mother's sulking but to respond only to reasonable requests made in a pleasant manner.

It was in her relationships with men that Ms. G. was least assertive. Once again the issue discussed was how to please others while satisfying her own needs. We also spent time considering ways in which Ms. G. could make new friendships with men and women. Ms. G. was invited to join a group as it would provide an excellent milieu for her to develop more adequate interpersonal relationships.

Drugs

Whenever I see a client who seems in need of medication, he or she is referred to a psychiatrist who acts as a consultant. It was my judgment that Ms. G. did not require medication, although I advised her to have a medical checkup to ensure that no physical complications were associated with her weight loss.

Discussion

Obviously, it is impossible to identify critical ingredients in any case lacking a reversal design and other controls. In the present instance, however, positive changes are unmistakable. Ms. G. lost a total of 80 pounds and showed other improvements, primarily in the affective and interpersonal modalities. At termination of therapy, she no longer was overly emotional and tearful, nor was she as distressed by normal frustrations incurred in the course of daily living. Although she continued to live with her parents, she made a number of new friends. She reported acting more assertively and was expressing more feelings toward her parents, colleagues, and friends. Several follow up sessions were held at two, six, and nine months following termination. Her measured weight was 140 or less at each meeting. In my opinion it is unlikely that such changes could have "spontaneously" occurred in the absence of therapy.

Ms. G.'s motivation to lose weight was certainly a necessary ingredient for success. Many clients cannot lose weight because they will not make the personal resolution to do so. Instead they hope for a magical pill or technique that will enable them to avoid necessary sacrifices and the intelligent use of self-control.

After approximately ten sessions, Ms. G. described what she believed to be the critical factor responsible for her success. She said that when she first saw me at our initial session, she said to herself, "Oh no, this won't do, he's much too young." She had hoped for an elderly man on whom she could become dependent and with whom she could discuss her feelings of inadequacy and incompetence. She was embarrassed to be seeking assistance for "personal problems" from someone younger than herself (who she thought, by implication of his role as a therapist, had no problems). She maintained that she would not have been uncomfortable discussing her own limitations and problems with a therapist who was older than herself. Therefore, instead of remaining overweight and discussing the negative feelings resulting from obesity (which would have been too embarrassing for her to do with a young therapist at the beginning of treatment), she convinced herself that she had to lose weight to save face.

Thus, it is quite possible that the behavioral techniques consciously applied were by no means the only active ingredients in the therapy. Complex "relationship factors" operating between Ms. G. and myself, as well as cognitions concerning her need to maintain self-esteem were of central importance. The single most important behavioral technique appeared to be the contract Ms. G. made (during the second session) to call me before going off her diet. It is likely that Ms. G.'s success stems largely from the interaction between her personal commitment (which involved her need to maintain self-esteem and her initial perception of the therapist as too young) and the explicit behavioral agreement between us. I made it clear in the behavioral contract that I wanted to know about any and all "infractions." Furthermore, the explicit understanding that this was "an agreement based on trust" made it very difficult for her to avoid calling me. Also of primary importance was the work focusing on the affective modality as well as the mutually positive relationship that developed between us. Ms. G. clearly wanted someone in whom she could confide and in whom she had sufficient trust and confidence to express her many pent-up feelings. She needed someone who was a good listener and who was able to communicate understanding. The client was able to form a close relationship with me, and my feelings and thoughts about her became very important to her. She stated in her Life History Questionnaire that she had never loved anyone, particularly a man, and that she had trouble expressing affection. I would not go so far as to say that food served for Ms. G. as a symbolic substitute for love. But I do believe that her ability to form a close therapeutic relationship with me was probably a significant factor responsible for her improvement. The evolution of our relationship became a crucial learning experience for Ms. G., facilitating the development of relationships with other men.

Conclusion

This case underscores the thoroughness of a multimodal approach in the treatment of a seemingly unitary problem. By exploring the BASIC ID we identified and rectified several distinct and interrelated problems that tied in with the presenting complaint. The chances of enabling Ms. G. to maintain her weight loss were thereby greatly enhanced.

References

Ellis, A. *Reason and emotion in psychotherapy*. New York: Lyle Stuart, 1962.

Ellis, A. The no cop-out therapy. *Psychology Today,* July 1973.

Ellis, A., & Harper, R. *A guide to rational living*. No. Hollywood, Calif: Wilshire Book Co., 1961.

Jacobson, E. *Anxiety and tension control: A psychobiological approach*. Philadelphia: Lippincott, 1964.

Lazarus, A. A. *Behavior therapy and beyond*. New York: McGraw-Hill, 1971.

Lazarus, A. A. *Multimodal behavior therapy: Treating the BASIC ID. Journal of Nervous and Mental Disease,* 1974, *156*, 404-411.

Lazarus, A. A. Multimodal therapy: BASIC ID. *Psychology Today,* March 1974.

Chapter 15

Clinical Notes on Paradoxical Therapy

Allen Fay

Therapists frequently are confronted by people with seemingly immutable problems (e.g., fixed delusions, encrusted obsessive ruminations, rigid character traits) which appear unresponsive to a comprehensive armamentarium of techniques. Many clinicians have had the experience of investing years of fruitless or only partially successful efforts with such cases. However, unusual approaches are often imperative when dealing with such refractory situations. Rosen's use of Direct Analysis (1962) in the treatment of psychotic individuals is one well-known example.

The clinical material presented here describes a technique in which the therapist, or any significant other, expresses agreement with the patient's irrationality ("siding with the resistance") (Sherman, 1961) and exaggerates his distortion. Often this will entail a concrete or bizarre intervention. Obviously, the use of paradoxical exaggeration must be but one part of a general regimen of multimodal treatment procedures. However, it is significant that in many instances seemingly refractory problems become less resistant following the introduction of one or more "absurd" interventions. In more than 30 cases I have treated with these methods, no untoward reactions have been observed.

Paradoxical methods cut across theoretical orientations and diagnostic boundaries. Therapists of backgrounds and persuasions as diverse as psychoanalysis, behavior therapy, hypnosis, existentialism, and communication theory have found them useful. Notable among those employing paradoxical techniques have been Coleman and Nelson (1957), Dunlap (1932), Frankl (1960), Haley (1963), Erickson (Haley, 1973), and Whitaker (1973). A number of behavioral techniques; e.g., negative practice (Dunlap, 1932), blowup (Lazarus, 1971), and implosion (Stampfl and

From *Psychotherapy: Theory, Research and Practice* (In press). Reprinted by permission of the author and publisher.

Levis, 1967) also involve exaggeration of the patient's symptoms. Even the term "exaggeration therapy" (Van Den Aardweg, 1972) has been used.

Many, if not most, therapists use these ideas at least intuitively, and, in fact, they are part of the common-sense repertoire of interpersonal exchange. For example, a twelve-year-old boy whose over-protective mother constantly peppered him with solicitous questions about his health, vociferously protested but to no avail. However, he virtually extinguished the undesired behavior when on several occasions, in response to her frantic "Are you all right?" he clutched his abdomen and said, "No, I'm not all right. I'm dreadfully ill and I don't think I can last much longer!" Therapists who invoke paradoxical techniques sometimes find immediate positive effects. Thus, in the treatment of a chronic schizophrenic woman who was inclined to lapse into prolonged suicidal verbalizations, the following dialogue ensued:

P: I want to die. I wish you would stab me.
T: (Gets up from chair and walks toward a desk) Let's see, I don't think I have a knife but I may have a pair of scissors. No, I don't see them, but here's a screwdriver. How's that?
P: (Startled, then whines with annoyance) Oh, come on.
T: (Persisting) You just tell me where you would like me to stab you and I will oblige. You know I studied anatomy and guarantee a good job.
P: (Laughing) No, thanks, I've changed my mind.

Years of experience with the more conventional responses of professional and family members, e.g., interpretation, reflection, support, inattention, distraction, reprimand, medication, etc., had failed to diminish this patient's maladaptive ploys. After the session described above, communications about dying, killing herself, or being killed did not recur, and progress in other areas also ensued.

Therapists may also advise their clients to employ paradoxical exaggeration in their own interactions. For example, a young woman snapped at her boyfriend who, trying to be helpful, put some salad on her plate. "Don't give me the salad, I'll take it myself!" adding a sprinkling of abusive expletives. Since he was upset by this incident, I instructed him to respond to her future outbursts as follows: "I'm so terribly sorry, I had no idea what a horrible thing I did. I might have completely destroyed you. Could you ever find it in your heart to forgive me?"

The following vignettes illustrate divergent ways of interrupting persistent pathological communication patterns.

Case I

A 30-year-old man with a 15-year documented history of paranoid schizophrenia and several hospitalizations, courses of ECT, and pharmacotherapy with phenothiazines, constantly asked people about him if he seemed "all right." He reported feeling that people were staring at him, that he appeared different, that everybody knew he was sick, and that he was going to suffer a relapse. His anxiety would be particularly marked if someone were to say, "How are you?" Although after a year in therapy (including phenothiazine medication) his global functioning was much improved, the particular symptoms persisted in attenuated form. At this juncture I invoked several "exaggeration" techniques: (1) The patient was encouraged to respond to, "Are you feeling all right?" by replying, "No, I've just come from the doctor and have some bad news. He said I have leukemia." (2) When the patient asked me if he was getting sick again, I answered, "Unquestionably! In fact we had better reserve a bed in the hospital immediately." (3) The patient's wife was instructed to handle his obsessive ruminations similarly. (4) I encouraged him to act in a deliberately bizarre manner with his family, who always treated him as a defective person in danger of breaking down at any moment. Although he experienced some difficulty with the assignments, the patient's ruminative tendencies significantly decreased.

Case II

A 22-year-old man, severely disturbed since early childhood, was referred by a psychiatrist from another city for comprehensive inpatient treatment in a structured milieu. There was a long history of severe anxiety, depression, and threats of violence to himself and others. Psychotherapy and a full range of psychotropic drugs in small to massive doses had been tried to no avail, and within the previous two years he had been hospitalized twice. When first seen, he was disheveled, disorganized, agitated, pacing, and showed marked facial grimacing as well as pressured speech. He could not stay with one subject. He carried two containers of mace, and paranoid ideas abounded, although a clearly defined thought disorder was not evident. His parents, with whom he lived, could not sleep at night for fear that he would kill them. He expressed suicidal and homicidal ideas but without apparent serious intent. Several months after treatment began, his anxiety level and capacity to relate to people in the hospital had improved, but discharge was difficult to effect. He would demand that we release him from the hospital and find a place for him to live. When a residence, school, or halfway house was made available, he would be enthusiastic until the day he was to begin, at which time with teeth and fists clenched he would refuse to leave. The following exchange, which took place during the last few weeks of hospitalization, illustrates the technique of promoting the desired response by frustrating it (Haley, 1973).

P: You have to find me a place so I can get out of here.
T: Well, there is a halfway house I know of but I don't think you would be interested.
P: Tell me about it.
T: (Tells him about it)
P: Will you make an appointment for me?
T: Okay, but it will only be a waste of time.
T: (A few days later) I can see that you are not really interested in the halfway house and it's perfectly okay.
P: What do you mean?
T: You seemed enthusiastic about getting an appointment last Thursday and here it is Tuesday and you haven't even mentioned it. But I don't think you would have liked it anyway.
P: Did you make the appointment?
T: Yes.
P: When?
T: For Friday, but I'll cancel it. It's no problem.
P: Well, wait a minute. Maybe I should go anyway.
T: But what's the point?

The interview at the halfway house went smoothly, and the patient started in the program shortly thereafter. Subsequent to his discharge, the following exchanges took place. The patient was a voracious reader and had studied a number of books about sex, including some that were replete with misinformation. His exposure to family attitudes about sex had been bizarre. At one time while sitting in my office discussing masturbation, he said, "I masturbate three times a day. Do you think that's too much, that is, can it cause any damage?" We had discussed this subject many times and he knew well that it did not cause any damage. However, I repeated the supportive, corrective, informative statements at which point he asked, "How about four times?" Realizing at this point that he knew the answer perfectly well, I said, "No, but I can tell you that with five times the most dire consequences can result including blindness, insanity, complete disintegration of the personality. . . ." He began to laugh, and immediately gained perspective on what he had been doing. He came to my office one day and said "I'm discouraged and tired of trying. I don't think things are going to work out and I'm ready to throw in the towel." I announced that I had a wonderful idea and promptly brought out two towels from the bathroom. I took the wastepaper basket, positioned it between us, gave him one towel and we proceeded to throw our towels into the basket. Again, this lightened his mood and enabled us to proceed with other issues. On another occasion he said, "Well, I think I'm having a relapse." I immediately replied, "Wait a second. You can't do that unless we plan it." I took out my appointment book and asked when he wanted to have a relapse. He was initially startled but planned one about a month in advance. After writing the date in my book I said, "All right, now we can dispense with that situation." On several subsequent occasions I reminded him that he was due for a relapse on October 29. It developed, not surprisingly, that he did not have a relapse, and a week after the scheduled date he said, "You know I just realized yesterday that it's been several weeks since I've had even the faintest suicidal thought." I responded, "Well, it's too late, you missed your chance. Last week was the week for the relapse." He once saw someone on the street who looked grossly disturbed and asked, "I can't get that way, can I?" Whereupon, I responded, "I don't see why not, if you really want to." At that time he was living in a residence, attending a halfway house, and working at a halftime job. He left the residence after two months to move into his own hotel room so that he could have sexual relations, which he had previously thought unattainable. He was working full time shortly thereafter.

Case III

A 61-year-old man who had been moderately paranoid for 40 years decompensated a few months before seeking therapy. After losing his job as a buyer, he tried working as a salesperson in a large department store, but left after a few weeks. He presented with a fullblown paranoid psychosis. He was convinced that the department store had agents spying on him and was about to initiate criminal proceedings against him because on one occasion his register was three dollars short. He was morbidly anxious, his speech pressured with repetitive questions related to this motif. At the end of the first visit he said that he would not be able to keep his next appointment with me because he was about to be arrested. Ignoring his dire prediction, I asked that his wife attend the next appointment with him.

His wife proved to be exhausted by her constant efforts to reason with him. These efforts had been along traditional supportive lines (reality-testing).

P: They are after me.

W: (Benevolently) No, Louie, they aren't. Why would a big organization like that worry about you? They have much more to do with their time than that. If they really wanted to get you they would have done something long before now. . . .

I suggested, in his presence that she respond as follows:

P: They are after me.
W: They certainly are. Not only are they after you from that store but they have notified other stores in the metropolitan area as well. A city-wide alert is out on you. The police have been notified and the conspiracy has already extended to the FBI. Country-wide agencies are focused on you and are trying to get you. Not only is the conspiracy nation-wide, but Scotland Yard and other international police organizations are interested in this case. There is no question that you are going to be arrested very soon.

One week later the patient announced that he was feeling much better. He seemed very comfortable and did not express the same delusional ideation, although he said that occasionally he had a paranoid thought. By the fourth session he was feeling well and this was fully corroborated by his wife who said that she had not implemented my suggestion because the paranoia had cleared after I had given her the instructions. Follow-up three and six months later indicated that he remained in remission. In several other cases amelioration of symptoms occurred following the mere description of the technique.

Case IV

A female patient of 30 was jealous of her husband. If the phone rang and the unknown caller hung up, she would accuse her husband of having a lover. I suggested to the husband, in front of the patient, that when she made one of these statements he should avoid becoming locked into a struggle in which he defends himself by saying, "I don't know what's the matter with you, I'm not involved with anybody, I'm here all the time, you're crazy, I can't stand your jealousy." An alternate response was recommended: "You know, I have been thinking about confessing for a long time. You are absolutely right. That was my lover on the phone and we were supposed to go out tonight but I told her to hang up if you answered. Not only do I have one lover but I have five. Do you remember last week when you wondered where I was? I was with one of my lovers from eight to nine and with another from nine to ten." Thus, the accused partner agrees with the deviation and amplifies it. The net result in this case, as in the others in which this method had been employed, was the elimination of destructive "games" and the opening of channels of authentic communication.

Case V

Lucy came for therapy in her senior year of high school. She was quite bright but never studied and invariably failed her examinations. She had to leave public school, and the parochial school she attended promoted her despite repeated failures. Her achievement-oriented family was unwilling to come to our sessions and kept pushing her to attend nursing school or college. My recommendation was that she get a job, but the family opposed this, and they prevailed. When she began college, I told her that it wouldn't be so bad because she knew in advance that she would flunk. We could, in fact, count on it and even plan it. My persistence with this theme, including actively discouraging her from studying so that she wouldn't be inconsistent, led to her becoming annoyed and resistant. She passed all of her subjects. This resistance was not generalized and we continued to have a very positive relationship.

Discussion

My use of paradoxical methods with more than 30 patients leads to the clinical impression that these interventions are effective. I do not know to what extent personal style is involved, but a good sense of humor in addition to empathic concern would seem to be important. If the paradoxical techniques are the agents of change, by what mechanism is the change produced? One possibility may be suggested by the following exchange with a 19-year-old man who had had a lifelong diagnosis of schizophrenia and marked impairment in global functioning since early childhood:

P: I am really worthless.

T: Yes, you are.

P: (Not angrily) I know what you're trying to do. It's a trick but it won't work.

T: It's interesting that when *you* say you are worthless, it doesn't sound ridiculous or like a trick, but when I say the same thing, it does.

Many people cannot recognize their own "irrationality" (as defined by the community) but when it is mirrored back to them, at times with an element of benevolent mimicry, they often do respond to it as inappropriate. By agreeing with and exaggerating the deviation, one incites the patient to take a stand against the irrationality of the imitator. This is consonant with Haley's idea (1963) that changing the predictable behavior of one member of a two-person game changes the game and forces the other person to change. In behavioral terms one might say that maladaptive responses are not being reinforced by interminable "reality-testing." The introduction of distortion into a rigid system may enable the system to reform along more adaptive lines and this idea would seem to be related to the notion of psychosis as a growth experience. The encouraging of circumscribed psychotic behavior with the participation of the therapist could help the patient master his fear of losing control or modify a rigid character pattern. The idea of the therapist as dramatizer is reminiscent of the court jester who reflects the irrationality of his surroundings through paradoxical communications. The concept of court jester as therapist in this regard is provocative (Rose, 1969).

The use of paradoxical techniques will often be associated with a modification of the patient's behavior and, in addition, can make life more tolerable for the people in his environment (including the therapist) while they are sharing his ordeal and trying to ameliorate his anguish.

Objections to the methods discussed above have been reviewed by others (Coleman and Nelson, 1957) and seem to center around three basic issues: violation of the concept of the therapist as an "ambassador of reality"; the undermining of trust because the therapist is not being "genuine" and is in fact deceiving the patient; and the use of these techniques as a vehicle for the expression of sadistic impulses by the therapist. Several points may be offered in response to these criticisms. (1) There is much more to human relationships (therapy included) than concrete, literal, predictable communications. Thus, there is no reason for therapists to be more restricted than others in the use of hyperbole and humor. In fact, therapeutic interventions are often more acceptable to patients when humorous and not stereotyped. (2) Genuineness of the therapist is more an attitude than it is a set of factual statements or interpretations about the patient and his behavior. Is the therapist's motivation to deceive the patient or to dramatize something about him? It is perfectly consistent with the successful use of these techniques to convey the intention to the patient. When the intention is not stated, the communication should be couched in a form that makes it obvious that the therapist is not being literal. If the patient fails to grasp this fact, the technique, in the author's view, has been applied incorrectly. Is it "honest" and "genuine" to tell the patient repeatedly something that he already "knows," or in any event has been told hundreds of times, e.g., "No, Louie, they are not after you," or is it, in fact, patronizing to do so? (3) The third objection probably has the most substance in the sense that mimicking the patient and creating humor from his problems may easily be used destructively. But so may any modality, technique, or style. Whether a caveat is sufficient or whether paradoxical methods should be interdicted will depend on the individual therapist.

Conventional therapy and "absurd therapy" are by no means mutually exclusive but in fact are complementary so that the basic serious concern of the therapist is evident. Haley (1963) describes therapy as "a peculiar mixture of play and dead seriousness" (p. 187). The author's experience is that the introduction of humor in general, and the kinds of distortion mentioned here in particular, actually bring the patient and therapist into a closer, freer, more spontaneous relationship. Learning to laugh at oneself is often a major achievement for the person in therapy. Identification with a therapist who can laugh at his own irrationality as well as that of the patient is seen as constructive. At times one may observe the patient deliberately making paradoxical statements to the therapist.

In conclusion, it would seem that the most appropriate intervention is the one that works. For many people, the one that works appears to be based on the hackneyed saying, "A foolish question deserves a foolish answer."

References

Coleman, M. L., & Nelson, B. Paradigmatic psychotherapy in borderline treatment. *Psychoanalysis,* 1957, *5,* 28.

Dunlap, K. *Habits, their making and unmaking.* New York: Liveright, 1932.

Frankl, V. E. Paradoxical intention. *American Journal of Psychotherapy,* 1960, *14,* 520.

Haley, J. *Strategies of psychotherapy.* New York: Grune and Stratton, 1963.

Haley, J. *Uncommon therapy: The psychiatric techniques of Milton H. Erickson, M.D.* New York: W. W. Norton, 1973.

Lazarus, A. A. *Behavior therapy and beyond.* New York: McGraw-Hill, 1971.

Rose, Gilbert J. King Lear and the use of humor in treatment. *Journal of the American Psychoanalytic Association,* 1969, *17,* 927.

Rosen, J. N. *Direct psychoanalytic psychiatry.* New York: Grune and Stratton, 1962.

Sherman, M. H. Siding with the resistance in paradigmatic psychotherapy. *Psychoanalysis and the Psychoanalytic Review,* 1961, *48,* 43.

Stampfl, T. G., & Levis, D. J. Essentials of implosive therapy: A learning theory-based psychodynamic behavioral therapy. *Journal of Abnormal Psychology,* 1967, *72,* 496.

Van Den Aardweg, G. J. M. A grief theory of homosexuality. *American Journal of Psychotherapy,* 1972, *26,* (1), 52.

Whitaker, C. A. *The psychotherapy of aggression: A special emphasis on psychotherapy of the absurd.* Talk given at Northshore Hospital, January, 1973.

Chapter 16

Multimodal Therapy and Mental Retardation

Carole Pearl and Vito Guarnaccia

Many professionals are under the impression that mentally retarded individuals do not experience the full range and depth of human feelings and emotions. They consider the idea of using similar therapy techniques with both retarded and nonretarded people as preposterous. As Slivkin and Bernstein (1970) have indicated, many educated people tend to characterize the retarded as inherently inferior since they cannot learn as rapidly as others. Furthermore, even among psychiatrists and psychologists, the attitude prevails that only intelligent and highly verbal people are good candidates for psychotherapy. Many of our colleagues (including educators, counselors, social workers, and parents) were surprised to learn that our method of treating the retarded involves the application of multimodal techniques which are very similar to those used with nonretarded individuals.

At a workshop on ''Sexuality and the Mentally Retarded'' we began our presentation by playing an audio tape of Lisa, a 17-year-old, mildly retarded girl with Down's syndrome who was responding to a story-telling test. The tape was selected to provide the workshop participants with the experience of hearing a retarded person discuss feelings about sex, marriage, being retarded, being different from other people, as well as needs for independence and freedom. We have used this tape at various lectures and seminars to dispel archaic and fallacious attitudes. The recording has been especially effective in training therapists to work with the retarded. A few excerpts from Lisa's picture story test are given below, so that readers who are not familiar with retarded persons can appreciate that the retarded have the same feelings, needs and desires as ''normal people.''

Examiner: Now look at this picture Lisa. Tell me a story with a beginning, a middle, and an ending. Tell me what the people are thinking about and what they are feeling.

Lisa: The lady is sleeping and the man is crying because he is unhappy because he can't walk right and talk right. He is half handicapped and half retarded and mental.

Examiner: How did he get that way?

Lisa: He was born that way. That's the way I was born.

Examiner: How?

Lisa: I was born retarded and that's why I go to a special school. People say it in school and they make fun of me.

Examiner: Who?

Lisa: People in school.

Examiner: The children?

Lisa: Yes, the kids.

Examiner: Are they retarded?

Lisa: No, not like I am. They call me handicapped, and I don't know what that means. I know what retarded means.

Examiner: What does it mean?

Lisa: Slow in learning. Can't learn fast like other people. Can't run fast. Can't read and talk the right way. Mental means stupid and dumb, and that's what they call me.

Examiner: Mental? How do you feel about being called those names?

Lisa: I don't like it.

Examiner: What do you say?

Lisa: Sticks and stones will break my bones, but names will never hurt me. But they keep saying it to get me mad, and they do it every day. They keep saying it.

Examiner: So, you can't get them to stop. How does that make you feel?

Lisa: I feel terrible.

Examiner: Can you think of a way to make them stop?

Lisa: If I bring a lunch box to school, I could hit them on the head and that would make them stop.

Examiner: What would happen if you did that?

Lisa: I don't know, but they will get mad at me and keep saying it to me.

Examiner: Sounds like a big problem. I can understand if you are feeling angry.

Lisa: They keep telling me that they have problems. They get seizures and they get sick and take medicine, and some people can't walk the right way, and they can't help it, and they were born that way. Like me.

Examiner: Some of the children are like you?

Lisa: There is another boy like me. His name is Mike. He can't walk right. Some people are deaf and they can't talk right and they can't hear.

Examiner: What do you think about when you see the other people with problems?

Lisa:	I feel kind of strange, but I go there because I am retarded. And that's how he feels. He feels terrible because he is retarded and people call him that. Sometimes I wish I was a boy so I wouldn't get my period. I had it twice a month last month.
Examiner:	Twice?
Lisa:	Yes. Once in the beginning and once at the end. I have it now. It started yesterday in school.
Examiner:	Do you take care of it yourself?
Lisa:	Yes, because I usually get blood stains on my underpants and I have to put a sanitary napkin on and I feel terrible when I wear it. It gets all gooked up and you have to take a shower. Can I finish the story?
Examiner:	Yes. How does it end?
Lisa:	He is crying because he is unhappy because he is retarded.

Multimodal Treatment of Mentally Retarded Children

In this chapter, we will describe some typical multimodal methods used in a group therapy program at a mental retardation institute.* The program was set up to teach assertive and appropriate social functioning to approximately 40 children who exhibited a wide range of problems and characteristics including extreme withdrawal behaviors. Many of these children were considered to be "nonverbal." The design of the program evolved from our previous experience in applying multimodal therapy to both retarded and nonretarded children, in which significant emotional and behavioral changes ensued. Although our experience had been limited to individual therapy, we felt that the variability and flexibility of techniques available in multimodal therapy would be especially suitable in a group setting.

Using multimodal therapy as our framework, we systematically concentrated on a variety of problems, while remaining aware that people experience themselves and their lives across many independent yet interrelated modalities.

In his book on mental retardation, Menolascino (1970) includes a number of articles supporting the view that psychotherapy for the retarded can effect notable gains in emotional development and social adaptive skills. He points out the need for consistently structured well-balanced groups led by active, alert therapists, and presents a broad eclectic approach as probably being the most beneficial. This may include any

* The group therapy program referred to in this chapter was developed and carried out at the Mental Retardation Institute of New York Medical College, Valhalla, New York.

technique that the therapist considers effective for his particular patient. Techniques ranging from remedial educational programs to operant conditioning (behavior modification) to psychodrama are suggested. The therapeutic use of drugs is also included as an adjunct to the process of psychotherapy. When this broad eclectic approach is applied, children, adolescents, and adult retardates show improvement in the following areas: "institutional adaptation, motivation for learning, peer group association, familial relationships, control of unacceptable behavior, resolution of conflicts with authority figures, return to the home and community, and personality modification and improving employability" (Menolascino, 1970, p. 245). But the multimodal orientation introduces better structure, greater precision, and a more thorough treatment plan. As we hope to show, coverage of the BASIC ID extends and sharpens Menolascino's general orientation. Before dwelling on precise multimodal procedures, however, numerous general points need to be underscored.

Group Selection

It is advisable for the selection of group members to be based on approximate homogeneity of age, intellectual functioning, social adaptive development, and "personality type." Within that context we find it useful to separate groups of children exhibiting withdrawal behaviors from those children habitually "acting out." Yet in every group both sexes should be fairly represented, and heterogeneity should be evident with regard to the children's ability to communicate and their levels of assertiveness, passivity, and activity. We recommend a number sufficiently small to allow each group member extensive individual attention. Each of our groups consisted of six to eight children and two therapists. Often we found it advantageous to include additional therapists to work with those children who presented special difficulties and required extra attention. For example, in one group a behavior modifier served as the third therapist, and applied operant conditioning techniques to control the disruptive and destructive behaviors exhibited by one particular child who was not yet ready for a group experience. Although we could have removed the child from the group and referred him to a strict behavior modification program, we believed that more durable results would be effected if his treatment was administered within the broader context of the multimodal framework. In fact, the child did improve, and a gradual increase in his ability to handle group interactions ensued.

Use of Therapist's Self

Probably the most significant function of the therapist who works with retarded children is that of role model. Therapist modeling of appropriate social skills affords the children an opportunity to observe behaviors directly that they can later copy and practice themselves while receiving reinforcement for these imitative actions from others. For example, in the presence of a few children, the therapist may interact with a child while demonstrating verbalizations such as "please" or "thank you," he may ask assistance from others, or he may pointedly share valued items in a cooperative and friendly way. If two therapists are present, both can act as models by interacting with each other in a constructive and appropriate manner. We have found it most effective for a male and female therapist to work in each group and to interact in such a way that they model cooperation, friendliness, respect for one another, a peaceful settling of differences, consistency, liking for one another, and so forth. In many ways, the therapists assume the function of parent figures by providing appropriate role-modeling and facilitating imitation.

Therapeutic consistency is crucial when setting limits on the children's aggressive behavior. It is vital that the children do not succeed in manipulating their two therapists, particularly by playing one against the other. (Frequently, when the child's manipulative ploys are successful at home, the parents resort to arguing, or the child may come to believe he has made a special contract with one parent. The wielding of this kind of power is generally too taxing for the child. Its consequences outweigh any positive gains a manipulative child may have expected.) The therapists must maintain open and direct communication with each other during the sessions so that they can monitor their own interactions and maintain consistency with the children.

Group Methods

Two basic assumptions guided our efforts in establishing child groups: (1) Many techniques effective in individual therapy could be used and amplified in a group setting. (2) Multimodal therapy, as used with non-retarded children, adolescents, and adults, could be successfully applied to retarded people as well. However, we felt some important distinctions had to be made or at least considered when working with retarded children. For example, Sternlicht (1964) pointed out the need for an extremely active therapist who could successfully structure a group session, especially when working with hyperactive children. Likewise, our first consideration was to emphasize the need for the therapist to initiate more of the activities during a session with retarded youngsters than might be necessary with a nonretarded group. In addition, we recognized the need for the therapist working with retarded children to use much more repetition and instruction, to verbalize more, to create simple tasks where applicable to insure easy success, and to take into account specific limitations as well as those in which normal functioning is evident.

Slivkin and Bernstein (1970) have suggested that the retarded need to learn to express themselves verbally. However, considering their limitations in functioning, the therapist has to be more directive in his approach and more instructive in teaching them not only how to communicate but exactly what to communicate in interpersonal situations. The following brief encounter between two boys participating in one of our multimodal groups illustrates the point.

Both boys were aggressive and had difficulties relating to their peers. David, the younger, was verbal and generally functioning in the mildly retarded range of intelligence. On the other hand, Richard could be described as "nonverbal," communicating only with grunts and gestures, and functioning in the moderate range of retardation. The situation involved both boys simultaneously running to a shooting gallery game that could accommodate only one person at a time. As a result of vying for first place, they began fighting in an effort to pull one another away from the game. Very little was communicated verbally by either boy.

What we did then as co-therapists was to model by playing "alter ego" for each boy. First, each of us stood behind one of the boys and verbalized the frustration each boy was feeling at not being able to have the game to himself and in not succeeding in getting the game away from the other. Our dialogue sounded something like this:

> (Speaking for Richard): "I am feeling angry, David, that you want the game. I want to play and you should stay away. Why don't you do what I want you to do? I am angry that I can't tell you in a way that would make you do what I want you to do."

> (Speaking for David): "Richard, I feel so angry, I want to push and hit you and make you go away from me. I feel mad at you because you won't go away and let me have the game. I should have the game because I want it. I get very mad and angry when I can't have the things I want and I feel like hitting you and pushing you away."

After repeating these and similar statements a number of times while the boys listened, we suggested to them how they might resolve the problem and find a way to share the toy, or at least share time playing with it. Our conversation sounded like this:

(Speaking for Richard): "OK, David, let's find a way that we both could use the toy without fighting, because I would feel better if we could play together and if we could understand each other better. Why don't we take turns playing with the game and we can ask Carole and Vito to help us do it so that it is fair for you and me."

(Speaking for David): "Okay, Richard, I feel good when we can both have a turn and we don't have to fight over the toy, and Carole and Vito can help us."

Speaking as ourselves, we then offered suggestions about how they could cooperatively use the shooting gallery, which they then proceeded to do within the time limitations that we had set up. It was therapeutically vital that we took over completely for them in directing, instructing, and verbalizing. We also role played appropriate behaviors and used behavior rehearsal techniques with them to insure success and continuation of what they had learned. Once cooperative behavior had been established, we reinforced the boys frequently with verbal praise and encouragement.

In our groups we maintained skepticism about the accuracy of the label "nonverbal child" which had been applied to several members. Many children can understand verbal material, although they have difficulty expressing themselves. It is important to know whether a child *cannot* or *will not* talk. Often there is a mixture of problems in both comprehension and verbal expression. As a result, it is critical to verbalize to the children, assuming that what one says is being understood; if not the words, then the gestures, actions, and expressions. It is also helpful to remember that children do not use words alone to express themselves. The therapist can utilize the nonverbal communications already used by the children who may draw on various modalities for expression.

Verbal Techniques

The freedom of the therapist to ask questions is crucial when working with retarded as well as non-retarded children. The best questions usually do not require a yes or no answer and are not too demanding. To help the patient to become more social-wise, the therapist is encouraged to make general statements about people and events. He readily makes suggestions and verbally sets limits. Setting limits might involve a statement such as "I won't let you hurt yourself or me or anyone else."

The therapist is also encouraged to make statements to a child which demonstrate that he understands what the child is experiencing or feeling at the moment, such as, "I know you are feeling angry, but I still can't let you do that." For example, during one group session, a child had to be physically restrained from deliberately breaking a plastic toy because another child had refused to play with him. As the therapist restrained the child, she helped him verbalize the feelings of anger he felt when the other child apparently rejected him. It was pointed out to him that he was expressing his frustration and anger by a direct aggressive action. The therapist then suggested to him that if he still felt angry he could take out his anger on the punching bag, and that when he felt better she would help work things out directly with the other child. Similarly, if a child lies down on the floor in a fetal position, the therapist might say, "I think you are trying to tell me that you feel like a baby right now." For the child who knows his colors but names a pink block blue, a permissive yet reality-oriented atmosphere can be created by saying to him, "Okay, you can call the pink block blue if you want."

As mentioned earlier, modeling appropriate behaviors (playing alter ego) is another important technique that can be especially effective for children with limited verbal communication skills. Essentially, the therapist speaks for the child. For example, if one child pulls a toy away from another, the therapist might say, "Give that back to me. I was playing with it," or "I don't like that." Especially when working with nonverbal children, statements such as "I think Johnny would like to play with you," can facilitate social interaction in a productive way, eliminating the necessity for each child to verbalize his feelings. However, it must be remembered that as therapists, our eventual goal is to teach the child to verbalize his own feelings.

In general, therapists can make direct statements about themselves and teach socially desirable behaviors as well. They can act as positive reinforcers of appropriate social behavior, and they can ignore or punish undesirable behaviors. At no point need therapists compromise personal integrity by allowing the occurrence of inappropriate behavior. In essence, they must come across as warm, caring, firm, and consistent individuals who are themselves socially-oriented.

Facilitating Group Interaction

The provision of structure in a group setting is extremely important for children who typically need guidelines and have difficulty initiating group activities on their own. One good approach is for the therapist to start an activity with one or more children, and, once momentum has been established, to involve other children, while either continuing or phasing out his/her own participation. For example, the therapist may have a few children join hands in a circle, ask others to join by directly placing their hands together, and then remove himself/herself from the circle. The therapist can further structure the group interaction by suggesting or insisting that the children take turns or by having one child assist another. Likewise, structure may be provided by asking the children to assist the therapist on a project, each child being responsible for a different aspect or part of the task.

Social interaction may be facilitated directly through role playing and fantasy techniques in which children are directed to act out various parts, such as buying things in a store, acting aggressively, playing school, rushing to a fire, engaging in a family quarrel, or going to the doctor. While individual children play different roles the others can observe the action. Props such as masks, puppets, toy guns, and dolls can be used.

Use of Equipment, Games, and Sports

The more active, lively, and stimulating the therapy sessions, the more effective they will prove. Competitive and noncompetitive games and sports which require more than one player should be encouraged, especially those demanding team cooperation and the taking of turns. In addition, the therapist can engineer situations to encourage interpersonal involvement. By engaging in a visually pleasant and enjoyable activity with one child, another child may be stimulated to join in. Limiting the number of toys available or dividing parts of games—so that one child must approach another for more toys or missing parts—is an excellent means of stimulating interpersonal interactions. When possible, it is best to initiate activities to which the children have active as well as similar reactions, e.g., musical activities such as singing, dancing, playing musical instruments (drums, cymbals, sticks, harps, etc.). The children will usually respond as a group if enough direction and structure are provided.*

Arts and Crafts

Arts and crafts materials (play dough, finger paints [not for aggressive children], lincoln logs, paper and paste, etc.) should be provided and

---

* These suggestions must be modified when working with children who have specific types of problems. For example, passive children are sometimes frightened by aggressive toys. When aggressive type toys are available for acting out children, careful supervision is required to see that they are not misused. Hyperactive and distractable children sometimes become over stimulated when presented with too large a variety of toys.

arranged on a table in such a way that will encourage the children to sit together, facing each other as they work. In addition to encouraging interaction, cooperation, and feelings of accomplishment, the resulting creations can provide insights into the fantasy life of the children and facilitate their expression of thoughts and feelings. They may provide excellent clues about the conflicts the children may be experiencing daily, but are unable to verbalize. For example, one boy consistently and compulsively used the lincoln logs to build a house over and over again. When we encouraged him to verbally express his feelings about building the house, his tremendous anxiety about his own house and his parents' imminent separation became evident. He appeared to be expressing a desire to hold things together and to exert, at least symbolically, some control over the situation.

Picture Taking

It is effective to have the children identify photographs of themselves and each other by name and to keep the pictures pasted or hung on the wall. The use of video tapes allows the children direct visual feedback. This is particularly helpful when modeling and behavior rehearsal techniques are employed, especially with children who need a great deal of repetition and practice.

Points of Particular Importance

1. *Necessity of constant verbalization*. Even if a child cannot initially correctly label his feelings, if the therapist identifies them verbally a sufficient number of times, the child will eventually make the connection and at some point may utilize verbalization as a new tool in communication.

2. *Prevention of children's manipulative behaviors*. Most assuredly the children will attempt to test the therapist for consistency to insure their safety and their expectations that destructive or isolating tendencies will not be tolerated. On the other hand, the therapist must always respect the individuality of each child's experience at the particular moment in time; it is neither always necessary nor desirable for a child to be sociable when he experiences feelings that are incompatible with such behavior. Nevertheless, as much as possible, limitations and contingencies should be made verbally explicit to the child. This would include rules, instructions,

explanations of contingencies, expectations, feeling statements, and reasons. According to Bandura (1969), although children's behavior can be shaped by traditional operant conditioning procedures, the learning process can be speeded up when verbal cognitive input, such as an announcement of the contingencies involved, is included in the conditioning program.

Multimodal Profile

Our attempts to work systematically on each child's individual needs within each modality were facilitated by the use of Lazarus's (1973) multimodal profile. In essence, the profile is a worksheet used by the therapist to identify the patient's particular problems as well as to specify a proposed treatment plan. We have extended the original profile to include not only the modalities, problems, and proposed treatment plans, but also the degree of severity of the problems, the frequency with which they occur, and, finally, a progress report. A five point functional rating scale for the frequency of occurrence is used with the breakdown as follows: constant (5), frequent (4), occasional (3), rare (2), and never (1). To indicate severity we ask the teachers and parents to rate each problem on a three-point scale with a number 3 indicating the problem to be a major difficulty, a number 2 indicating a moderate difficulty and a number 1 a mild difficulty. This rating procedure proves extremely valuable in charting each child's progress to determine the results of treatment and to help guide the therapist in selecting those problems on which he will focus.

The information and data we include in the profile are derived from six basic sources: general observations of the children in their classrooms; interviews and discussions with teachers; interviews and discussions with parents; information obtained from available diagnostic material and records; interviews with the children; ongoing observations and impressions obtained during actual therapy sessions. Although the rating information included in the severity, frequency, and progress columns is subjective in nature, we believe that subjective experiences can be valid, especially if the children remain in the same environment. In effect, our version of the profile is a functional worksheet used to describe not only problem areas but also an entire treatment program with an evaluation of the results.

Case Presentation

To demonstrate the use of the multimodal profile, we present the following case:

A 16-year-old severely retarded girl named Susan was involved in our group program for approximately eight months. She could be described as a rather depressed, unassertive youngster, who besides talking to herself, would on occasion engage in angry behavior and verbalize psychotic-like hallucinations. Nevertheless, despite these difficulties and the others outlined in her profile, Susan exhibited a number of strengths. For example, she usually acted nonaggressively, demonstrated a long attention span, did not engage in hyperactive behaviors, could understand verbal directions as well as express herself verbally, and had developed most ADL skills (Activities of Daily Living). Except for occasional overreactive outbursts, even the direction and quality of her emotional reactions were generally appropriate. Although she did not initiate contact, she appeared to enjoy physical contact initiated by others. Susan liked to play with dolls and play house, and she was usually coherent and reality-oriented. Intellectually, her reasoning ability was intact at about the seven-year level. She was well oriented in time and space and had a good memory for everyday events. Interpersonally, Susan exhibited cooperative behaviors, and, at times, related to others on a positive feeling level. Keeping in mind these assets, as well as her problems and limitations, we developed for her a multimodal profile (Table 1).

In addition to the improvement noted in Susan's profile, further progress was made by working with her mother and sister who attended a multimodal parent group consisting of parents whose children were participating in our group program. The ongoing therapy for the mother and sister centered around their difficulties in handling Susan's expression of feelings at home, especially her reactions to the father's separation and abandonment of the family. Both mother and sister responded positively to the therapist's suggestions that they encourage Susan to freely express herself, and that they treat her more respectfully by giving her needed information:

> Susan would often talk to herself when her father, without calling to explain, broke his promise to visit her on weekends. In the past, the mother and sister used to make excuses for him and try to dispell her negative feelings. After their involvement in the parents' group, they became honest with her, and joined her feelings, admitting that they too, had similar reactions. Susan stopped talking to herself on such occasions because she felt more comfortable relating to the others.

Table 1. Multimodal Profile for Susan, Age 16

Modality	Problems	Treatment Plan	Severity	Frequency	Progress (8 months later)
Behavior	B1 Rocking	Substitute other acceptable stimulation to satisfy rocking; "time out" when very disruptive; give selective attention to others more appropriately engaged.	Moderate	Frequent (4)	Occasional (3)
	B2 Self-talk as if hallucinating	Interview for information; translate into words what you think she is expressing; role play the different parts; use cognitive restructuring (explain about reality, especially consequences for that behavior).	Moderate	Occasional (3)	Occasional (3)
Affect	A1 Extreme anger (Manifested behaviorally mainly by sulking and withdrawing)	Cognitive restructuring (RET) change belief system (shoulds and demands); substitute assertive responses for aggressive reactions; ask about feelings; help verbalize and give positive reinforcement for appropriate expression of feelings; teach alternatives with modeling and didactic instruction.	Mild	Occasional (3)	Occasional (3)
	A2 Depression	Increase self-worth by using time projection (imagining self feeling better); encourage her to verbalize her emotions, especially her anger; join the depression in an exaggerated fashion; suggest and teach alternatives to her depression; positively reinforce her when she is not acting depressed.	Major	Frequent (4)	Occasional (3)

Table 1. Multimodal Profile for Susan, Age 16 (Continued)

Modality		Problems	Treatment Plan	Severity	Frequency	Progress (8 months later)
Sensation			Not Applicable in This Case			
Imagery	I1	Gets upset at sight of mother (covers ears and eyes sometimes). May hallucinate mother being present when angry and upset.	Use of desensitization techniques around being with mother; parent counseling; assertive training. Also join the feelings and then suggest alternative solutions to her problems; suggest that she can talk to you; give her positive reinforcement when she stops hallucinating. Ask if there is really someone there. Model (verbalize that you see no one).	Moderate	Occasional (3)	Rare (2)
Cognition	C1	Has low self-worth and poor self-concept.	Give attention and positive reinforcement for her positive qualities; model for children and coax them to reinforce each other; challenge internal sentences in which she puts herself down (cognitive restructuring).	Major	Constant (5)	Frequent (4)
	C2	Feels she must keep her thoughts to herself.	Verbalize over and over that it is okay and important to say anything she wants to say during the sessions. Reward her for expressing her feelings and model the same for her by expressing your own feelings and what you think may be her feelings.	Major	Constant (5)	Frequent (4)
	C3	Intellectual Retardation Severe (AAMD Classification). Adaptive Behavior Functioning Level II— Moderate Retardation	Special school for mentally retarded			

Table 1. Multimodal Profile for Susan, Age 16 (Continued)

Modality	Problems	Treatment Plan	Severity	Frequency	Progress (8 months later)
Interpersonal	IP1 Never asserts herself with teachers, parents, siblings, and peers.	(Assertive Training) Use of role-playing and behavior rehearsal; use of coaching and modeling of assertive behavior; use of cognitive restructuring (demands, rights, rules, shoulds, etc.). Give positive reinforcement for assertive acts and get children to reinforce each other; use puppets and dolls to act out assertive behavior.	Major	Constant (5)	Occasional (3) Asserts herself more in group, in class, and at home.
	IP2 Poor socialization skills	Fantasy trips concerning social events; use of assertive training and positive reinforcement.	Major	Constant (5)	Frequent (4) She will make attempts to relate to the other children.
	IP3 Difficulties and conflicts with mother	Assertive training with use of role-playing, role-reversal. Also use puppets, self, and other children. Parent counseling.	Major	Frequent (4)	Occasional (3)
Drugs		Medical consultation to be considered if hallucinatory responses do not diminish.			

Susan is now being groomed in more appropriate behaviors for her age and is being treated by her family in a less overprotective and infantilizing manner.

Multimodal Therapy with Older Retardates

Already proven effective in treating a retarded child population, multimodal therapy can be applied to retarded adolescents and adults as well. Recommended techniques are the same as those used successfully with a normal population. However, more repetition, direct suggestions, modeling, and verbal connections have to be made. The therapist must pay special attention to psychosocial-sexual developmental problems—an area often overlooked in the treatment of retardates, but one that creates many critical issues for them. Finally, the therapist can teach the retardate who has come to overvalue and to accept uncritically the opinions of his parents and other authorities, to think divergently and exercise his own judgment in decision-making. Since decisions cannot be made without choices, divergent thinking is taught to the patient by presenting very concrete step by step alternatives to problems. Similarly, by discussing the outcomes that may result from a variety of alternative choices, consequential thinking is encouraged. This is coupled with reinforcement of appropriate value systems. When the patient begins to make more independent decisions, or expresses an interest in doing so, we find it especially helpful to involve the family or relevant authorities in the treatment plan. The goal is to better enable others to accept the retarded adult as a responsible decision maker so that they are more likely to support rather than challenge or undermine the patient's attempts at asserting his own rights.

References

Bandura, A. *Principles of behavior modification*. New York: Holt, Rinehart and Winston, 1969.

Lazarus, A. A. Multimodal behavior therapy: Treating the "BASIC ID." *The Journal of Nervous and Mental Disease,* 1973, *156,* 404-410.

Menolascino, F. J. *Psychiatric approaches to mental retardation*. New York: Basic Books, 1970.

Slivkin, S. E., & Bernstein, N. R. Group approaches to treating retarded adolescents. In F. J. Menolascino (Ed.) *Psychiatric approaches to mental retardation*. New York: Basic Books, 1970.

Sternlicht, M. Establishing an initial relationship in group psychotherapy with delinquent retarded male adolescents. *American Journal of Mental Deficiency,* 1964, *69,* 39-41.

Chapter 17

Sex Therapy and the BASIC ID

Arnold A. Lazarus

Leon and Carol were in love. They had been dating for the past year, and they planned to marry soon. Both were virgins eager to have premarital sex. Although Leon had been seeing various girls for five years, Carol was his first serious involvement. He enjoyed kissing and caressing her, but as soon as their amorous activities became more serious, he became tense and agitated. Leon was impotent.

They were sophisticated enough to realize immediately that they needed professional help. Through a referral, they attended a clinic and underwent a Masters and Johnson treatment program. They cooperated fully with the male-female cotherapy unit for about 96 hours of sexual retraining. Leon obtained an erection on one occasion, but lost it.

In their desperation, the couple went shopping for expert advice and encountered a bewildering array of contradictory opinions. They read books on everything from hypnosis and psychosynthesis to hormone treatments and existential philosophy. Some therapists said that Leon's problems obviously were deep-seated, and that after several years of psychoanalysis, he might obtain sufficient insight to restore his normal functioning. One of Carol's friends was a firm believer in Primal Therapy; she insisted that nothing less than gut-rending screams could unhook Leon from his childhood agonies. Someone else suggested that Carol probably had a castrating personality.

The couple's confusion and uncertainty escalated, and Leon entertained suicidal thoughts. An "expert" who indicated that Leon might be a homosexual and should join the Gay Liberation Movement did not improve his state of depression. About this time, Leon discovered modality training and began therapy with me. . . .

Reprinted with changes, from *Psychology Today* Magazine, March 1974. Copyright © 1974 Ziff-Davis Publishing Co. All rights reserved.

Before his initial interview with me, Leon filled out a life history questionnaire. His parents were shy and retiring people who had over-protected their only child. Consequently, he was socially inept, timid, and anxious. Leon impressed me as a bright but introverted young man who was a perfectionist. Currently, at the age of 24, he was completing his degree in architecture.

Since Leon had undergone a Masters and Johnson treatment program, I explored the imagery modality with him. While Masters and Johnson use most of the other modalities with their patients, imagery techniques are not part of their usual therapy. In their program, they deal with the *cognitive* modality through round-table discussions during which clients' faulty attitudes come out into the open. The *sensory* modality is covered by what Masters and Johnson call the ''sensate focus''—clients explore various sensory pleasures, examining each sense as a separate experience. The *behavioral* modality is monitored by training clients not to regard sex as a pressured test of their ability to perform. The *affective* modality is dealt with during the round-table discussions and history-taking, when basic feelings are sensitively explored and intimate disclosures are encouraged. The *interpersonal* modality is central to Masters' and Johnson's main thesis that ''there is no such thing as an uninvolved partner in any marriage in which there is some form of sexual inadequacy.'' However, *imagery* appears to receive only transient or indirect attention, and this might explain their high failure rate for certain conditions, notably impotence, a rate they have themselves deplored.

In Leon's case, the most logical imagery technique was systematic desensitization. If one pictures a progressive series of subjectively more threatening events until the anxiety dissipates (e.g., by allowing relaxed feelings to win out over tension) the actual situations no longer will evoke fear or anxiety. I lent Leon a series of cassette recordings on deep muscle relaxation so that he could learn how to relax his entire body. Meanwhile, I asked him to picture a range of nonthreatening images; they included seeing Carol, dancing with her, holding her hand, rubbing her back, and stroking her hair.

We began the desensitization process by asking Leon to imagine himself fondling Carol's breasts while she was fully clothed. He pictured this image clearly and reported no anxiety. I then asked him to imagine kissing, hugging, fondling of naked breasts while otherwise fully clothed; mouth contact with breasts; undressing completely; lying together in the nude; touching Carol's genitals.

We could not proceed beyond the last item without evoking high levels of anxiety in Leon. This block prevented me from adding progres-sively more intimate images. I switched to those that involved Carol as the more active partner; Leon was soon able to visualize her caressing *his* genitals without anxiety. But the moment *her* genitals came into the picture, Leon became highly anxious. Clearly, he found female genitalia inherently charged with anxiety. At the cognitive level, Leon and I searched vainly for reasons to account for his overwhelming aversion. Reverting to imagery once more, I asked him to picture his mother's genitals, an item from Akhter Ahsen's Eidetic Parents Test. He found the idea abhorrent. "I feel like throwing up. It's horrible! Ugh!"

I advised him to relax for a few moments and try the image again. He found it difficult to believe that I was serious, and he continued to block it from his mind. I asked him if her genitals would feel warm or cold. "Sticky!"

This reaction proved to be a wedge that pried open a series of memories, events, and associations that accounted for much of his impotence. At subsequent sessions, he recounted myths about masturbation that had made him fearful and guilty during adolescence. He recalled that his mother always reacted negatively toward pregnant women. He also remembered her saying, when he was about six, that his birth had been so traumatic for her that she absolutely refused to have more children. Leon and I discussed his thoughts and feelings about these memories of his mother. He then recalled the following incident:

Leon:	My mom and dad had a double bed and I used to cuddle with them on Sunday mornings. One day I noticed an unpleasant odor and saw blood on the sheets.
Therapist:	How old were you at the time?
Leon:	About eight or nine.
Therapist:	What did you think had happened?
Leon:	What *do* I think or what *did* I think?
Therapist:	I mean how do you view it today?
Leon:	Oh, I guess that she was menstruating.
Therapist:	But at the time you must have had a very different impression.
Leon:	God knows what I thought.
Therapist:	Well, can you get into that image? Pretend you are eight or nine years old. It is a Sunday morning and you are cuddling in bed with your parents. Can you picture that vividly?
Leon:	(pause) Yes.
Therapist:	Now you mentioned an odor.
Leon:	Yeah. Carol sometimes smells like that.
Therapist:	When she menstruates?
Leon:	I don't know.
Therapist:	Okay. Let's get back into the image.

Leon had difficulties suspending his adult faculties at this point. I then asked him to imagine himself in bed with Carol when she was menstruating. ''That makes me uptight.''

I instructed Leon to relax and go through the last scene several times. At the next session, Leon was able to visualize himself touching and caressing Carol's genitals without experiencing anxiety, even with the imagery of menstruation added. The desensitization proceeded swiftly.

Leon and I had met ten times over a period of six weeks; it was now time to bring Carol into therapy. She appeared tense but eager to help by going through a modified Masters and Johnson program with him. I decided to work on their problems in the *sensory* modality by applying Masters and Johnson's method of ''sensate focus.'' I instructed them to examine and to explore each other's bodies, and to report their reactions over a range of nonerogenous intimacies. I suggested that they examine their respective feelings and sensations while one gave the other a back rub for 20 minutes. Next, I suggested head scratching, ear tickling, shoulder massaging, or whatever gave them a relaxed and pleasant feeling. The emphasis was on a catalogue of pleasant sensations that were sensual rather than sexual.

One week later, they reported that they both had become aroused during noncoital sensual exchanges, and that they had had sexual intercourse on three separate occasions. They were jubilant. Carol had found the defloration somewhat painful, but she had experienced considerable pleasure anyway. By the third occasion, she had had no pain, although she was disappointed; she thought that she might be frigid since she had achieved only clitoral orgasms. I referred them again to the Masters and Johnson's book. It emphasized the normality of women who require direct digital stimulation, and stressed the myth of the purely vaginal orgasm. This restored Carol's confidence. Leon stated that his sexual prowess exceeded his wildest dreams. Carol had discovered several copulative positions that permitted simultaneous penile-vaginal and clitoral stimulation; she found them very satisfying. They had set a date for their wedding, and had replaced the initial atmosphere of gloom and desperation with one of joy and optimism in less than four months of therapy. Many clinicians might have terminated therapy at this point. I knew, however, that more discussions with the couple were necessary to consolidate their sexual relationship.

My latest follow-up studies would lead me to predict that if I had discharged Leon and Carol from therapy at this stage, there would be a high probability that after one to three years, Leon would be impotent again, but with more serious consequences. During the past four years, I have followed up more than 200 people who successfully underwent treatment programs with techniques similar to those used with Leon and Carol. About 36 percent relapsed or developed new problems within one to three years. These follow-ups were not limited to persons who had overcome sexual problems; they covered the gamut of neurotic disorders from phobias to obsessive-compulsive disorders. The relapse rate for people with sexual disturbances was closer to 60 percent. Psychoanalysts might argue that these results support the idea that unless deep, unconscious processes are unraveled, we may predict relapse or substitution of symptoms. This is not true. Researchers know that understanding *why* one's emotions and behaviors are maladaptive does not necessarily mean that a person will be able to do anything constructive about it. In order to achieve fundamental recovery and to prevent relapse, one must treat the spectrum of problem areas represented by the BASIC ID. And this is precisely what my multimodal therapy does.

Although Leon and Carol had made spectacular gains in their sexual adjustment, I pointed out a number of additional trouble spots that I had observed during our sessions. For example, Leon was inclined to be too unassertive and self-critical. Carol mothered him and submerged her own needs while playing the stereotyped role of the dependent and hypersensitive female. Unless we eliminated these and other areas of potential friction, the two were set on a collision course. I pointed out some of my observations and misgivings to Leon and Carol; both of them agreed that the therapy was incomplete.

I conducted a BASIC ID analysis on the couple, and asked them to prepare a list of undesirable behaviors that they noted in themselves and in each other. Together, we discussed situations, settings, people, and events that produced undue tension, anxiety, unhappiness, or anger in each of them. I asked them to observe unpleasant sensations, and to record any fantasies and images that seemed noteworthy. It was easy to spot their main cognitive blocks. They each had a headful of categorical imperatives ranging from absolute shoulds to must-nots. During our next session, I constructed their BASIC ID profiles (shown below). The BASIC ID profile provides a blueprint for client and therapist to set clear objectives for change. Both therapist and client add new items to the profile as therapy progresses and as new difficulties come forward. Carol, for example, became aware of her fear of the responsibilities of motherhood. She wanted children, but felt incompetent as a mother. Here again we used imagery procedures. She pictured herself pregnant, giving birth, nursing the baby, and going through routine procedures such as changing diapers and bathing the child. I asked her to picture herself coping with the demands of raising a child. By analyzing the overwhelming concept of motherhood into its various components, she lost her fear; she felt relaxed and confident at the prospect of having a child within a year or two.

We also overcame Carol's inclination to play the helpless female role. First, I asked her to monitor her own behaviors and thus to become aware of each occasion that she lapsed into this tendency. Leon whispered "H.F." (for helpless female) whenever he noticed Carol playing the role. In the consulting room, we rehearsed alternative ways in which Carol could behave independently and assertively. While expressing forthright feelings, Carol reported an unpleasant constriction in her throat. I asked her to relax and to breathe slowly in and out of her mouth. This, however, elicited an image of her father grabbing her mother by the throat. As we explored the feelings, sensations, and thoughts associated with this image, it became clear that by always deferring to Carol's father, her mother had taught her that females were inadequate. I then played the role of Carol's father by

	Leon	*Carol*
Behavior	Is timid and reticent with authority figures	Uses tears as a manipulative device
	Is excessively retiring in social situations	Too often plays the "helpless female" role
	Refuses to talk to Carol when annoyed with her	Lies to her parents instead of standing up for her rights
Affect	Is afraid of expressing anger	Is easily made to feel guilt and self-condemnation
	Feels anxious in crowds	Is made anxious by formal dinners
		Is anxious when exceeding 50 mph in a car
Sensations	Has frequent lower-back pain	Is prone to tension headaches
Imagery	Has vivid pictures of ridicule from peers in high school for poor athletic performance	Has images involving desertion and abandonment
Cognitions	Has perfectionistic standards	Wishes to be liked by everyone
	Has tendency to evaluate his self-worth according to extrinsic standards	Regards minor mishaps as "awful" and "dreadful"
Interpersonal	Has a general deficiency in assertive skills	Tends to reinforce Leon's petulance
		Resorts to manipulation rather than direct confrontation
Drugs	No need for medication	No need for medication

insisting that women are weak and inferior, and that they should turn to men for help at every opportunity. I encouraged Carol to dispute these contentions, to argue with me, to stand up for women's rights. We rehearsed these arguments several times and tape-recorded each sequence. Carol listened to the playbacks and realized that she remained unconvinced and unconvincing. With continued practice, however, she rapidly overcame her verbal hesitations and began to sound really self-confident. She was afraid, however, that her new-found assertiveness would threaten Leon and also compromise her femininity. We then explored what would happen if she elected habitually to suppress her feelings in order to placate Leon. We also spoke at length about the idea that strength and independence are not incompatible with femininity. I knew that Carol had really changed when she expressed direct anger at me for making a comment that seemed to reflect my "male chauvinism"!

An effective therapist needs dozens of techniques at his disposal to offset the problem areas that call for modification or elimination. Therapy sessions, depending upon the specific needs of the moment, can range from quiet conversations to the uncontrollable laughter that sometimes follows relief from undue tension.

Perhaps the most important modality-training technique is to encourage clients to rehearse new ways of responding to old situations. Thus, Carol agreed to stop deceiving and placating her parents. When this led to a serious altercation, a few meetings with Carol, her parents, Leon and me was necessary. A modality therapist does whatever seems most productive, and he will swing his focus from the individual to his or her social setting. He works with individuals, couples, families, and groups as the needs indicate.

Carol and Leon were in therapy with me for less than eight months. Scientists can justifiably ask what hard data I have to support my contention that modality training helped this couple. It is fair to ask whether psychoanalysis, meditation, or nude marathon encounters may have produced the same results. But my students and I consistently find that the multidimensional methods of modality training are inclined to succeed where other methods fail. The therapist's essential role, after all, is to restore the client's ability to function successfully in almost any situation. And the comprehensive approach of BASIC ID has been successful in doing just that.

Concluding Commentary

Arnold A. Lazarus

Who is most likely to respond favorably to this book? Active practitioners interested in broadening their ranges of technical and clinical expertise will, we hope, discover a stimulating and practical array of effective methods and strategies. Research-minded therapists will probably subject many of these procedures to clinical investigation with resulting innovations. And it is even conceivable that laboratory-minded scientists may test our claims of efficacy through controlled study, since one of the advantages of multimodal assessment and treatment is that they are amenable to verification or disproof.

We anticipate a negative reception from doctrinaire theorists and therapists of all persuasions. Psychoanalysts and the more conventional S-R oriented behavior therapists will find little merit in the ideas espoused by multimodal therapists—each for entirely different reasons. But most clinicians and scientist-practitioners are neither purists nor extremists. Along with the positive properties of a multimodal approach, they are likely to find *legitimate* faults, drawbacks, and shortcomings that warrant serious consideration.

A first and obvious issue to which we must address ourselves is whether the multimodal orientation falls outside the compass of "behavior therapy." To equate *any* effective therapeutic technique with "behavior therapy" clearly results in the loss of identifiable boundaries for procedures that are distinctly "behavioral" as opposed to useful "non-behavioral" strategies and techniques. If behavior therapy is limited to principles and methods *derived from research in experimental and social psychology* (a notion to which the Association for Advancement of Behavior Therapy subscribes), a considerable range of the treatment strategies employed by multimodal therapists clearly lies outside the realm of "behavior therapy."

For example, it is evident that in using certain imagery techniques and exercises in sensory awareness, or in exploring cognitive judgments and philosophical viewpoints, one is *not* employing techniques derived from experimental and social psychological research. Nevertheless, the efficacy of these procedures may be *explained by* experimental and social-psychological principles. And each contributor to the present volume prefers to place his or her empirical observations into the testable framework of social learning theory and cognitive behavior therapy rather than resort to "explanations" based on putative complexes or units of psychic energy.

But why incorporate methods into one's clinical repertoire that have not stemmed directly from research in experimental and social psychology? In other words, why go beyond behavior therapy? Simply because we find "behavior therapy" too limited and narrow to alleviate many facets of human suffering that we encounter in our daily practices. More than 20 years have elapsed since I first stressed that "the emphasis in psychological rehabilitation must be on a *synthesis* which would embrace a diverse range of effective therapeutic techniques, as well as innumerable adjunctive measures, to form part of a wide and all-embracing re-educative program" (Lazarus, 1956). Two years later I emphasized that the "objective psychotherapist employs all the usual psychotherapeutic techniques, such as support, guidance, insight, catharsis, interpretation, environmental manipulation, etc., but in addition to these more "orthodox" procedures, the behavior therapist applies objective techniques which are designed to inhibit specific neurotic patterns" (Lazarus, 1958).

Eysenck (1960) saw fit to reprint the entire article from which the previous quotation is taken, but ten years later, he took me severely to task for implying that "orthodox" techniques can possess any clinical merit (Eysenck, 1970). Academicians can afford to revel in solipsistic splendor, but practitioners face moral and litigious consequences when withholding action that may enhance human welfare. As practitioners we cannot afford to eschew methods that may save human lives—even when these methods are not well-grounded in immaculately controlled experimental trials. In this regard, it is essential to realize that "many of our greatest advances in therapeutic theory and practice come through clinical experimentation and innovation, rather than through laboratory research or controlled field trials across large samples of cases" (Lazarus and Davison, 1971, p. 196).

However, a spate of legitimate criticisms directed at multimodal therapy emanates from a source that is neither frenetic nor ill-conceived. If Eysenck typifies the destructive critic, Franks and Wilson (1975) represent the views of forward-looking, scientifically minded theoreticians fully familiar with the realities of clinical responsibility and the complexities of patient care. They call for more explicit criteria concerning the choice of different techniques, coupled with less reliance upon subjective judgment. They also correctly stress the need for data-oriented findings, and for empirical and rational, rather than notional, intervention. Many of these issues are addressed in this book, but only a series of well-conceived and properly executed clinical studies can establish the proper value and limitations of the multimodal orientation. There are many options to pursue in this regard. One acceptable method is to obtain further reports from practitioners who apply the BASIC ID to their own patients. It is significant when therapists of somewhat diverse persuasions, with differing backgrounds and training, discover that multimodal therapy yields significant gains in diagnostic accuracy and enhances clinical creativity. And when the consensus points to more positive and durable treatment outcomes following multimodal therapy, one is entitled to conclude that factors other than bias and chance may be responsible for these encouraging results.

References

Eysenck, H. J. (Ed.) *Behavior therapy and the neuroses*. New York: Pergamon, 1960.

Eysenck, H. J. A Mish-mash of theories. *International Journal of Psychiatry*, 1970, *9*, 140-146.

Franks, C. M., & Wilson, G. T. (Eds.) *Annual review of behavior therapy: Theory & practice*. New York; Brunner /Mazel, 1975.

Lazarus, A. A. A psychological approach to alcoholism. *South African Medical Journal*, 1956, *30*, 707-710.

Lazarus, A. A. New Methods in psychotherapy: A case study. *South African Medical Journal*, 1958, *32*, 660-664.

Lazarus, A. A., & Davison, G. C. Clinical innovation in research and practice. In A. E. Bergin & S. L. Garfield (Eds.)*Handbook of psychotherapy and behavior change: An empirical analysis*, pp. 196-213. New York: Wiley, 1971.

Appendix

Life History Questionnaire

LIFE HISTORY QUESTIONNAIRE

Purpose of this questionnaire:

The purpose of this questionnaire is to obtain a comprehensive picture of your background. In scientific work, records are necessary, since they permit a more thorough dealing with one's problems. By completing these questions as fully and as accurately as you can, you will facilitate your therapeutic program. You are requested to answer these routine questions in your own time instead of using up your actual consulting time.

It is understandable that you might be concerned about what happens to the information about you because much or all of this information is highly personal. Case records are strictly confidential. *No outsider is permitted to see your case record without your permission.*

If you do not desire to answer any questions, merely write "Do not care to answer."

* * * * * * * * * *

Date _____

1. *General*

   Name: _____

   Address: _____

   _____

   Telephone numbers: (day) _____ (evenings) _____

   Age: _____ Occupation: _____

   By whom were you referred? _____

   With whom are you now living? (list people) _____

   _____

   Do you live in a house, hotel, room, apartment, etc.? _____

   Marital status: (circle answer)

   Single; engaged; married; remarried; separated;

   divorced; widowed.

If married, husband's (or wife's) name, age, occupation?

_____

Religion and Activity:

   a) In childhood _____

   b) As an adult _____

2. *Clinical*

   a) State in your own words the nature of your main prob-
       lems and their duration:

   b) Give a brief account of the history and development of
       your complaints (from onset to present):

   c) On the scale below please estimate the severity of
       your problem(s):

       mildly upsetting _____

       moderately severe _____

       very severe _____

       extremely severe _____

       totally incapacitating _____

   d) Whom have you previously consulted about your present
       problem(s)? _____

   e) Are you taking any medication? If "yes," what, how
       much, and with what results? _____
       _____

3. *Personal Data*

   a) Date of birth: _____ Place of birth: _____

b) Mother's condition during pregnancy (as far as you
    know): _____

    _____

c) Underline any of the following that applied during
    your childhood:

    Night terrors   Bedwetting   Sleepwalking

    Thumb sucking   Nail biting   Stammering

    Fears   Happy childhood   Unhappy childhood

    Any others:

d) Health during childhood?

    List illnesses:

e) Health during adolescence?

    List illnesses:

f) What is your height?_____ Your weight?_____

g) Any surgical operations? (Please list them and give
    age at the time)

h) Any accidents?

i) List your five main fears:

    1.

    2.

    3.

    4.

    5.

j) <u>Underline</u> any of the following that apply to you:

headaches	dizziness	fainting spells
palpitations	stomach trouble	anxiety
bowel disturbances	fatigue	no appetite
anger	take sedatives	insomnia
nightmares	feel panicky	alcoholism
feel tense	conflict	tremors
depressed	suicidal ideas	take drugs
unable to relax	sexual problems	allergies
don't like week-ends and vacations	overambitious	shy with people
can't make friends	inferiority feelings	can't make decisions
can't keep a job	memory problems	home conditions bad
financial problems	lonely	
excessive sweating	often use aspirin or painkillers	unable to have a good time
		concentration difficulties

Others: Please list additional problems or difficulties
          here.

k) <u>Underline</u> any of the following words which apply to you:

Worthless, useless, a "nobody," "life is empty"

Inadequate, stupid, incompetent, naive, "can't do
  anything right"

Guilty, evil, morally wrong, horrible thoughts, hostile,
  full of hate

Anxious, agitated, cowardly, unassertive, panicky,
  aggressive

k) (cont.)

Ugly, deformed, unattractive, repulsive

Depressed, lonely, unloved, misunderstood, bored, restless

Confused, unconfident, in conflict, full of regrets

Worthwhile, sympathetic, intelligent, attractive, confident, considerate

Others:

l) Present interests, hobbies, and activities: _____

_____

m) How is most of your free time occupied? _____

_____

n) What is the last grade of school that you completed?_____

o) Scholastic abilities; strengths and weaknesses:_____

_____

p) Were you ever bullied or severely teased? _____

q) Do you make friends easily? _____

Do you keep them? _____

4. *Occupational Data*

a) What sort of work are you doing now?

b) Kinds of jobs held in the past?

c) Does your present work satisfy you? (If not, in what ways are you dissatisfied?)

d) What do you earn?_____

How much does it cost you to live?_____

e) Ambitions _____

Past: _____

_____

Present: _____

_____

5. *Sex Information*

a) Parental attitudes toward sex (e.g., was there sex
instruction or discussion in the home?)

b) When and how did you derive your first knowledge of sex?

c) When did you first become aware of your own sexual
impulses?

d) Did you ever experience any anxieties or guilt feelings
arising out of sex or masturbation? If "yes" please
explain:

e) Any relevant details regarding your first or subsequent
sexual experience:

f) Is your present sex life satisfactory? (if not, please
explain)

g) Provide information about any significant heterosexual
    (and/or homosexual) reactions:

h) Are you sexually inhibited in any way? _____

6. *Menstrual History*

Age at first period? _____

Were you informed or did it come as a shock? _____

Are you regular? _____ Duration: _____

Do you have pain? _____ Date of last period: _____

Do your periods affect your moods? _____

7. *Marital History*

How long did you know your marriage partner before engagement?

How long have you been married? _____

Husband's/Wife's age _____

Occupation of husband or wife: _____

a) Personality of husband or wife (in your own words):

b) In what areas is there compatibility?

c) In what areas is there incompatibility?

d) How do you get along with your in-laws? (This includes
    brothers and sisters-in-law)

How many children have you? _____

Please list their sex and age(s). _____

_____

e) Do any of your children present special problems?

f) Any relevant details regarding miscarriages or abortions?

g) Comments about any previous marriage(s) and brief details.

8. *Family Data*

a) Father:

Living or deceased? _____

If deceased, your age at the time of his death? _____

Cause of death? _____

If alive, father's present age? _____

Occupation: _____

Health: _____

b) Mother:

Living or deceased? _____

If deceased, your age at the time of her death? _____

Cause of death? _____

If alive, mother's present age? _____

Occupation: _____

Health: _____

c) Siblings:

Number of brothers: _____ Brothers' ages: _____

Number of sisters: _____ Sisters' ages: _____

d) Relationship with brothers and sisters:

1) past: _____

_____

2) present: _____

_____

e) Give a description of your father's personality and his attitude toward you (past and present):

f) Give a description of your mother's personality and her attitude toward you (past and present):

g) In what ways were you punished by your parents as a child?

h) Give an impression of your home atmosphere (i.e., the home in which you grew up. Mention state of compatibility between parents and between parents and children).

i) Were you able to confide in your parents? _____

j) Did your parents understand you?_____

k) Basically, did you feel loved and respected by your
    parents? _____

    If you have a step-parent, give your age when parent
    remarried: _____

l) Give an outline of your religious training:

m) If you were not brought up by your parents, who did bring
    you up, and between what years?

n) Has anyone (parents, relatives, friends) ever interfered
    in your marriage, occupation, etc.?

o) Who are the most important people in your life?

p) Does any member of your family suffer from alcoholism,
    epilepsy, or anything which can be considered a "mental
    disorder"?

q) Are there any other members of the family about whom
    information regarding illness, etc., is relevant?

r) Recount any fearful or distressing experiences not
    previously mentioned:

s) List the benefits you hope to derive from therapy.

t) List any situations which make you feel calm or relaxed.

u) Have you ever lost control (e.g., temper or crying or aggression)? If so, please describe.

v) Please add any information not tapped by this questionnaire that may aid your therapist in understanding and helping you.

9. *Self-Description*   (Please complete the following):

a. I am a person who _____

b. All my life _____

c. Ever since I was a child _____

d. One of the things I feel proud of is _____

e. It's hard for me to admit _____

f. One of the things I can't forgive is _____

g. One of the things I feel guilty about is _____

h. If I didn't have to worry about my image _____

i. One of the ways people hurt me is _____

j. Mother was always _____

k. What I needed from mother and didn't get was _____

l. Father was always _____

m. What I wanted from my father and didn't get was _____

n. If I weren't afraid to be myself, I might _____

o. One of the things I'm angry about is _____

p. What I need and have never received from a woman (man) is _____

q. The bad thing about growing up is _____

r. One of the ways I could help myself but don't is _____
_____

10. a) What is there about your present <u>behavior</u> that you would
        like to change?

    b) What <u>feelings</u> do you wish to alter (e.g., increase or
        decrease)?

    c) What sensations are especially:

        1) pleasant for you?

        2) unpleasant for you?

    d) Describe a very pleasant image of fantasy.

    e) Describe a very unpleasant image of fantasy.

    f) What do you consider your most irrational thought or
        idea?

    g) Describe any interpersonal relationships that give you:

        1) joy

        2) grief

    h) What personal characteristics do you think the ideal
        therapist should possess?

     i) How would you describe an ideal therapist's interactions with his clients?

     j) What do you think therapy will do for you and how long do you think your therapy should last?

     k) In a few words, what do you think therapy is all about?

11. With the remaining space and blank sides of these pages, give a word-picture of yourself as would be described:

     a) By yourself

     b) By your spouse (if married).

     c) By your best friend

     d) By someone who dislikes you

Author Index

Subject Index